THE
GREAT WESTERN
AT WORK 1921-1939

Patrick Stephens Limited, a member of the Haynes Publishing Group, has published authoritative, quality books for enthusiasts for more than 25 years. During that time the company has established a reputation as one of the world's leading publishers of books on aviation, maritime, military, model-making, motor cycling, motoring, motor racing, railway and railway modelling subjects. Readers or authors with suggestions for books they would like to see published are invited to write to: The Editorial Director, Patrick Stephens Limited, Sparkford, Nr Yeovil, Somerset, BA22 7JJ.

THE
GREAT WESTERN
AT WORK 1921-1939

ADRIAN VAUGHAN

PSL

Patrick Stephens Limited

**Dedicated with admiration and affection to
The men and women who ran the Great Western Railway**

First published in 1993

British Library Cataloguing in Publication Data
A catalogue record for this book is available from the British Library.
ISBN 1 85260 300 3

Patrick Stephens Limited is a member of the Haynes Publishing Group P.L.C.,
Sparkford, Nr Yeovil, Somerset, BA22 7JJ.

Typeset by Character Graphics, Taunton, Somerset
Printed by Butler and Tanner Ltd, London and Frome

Contents

Acknowledgements

The research for this book was undertaken mainly in the Great Western Railway's internal reports which can be read at the Public Record Office (PRO), Kew, London. The full list of papers consulted in the preparation of this book would be very lengthy, but included the following:

'General Manager's Fortnightly Reports to the Board of Directors', 1921-39 (PRO RAIL 250/448-66). The chapters on labour matters and the General Strike used material to be found in RAIL 250/472, 'The General Manager on Labour Matters', and RAIL 250/451 'Management of Railway during General Strike'. I have also included eye-witness accounts given to me by men with whom I worked on the railway.

The chapters on signalling used material found in the Signal & Telegraph Department Reports, 1935-31 (RAIL 258/406), and information from GWR papers collected by the learned Signalling Record Society. A vast amount of information on the running of the railway can be found in 'Minutes of the Fortnightly Meetings of Divisional Superintendents', 1922-26 (RAIL 250/724) and 1931-42 (RAIL 250/772), and the 'Superintendent of the Line's Report on Branch Lines', 1926 (RAIL 267/365). The 'Minutes of the Divisional Traffic Research Committees' are also in RAIL 250; piece 710 is for the Shrewsbury Division in 1937. Papers concerning GWR air services are in RAIL 258/511-6. I also consulted the Railways Act 1930 and 1933. Hugh Mytton's play about rating mentioned in chapter 2 can be found in RAIL 268/249.

The major input came from these GWR internal papers, but some printed books were consulted: *The Great Western at Swindon Works* by Alan Peck (OPC); *Great Western Engines*, Vol 2, by J. H. Russell (OPC); *Locomotives of the GWR* (RCTS); *Traffic and Transport* by Dr Gerald Turnbull (George Allen & Unwin); *British Railways: a business history* by Dr Terry Gourvish (Cambridge University Press); and *The Great Western Railway under the British Railways Act of 1921* by Dr Geoffrey Channon (Journal of Transport History).

In addition to this documentary material I was given much assistance by dedicated and expert researchers, and I am pleased to acknowledge the help I received from David Collins Larry Crosier and John Morris of the Signalling Record Society on signalling matters, Alan Peck concerning locomotive matters, and Dr Michael Bonavia and Prof Philip Bagwell concerning finance and labour matters. I would also like to thank my Editor, Will Adams, for his hard work and patience in sorting out the typescript, and my friend Paul Dye for his help with Bristol Temple Meads.

Most of the research was carried out at the PRO at Kew, but also at the University of East Anglia library, and I would like to thank the staff of both places for their kindness in helping to get the books and papers I required.

I would also like to thank my sister and brother-in-law, Frances and Camilus Travers, and my friends Ron and Jo Price for generously providing accommodation when I was working at Kew, and last but not least my dear wife Susan for her support and planning which have enabled me, yet again, to complete this book.

Introduction

I had two good reasons for writing this book - apart from having to earn my living, that is. I have always admired the Great Western Railway and therefore want to know as much about it as possible. It was for the same reason that I set out to write my biography of I. K. Brunel, and the book now in your hands, like the Brunel biography, seeks to discover what the *real* history was - there is no place for nostalgia here.

I have spent something over two years in this quest and I hope that I have been successful in pointing out the Company's problems, successes and failures. The problems that faced the management of the GWR throughout the period were a lack of money, ever-increasing costs, declining receipts, a developing competition from the roads, and a lack of support from the Government. The Railways Act of 1921 discouraged competition and, indeed, the companies were in no shape to compete, since that would mean reducing fares. Competition with road hauliers and the private car kept the fares down.

Three of the four 'Grouped' railways were in pretty close co-operation by 1930 - pooling freight revenue, for instance - and gradually involved themselves in passenger and freight road haulage by obtaining shares in some large bus companies and buying such large freight carriers as Hays Wharf Cartage, which included Pickfords. A more of less co-operative transport network of private companies had been achieved by 1933, but still the GWR became less and less profitable - the Company could not buy up every road haulier.

I have now arrived at the second reason for writing this book. It began in 1990 when the present course now chosen by the Government for our railway system was plain enough to foresee. I wanted to show, by a study of what has gone before (and that is, after all, what 'history' is for), how those truly great railway managers had coped with their transport problems - in those days of private enterprise, under-funding, and recession. Whilst there is no room for nostalgia here, there is plenty of room for admiration of the fighting spirit of the people in charge of railways in those days. Surrender was not on their minds.

If I can show the course that they took, I hope that I can also demonstrate that what is proposed by the 1993 Bill on railways is completely irrelevant to the needs of a nationwide transport system of co-ordinated road and rail.

Adrian Vaughan
Barney, Norfolk, 1993

Chairmen of the Great Western Railway Board 1921-1939

Viscount Churchill GCVO Feb 1908-Jan 1934 (the longest serving Chairman of any railway)
Sir Robert Horne PC GBE (Viscount May 1937) Jan 1934-Sept 1940

Officers of the Company 1921-1939

General Managers
Charles Aldington July 1919-June 1921 (retired ill)
Felix John Clewett Pole June 1921-June 1929 (knighted 1924)
James Milne KCVO CSI, June 1929-31 Dec 1947 (knighted 1932; offered post of Chairman, Railway Executive, but refused it)

Chief Engineers
W. W. Waddell retired 1925
J. C. Lloyd 1925-1929
R. Carpmael 1929-1940
Sir Allan A.S. Quartermaine 1940-1947

Chief Mechanical Engineers
George Jackson Churchward OBE retired December 1921
Charles Benjamin Collett CBE Jan 1922-July 1941

Chief Signal & Telegraph Engineers
Alfred Thomas Blackall retired 1923
Robert James Insell 1923-1928
Charles Mark Jacobs 1928-1936
Frederick Harold Dunn Page 1936 - 1947

Superintendents of the Line
R. H. Nicholls 1919-1932
H. L. Wilkinson 1932-1936
F. R. Potter 1936-1940
G. Matthews 1940-1947

1
Aftermath of war

Between 1900 and 1914 the Great Western Railway had constructed 400 miles of brand new railway together with 'state of the art' standardised locomotives and new coaching stock. But just as the Company was beginning to reap the benefits of this enormous investment the Great War broke out and the GWR, with all the other railways in the land, was taken over by the Government under the 'Defence of the Realm Act'.

Under this arrangement, made public by the Board of Trade on 15 September 1914, the shareholders were paid a fixed dividend and the Company was paid a fixed amount for the use of its facilities. The terms amounted to a guarantee by the Government to maintain the GWR's income at its 1913 level, and these payments were also to cover 'all special services such as those in connection with military and naval transport'. The railway therefore carried a vastly increased traffic free of charge since it was only receiving revenue based on peacetime traffic.

Meanwhile, the cost of labour and materials rose sharply while the Company's fares and freight rates were held down by government decree. The locomotives and rolling-stock were not repaired or renewed at the usual rate - either because they could not be spared from traffic or the Works's capacity was diverted into armaments manufacture - so the rolling-stock fleet became relatively run-down.

This government control during wartime effectively nationalised all Britain's railways, and this also demonstrated that economies in operation could be made since all facilities and rolling-stock were 'in common use'. Generally speaking, engines could be serviced on any loco shed, and engines and rolling-stock could go almost anywhere - there were of course some limitations due to the width, weight or length of certain GWR engines and carriages over some other lines. In addition, parcels delivery services for an area did not have to be run perhaps in triplicate by three separate companies.

The Government set up a Parliamentary Committee to investigate these 'economies of scale', and this reported on 14 November 1918. The Committee was chaired by Sir Eric Geddes, who had been Deputy General Manager of the very efficient North Eastern Railway and was recognised as being a forceful and highly capable organiser. During the Great War he had been Minister of Munitions, afterwards organising the demobilisation of the armed forces before addressing the problems of post-war transport.

Geddes's railway experience before the war convinced him that it would be folly to go back to the pre-1914 situation - a multiplicity of companies with competing lines and duplicated services. Even though pre-war competition had been tempered by many no-competition pacts between the companies, it was still wasteful of resources and tended to reduce profits to uncommercially low levels.

Six possible paths to follow were suggested, all of them involving amalgamations, and one of them being nationalisation; in Dundee, in December 1918, Winston Churchill made a speech suggesting that this was the best course of action. The following year the Ministry of Transport Act established that Ministry, with Geddes as the first Minister. This was thought of as a first step towards a properly co-ordinated and nationalised transport system in Britain.

Battle was then joined, with the companies' lobbying hard against nationalisation, and the Great Western's Chairman, Lord Churchill, very much in the vanguard of that opposition. Even the Trade Unions opposed nationalisation, as part of the proposal was to have 'Worker-Directors' on the Board of Management.

As an outcome of intense lobbying from all sides, the decision was taken in Cabinet to group the 120 companies into four under private ownership. Economies of scale would result, competition amongst so few would be difficult, and clauses in the enabling Act would restrict further the opportunities for the debilitating competition so feared by the experienced railwayman, Eric Geddes. The Grouping solution was also a cheaper option than nationalisation which would have required the Government to buy the entire network – and after the most exhausting war in history that amount of money was not available.

The Grouping brought about by the 1921 Railways Act was, therefore, a compromise between privatisation and nationalisation. It was essential to the life of Britain that the railway network be pre-served, so the smaller, less profitable companies had to be brought under the protection, so to speak, of their larger brethren, and profit-cutting competition between the four large groups had to be prevent-ed.The Railways Act obliged the railway companies to send their passenger and freight traffic by the shortest route and not by the route which kept it on the originating company's metals for the longest mileage to earn the greatest share of the fare. It also laid down what would be a reasonable profit for the railways to make, and then set the prices which the railways could charge in order to earn that revenue – known as 'the Standard Revenue'. At some time in the future, on what the Act called 'The Appointed Day', the companies would be assessed as to their efficiency and as to whether or not they were actu-ally earning their 'Standard Revenue'. If they were earning more than their 10 per cent they would be obliged to reduce their fares. In this respect it was a re-run of the 1844 Act.

Meanwhile, by 1919 it had become obvious even to the Government that the railway companies had a right to expect compensation, over and above the original agreement, for the abuse that their perma-

nent way and rolling-stock had suffered. Between December 1913 and November 1923 the GWR had spent £433,853 on major enlargements and improvements to Swindon Works, which had been promptly taken over for Government munitions manufacture, the Company receiving no benefit from their investment.

Thus a Ministry of Transport Committee was appointed in September 1920 to investigate 'the possible extent of outstanding liabilities of the State' to the railway and, if such extra liability was found to exist, whether the Government ought to pay up - 'having due regard to the cost'.This Ministry Committee discovered that, due to 'Arrears of Maintenance to track, rolling-stock, buildings and machinery, due to abnormal wear and tear and abnormal consumption of stores' incurred as a result of the Government's use of the British railway sys-tem during the war, the Government had a moral (but not legal) obligation to pay to the combined railways of Britain the sum of £150,000,000. This figure, coming from a Government department, was without any shadow of a doubt an under-estimate.

What the four companies got, through the 1921 Railways Act, was £60,000,000 between them. Thus with compromise, good intentions and with less than half the compensation to which they were entitled, the re-constituted companies were released to private ownership and sent on their under-funded way.

The management structure of the GWR had developed piecemeal out of the original system for operating the London–Bridgwater line of 1841 when a 'London' and a 'Bristol' Divisional Superintendent organised the train running, sig-nalling and booking office side of things, answering to the 'Superintendent of the Line' who was respon-sible to the Directors. As the railway extended, so more Divisions were added to the original plan. It was not until 1850 that the GWR Directors decided that they needed a 'Goods Manager', and the posi-tion of General Manager was not created until 1866, when it was held by James Grierson. However, he was not in command of all departments since the Chief (Civil) Engineer, the Locomotive Superintendent and the Accountant reported direct-ly to the Board.

In 1921 there were still independent Committees of Directors to control the GWR's Traffic, Engineering or Locomotive Departments, for exam-ple, and the Heads of these Departments reported direct to their Directors' Committee. These

The GWR in 19th-century mode - relaying the main line/Windsor branch junction at Slough. The trackwork was prefabricated at the lineside and was then levered and slewed - in pouring rain - over signal wires and point rodding and along the rails to reach its operating site. Note the screw jacks on the sleepers which will be used to lift the assembly for ballasting. 29 March 1936. (British Rail)

Directors considered Departmental requests for money and authorised expenditure as they saw fit. Liaison between Committees was limited or non-existent. This ancient system was conservative and insular, even secretive, full of departmental loyalties - and jealousies - time-consuming when decisions were required, and difficult to control. The worst result was that the 'spending' departments like those of the Civil or Chief Mechanical Engineer were not in contact with the revenue-earning side of the business - nor under the control of that side of the business.

The freight business of the GWR was organised by Districts under the District Goods Managers; they reported to the Chief Goods Manager, who ran his own show, one rank below the General Manager. The Goods Department was the single largest earner of revenue on the GWR. It canvassed for and obtained freight traffic, its porters loaded wagons, and it had its own accountancy to cover all this business.

The daily supply of freight rolling-stock to the stations and yards was under the control of the Superintendent of the Line, which was 'Traffic Department'; the Traffic Department was responsible for setting the rates for goods and passenger traffic as well as running the trains, stations and signal boxes, and was also responsible for settling claims for damage to goods *en route*. The engines to haul the trains were the responsibility of the Locomotive Department, while the repair of the goods wagons was carried out by the Carriage & Wagon Department under the Chief Locomotive Engineer. The Great Western divided its territory into Districts or Divisions for its various activities, the main ones being Locomotive, Traffic, Engineer and Goods, with a 'Divisional Superintendent' or 'District Manager' for each. Nowhere, however, did the boundaries of the Divisions or even Districts coincide. For instance, the Bristol Divisional Locomotive Superintendent's area covered the Divisional Traffic areas of Bristol, Exeter and Plymouth. Not until 1938, and then only in the Plymouth and Central Wales Divisions, were the functions of Divisional (Passenger) Traffic Superintendent and District Goods Manager merged into the one post of District Traffic Manager.

The Chief Mechanical Engineer, G. J. Churchward from 1902 to 1921, ran his own empire from Swindon, controlling not only the construction and repair of locomotives, carriages, wagons and locomotive sheds and factories, but also, through his Divisional Running Superintendents, the day-to-day running and maintenance of the

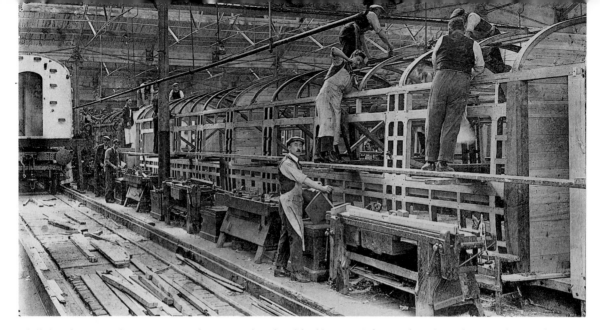

Skilled craftsmen in the Carriage Works at Swindon, hand-building a 70-foot coach with much painstaking and intricate carpentry during the Churchward era, circa 1921. It was magnificent, but it was not profitable. (British Rail)

engines, and the employment and disciplining of all the staff employed therewith. He was generally considered 'top dog' by himself and by the Directors.

James Inglis, General Manager from 1903 to 1911, had tried to bring some co-ordination to the Departments under his direction - to save money - but without success. His successor, Frank Potter, also tried in 1913 with his 'Chief Officers Conference', but the war came the following year, the railway was taken over by the Government and the idea was still-born.

Churchward viewed these entirely laudable attempts to curb egos in the name of economy as 'outside interference' with his Locomotive Department, as if it was something separate from the rest of the GWR. So the Chief Locomotive, Carriage & Wagon Superintendent continued to be considered 'top dog' by himself, and always got the money he wanted - and more than he needed, for Churchward had an extra fund, put aside against the day when his power just might be restricted. The Superintendent of the Line (SoL) met fortnightly with his 12 Divisional Traffic Superintendents to discuss all aspects of working the traffic, and these men assessed the timetable requirements for each summer/winter service; the Superintendent's

Erecting the frames of a four-cylinder engine in Swindon Locomotive Works at about the same date. In the foreground a bowler-hatted Foreman and cloth-capped Chargemen examine the plans. (British Rail)

timetabling staff then produced the timetable. The Chief Mechanical Engineer (CME) took no part in this, but supplied the locomotives to work the schedules thus presented to him and tried to arrange his engines' and mens' workings in the most economical way.

This was a situation typical of many large railways, but one which the Great Eastern Railway, under its American General Manager, Henry Worth Thornton, had seen fit to revise before 1914. Thornton had taken the responsibility for day-to-day running of locomotives out of the hands of the CME, but the old system's prolongation on the GWR through to 1921 and beyond was due partly to the granite personality of George Jackson Churchward, partly to the Directors and partly to GWR tradition.

Churchward was a great locomotive engineer, perhaps the greatest of his era, but he was also a great autocrat who seems to have viewed humans as an inferior sort of locomotive. Neither he nor the Great Western as a company had ever 'recognised' trade unions as such. The men could come to him with complaints, but only as individuals - not as delegates. The unions were only 'recognised' by the Government after the 1914 take-over, so Churchward and the Company were presented with the accomplished fact in 1921. Churchward found the experience of enginemen and factory workers facing him as equals, laying down their terms for negotiation, hard - indeed impossible - to tolerate.

Further shocks were in store. When Felix Pole became General Manager in June 1921 he set out to modernise the GWR and make the Company run more economically. He began in the right place - at the top - and set out to modernise the GWR's antique, gentlemanly - and inefficient - management structures. What Pole had in mind for the GWR was the American, Pennsylvania Central Railroad, system, where a 'Division' meant an autonomous unit where all departments were co-ordinated under one head for daily operational and financial decisions, while a head office took the main expenditure and policy decisions.

Pole began by reviving Frank Potter's 'Chief Officers Conference' of 1913. By this means he hoped to establish his authority over all departments, not for the sake of his ego but for economy, to co-ordinate and control the financial activities of all departments of the railway, rather than allow each department to spend whatever it thought was right. Under Pole's systemeach 'Chief' would be told what he could spend - and what money he had to save.

George Churchward, faced on the one hand with the new breed of non-subservient engine drivers and factory hands who formed the trade union delegations, and on the other by the modernising General Manager, also seeking to curb his power, saw that 'it was time for the Old Man to go'. He would, in any case, be 65 in March 1922 and due for retirement, so he retired early, on 31 December 1921, unable, or unwilling, to cope with conditions in a changed industrial world.

He was succeeded by C. B. Collett, a very different character, a gentler person, but still no 'pushover'. Collett, too, successfully resisted Pole's attempt to break the autonomy of the Locomotive Department. This can be seen in the prevaricating 'Minute' of 6 January 1922, which ordered that the Divisional boundaries should be synchronised - but not at once, only 'as and when opportunity offered', so as not to offend departmental loyalties. This same Minute's orders, regarding liaison between locomotive and traffic sides, seem to be the ruins of a far more positive proposal to bring all the Locomotive Department's daily running matters under the control of the Superintendent of the Line's office, whilst leaving to the Locomotive Department responsibility for the construction and repair of engines, carriages and wagons. All the Minute was able to do was to *ask* for the *co-operation* of the Chief Mechanical Engineer's Department with the Superintendent of the Line's office in:

1. The allocation and distribution of engine power
2. The preparation of engine working diagrams
3. The timing and alteration of trains
4. The examination of enginemen's records, and
5. The hours of duty of enginemen

That such an obvious course had to be made the subject of an official Minute is itself a commentary on the odd way that the GWR had organised its affairs. But even this was 'watered down' by Collett, thus avoiding the 'humiliation' of being subjected, even to this small degree, to the despised 'Traffic'. The Superintendent of the Line, mighty official though he was, never even gained sole control of locomotive rostering to work his trains, but had to share the responsibility with the CME. It seems likely that it was Pole's inability to modernise GWR management that caused him to resign on 6 June 1929.

2

A square deal?

Pole was sorely distressed by the confused organisation he found on the GWR generally and in South Wales in particular, now that the GWR had taken over a lot of small companies as a result of the Grouping. Again, the time was ripe for some drastic reorganisation, as all these companies with their various methods had to be smoothly absorbed into the larger body.

On 4 May 1922 Pole proposed to the Directors that there should be a Cardiff Valleys Division comprising all the old Rhymney and Cardiff railways and parts of the Taff Vale, Barry and Alexandra Docks systems, with headquarters in Cardiff. He also proposed a Central Wales Division to control what

No 3266 Amyas, *an 1896-built 'Duke of Cornwall' Class locomotive, with carriages hardly any younger, on a train 'over the Alps' from Didcot to Southampton, running into Winchester on 20 May 1935. The train is short, even for this route, suggesting a lack of traffic for this particular service, while the lack of activity on the platform - apart from the Station Master greeting the train - seems to confirm this. A beautiful but unprofitable scene.*

All over the GWR from Afon Wen to Yealmpton similar situations existed. The railways had been built when money and enthusiasm were available; by the time they became outdated, enthusiasm for railways (as investments) had passed and modernisation was very difficult. The more outdated the railways became the less profitable they were, and the more enthusiastic the railway enthusiasts became! (H. C. Casserley)

'Metro' Class 2-4-0T No 1499 of 1899 at Marlborough High Level with the branch passenger train on 23 May 1929. The 15-lever signal box dated from 1892 and was taken out of use on 17 July 1933 when the ex-M&SWJR station and route took over the functions of the GWR station and branch. The branch locomotive's headlamp is in the 'J' position for a slow, loose-coupled freight, but perhaps it was placed in its proper position for a local passenger train - at the base of the chimney - before the train started. (H. C. Casserley)

had been the Cambrian Railways. These new Divisions he intended to become true Divisions, decentralised and autonomous, prototypes for the way he intended to re-organise the entire Great Western, but nothing came of this until 1938.

The conservative and unimaginative management

The locomotive 'runs round' its brake-van at Marlborough High Level - although the van appears to have been left 'foul' of the loop line. The ex-M&SWJR tracks can be glimpsed on the right with that company's staff housing 'semi' marking the site of the Low Level station.

The cost of keeping two establishments running was well known to the GWR but nothing could be done to improve the situation until the Company obtained the permission of the landowner, the Marquis of Ailesbury. Circa 1925. (Clinker Collection, courtesy Brunel University)

men in South and Central Wales infuriated Pole, who wrote of them:

> '"Live" men are not very conspicuous among them and it would be best to remove them. Compensation would be cheap compared with the cost of keeping inefficient Officers.'

In tandem with the increasing depression of trade came the rise of road motor competition which provided a cheap transport service of a relatively local nature – 30 to 50 miles – at first, but which rapidly took on long-distance haulage from 1924 as roads and lorries improved.

Economies in railway running costs had to be made – but this had to be done without giving large offence to the local population. In the God-fearing 'Eastern' and 'Western Valleys' lines of South Wales – from Newport to Pontypool (Crane Street) and Blaenavon, and from Newport to Bargoed and Dowlais Top respectively – the GWR was, in 1921, rashly running a Sunday train service when the LMS sensibly did not. The GWR Sunday service cost £23 more to run than was gained in revenue, and was withdrawn from 1 January 1922. It was, however, later restored.

As another example, Worle station on the Weston-super-Mare loop was closed completely on 1 January 1922. No freight traffic was dealt with there and the passengers could be dealt with at Puxton, 1¼ miles east, or at Weston-super-Mare, 2

miles westwards. Takings at the station for the 12 months ended September 1921 had amounted to £468, while the salary of the Station Master – the only man employed – and the cost of clothing and stores came to £330; when rates on the station were taken into account, the place operated at a complete loss.

In addition, a number of halts were closed during the war and were not re-opened; it was also decided to close Brook Street, Rhos, and Wynn Hall, Pant, on the Rhos branch and use their materials elsewhere. Indeed, throughout the Depression years, as halts were closed at uneconomic sites, others, using second-hand materials, were erected elsewhere to make it easier for the GWR's potential customers to get on trains.

From 2 January 1917 ordinary 10-ton open wagons became 'common user' and covered vans were 'pooled' from 3 March 1919. The GWR was not pleased with the arrangement, forced on it by government regulations, for whilst the Company's officers could appreciate the advantage of 'pooling' – the reduction in shunting because each company's wagons were no longer sorted and returned – they felt even more strongly, just as Brunel had felt in 1838, that GWR wagons ought not to be mixed with those from other companies. Pooling would be disadvantageous to the GWR because of 'the high standard of Great Western stock compared with that of other Companies'.

In 1922, therefore, the GWR gave notice to the

Bradford-on-Avon, a town of declining textile industry, photographed in 1939. The Brunellian goods shed in the left middle distance is no 'toytown' architecture, but a sympathetic addition to a mediaeval foreground. Very sadly, Brunellian good taste and GWR gentlemanliness was no cure for a declining local economy and no match for its competitors, running on their government-subsidised roads. (John Pepler FRPS/Adrian Vaughan Collection)

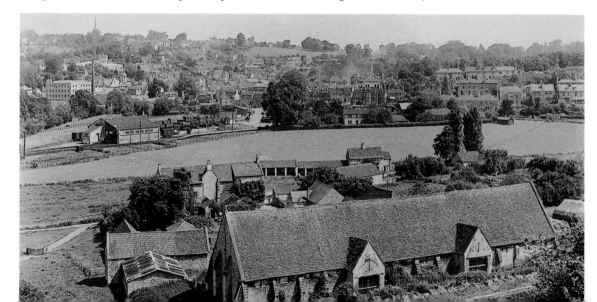

The terminus of the 6½-mile Dauntsey-Malmesbury branch, opened on 17 December 1877 with 1840s 'Brunel-style' architecture and unchanged in any significant way until since then. In 1925 the line earned a gross income of £20,295 and cost £8,552 to run - 42 per cent of the income. At that time there were seven round trips per day, all conveying passenger and freight vehicles with the main traffic being bacon, grain, hay, milk and cattle outwards, roadstone, coal and feedstuff inwards: 68,040 cans of milk and 139 trucks of cattle were dispatched during 1925. Milk churns on the platform and 'Siphons' in the siding testify to the traffic. The nearest wagon on the right carries pressurised cylinders of gas, proving that the branch train at this time consisted on gas-lit 19th-century (and possibly Four-wheeled) carriages.

The GWR considered the use of a steam railmotor to replace the locomotive and coaches and also considered running it as a 'light railway', but nothing was done. The 'South Wales Direct' line opened from Wootton Bassett to Patchway in 1903, crossing above the Malmesbury branch just west of Little Somerford station. From 17 July 1933 the branch was diverted up into this station and the 2¾ miles of track to Dauntsey was closed to traffic, although retained for some distance for wagon storage. (Clinker Collection/courtesy Brunel University)

Railway Clearing House that it would withdraw from the pooling system. This would, however, have brought about the collapse of the entire system, and very strong pressure was brought to bear on the Company. As a result, the GWR reluctantly agreed to allow its high-quality wagons to be used on 'foreign' lines and to take in exchange the inferior wagons of 'other lines'. As the Depression of trade deepened, the grand old GWR snobbery died and by 1929 the Company was downright anxious to merge its wagon fleet with other railways in money-saving 'pooling' arrangements.

Meanwhile, Felix Pole tried to 'sell' the American idea of large-capacity coal trucks. He wanted the collieries to use 20-ton steel trucks and offered a 5 per cent reduction in his charges to any colliery that would take up the idea. The use of 20-tonners would benefit the railway by:

1 A reduction in the number of wagons to be handled
2 Less dead-weight to be hauled

3 At least 10 per cent less shunting required, and
4 A saving of 35 per cent of the present siding accommodation for the wagon fleet.

The GWR was so keen to make these large savings that on 8 October 1925 not only did it promise the 5 per cent reduction in rates to any colliery using 20-ton coal wagons, but the Company took out of circulation 200 10-ton wagons from the Tredegar Associated Collieries fleet by hiring them at 5s 6d per wagon per week in the hope that the collieries would replace the little wooden tubs with the steel 20-tonners.

The wooden 10-tonners were re-hired to the Cornish china-clay companies, where there was a shortage of wagons. One hundred went to Toyne Carter & Co and 100 to Hannen Samuel & Co, all at 6 shillings per wagon per day. But having got the wagons to the clay works it was discovered that some of them were too high to go under the shoots at the clay drying plants, and the GWR was left with a lot of useless 10-ton tubs - representing a

potential income of £1,555 per annum – and made
a loss of £978 on the deal. However, the Company
was not downhearted as the Tredegar Collieries did
indeed hire 100 GWR 20-tonners and, being
impressed with the savings they made, placed an
order for 100 more to be built as 'Private Owner'.

The Company had not only the cost of maintaining its vast network of rolling-stock, rail-roads, stations, signalling and other fixed plant and buildings,
but it was also encumbered with paying rates to each
parish through which its line passed.

The Great Western's rates bill in 1925 was a sum
equivalent to 1 per cent of the annual dividend paid
to ordinary shareholders. Since a lot of the money
paid as rates went towards the upkeep of roads for
the benefit of the GWR's competitors, the
Company was not best pleased, and waged a
vigourous campaign of pamphlets against this unfair
governmental bias in favour of its road motor competitors.

In 1926 the GWR published a play by Hugh
Mytton, who worked in the Estate Surveyor's office
at Paddington. The action took place in the house
of a certain 'Colonel Rallaway – also known as
'Squire Western' or the 'Great Squire' (get it?) –
who lived in a vast house with his housekeeper, Mrs
Britain. The Squire's appearance was, according to
the parable, 'strangely contradictory', for, with all his
characteristics of vigorous youth, his face was lined
and had the look of profound care.

The play opens with him telling Mrs Britain to
prepare to live without him because he can no
longer afford to keep up his vast establishment, and
warning her of the serious consequences for the village of his departure, since he is the major employer.
At this point a deputation of villagers arrives at the
door demanding an interview. They are ushered
into the Squire's presence where they somewhat

rudely demand that he pay an even greater contribution to the local rates.

'Why should I?' asks the Squire. 'What do your
rates do for me? My house isn't even in your parish.
It is true my drive runs within your boundaries but
it is more than two miles from your village and you
do not pay for its repair.'

He offers to pay the same as the highest-rated vil-
lage trader – £26 – but the villagers are horrified.
The total sum to be raised is £3,788 and the Great
Squire has always paid £3,236 of this.

The example used in the play was taken from real
life – and there were plenty of places where plain
line, without so much as a signal on it, passed
through the fields of a parish, remote from the village, and yet the GWR had to pay, typically, 80 per
cent of local rates. Whilst the local rates made no
financial contribution whatsoever to the upkeep of
the railway, in 1920-21 £30,157,683 from the total
of money raised (from all sources) for local rates
went into the upkeep of local roads.

A fascinating feature of the play is to learn how
the Directors of the Great Western Railway saw
themselves and their Company in relation to the rest
of the country. Many of them were aristocrats, and
all of them possessed well-run country estates surrounded by their obedient, loyal and long-serving
staff.

The GWR kept up its campaign for some relief
from rating and in 1928 their assessment was
reduced by Act of Parliament. Its contribution to
the rates fell from £1,529,000 in 1927 to £734,000
by 31 March 1937, but the difference had to be
applied to a reduction of freight rates. In addition,
the duty payable on passenger tickets sold was abolished in the April 1929 Budget, but this again was
conditional on the saving being used to make
improvements such as building new stations.

3

Against the odds

The Company's working expenses had increased annually, without a break, since at least 1850. In 1890, 51.56 per cent was spent on running the business - this was first year that expenses had exceeded 50 per cent of gross revenue - and by 1912 working costs swallowed 64 per cent of income. In 1913 the staff took 40 per cent of income and the shareholders 22 per cent.

In 1923 staff wages took 60 per cent of the Company's income and the shareholders' took 10 per cent. The total pay-out to the shareholders in that year was £3,612,605, the total paid to all staff being £21,700,000, a sum equal to the Company's gross revenue from 1 January to 31 August. The railway's fixed charges - rents, rates, interest repayments - swallowed the next two months' income and the shareholders got the income of the last two months of the year. This was, however, at a time of declining revenue; although passenger travel increased in 1923 and 8 per cent more passenger trains were run, freight traffic declined, and at the end of 1923 the GWR was £784,000 worse off than in 1922.

In spite of this, the Company still paid a dividend to its Ordinary shareholders of 7½ per cent when the real figure, according to earnings, was 5 per cent, the balance being made up from the Company's savings and from interest on investments.

Because of this shortage of income and the need to maintain a reasonable dividend, the buildings, communications, locomotives and rolling-stock of the railway were not replaced or renewed as they ought to have been. Some new engines and carriages were, of course, being built every year, and plans were made for enlarging and rebuilding stations, but the amount of money available for replacements and maintenance was less each year as profits declined. The Company did its best to maintain a good standard, but did so at the expense of the dividend - and if the dividend was lower than could be obtained elsewhere, why should anyone, following their own best interest in the approved manner, invest their money in the GWR?

The railway was fighting for its life and without a thorough modernisation this was a battle that could not be won. The *Great Western Railway Magazine* carried an article in 1926 part of which stated that:

'£800,000,000★ of new money is needed for the railways if they are to employ the same number of men in 1956 and 1926 - but where is this money to come from? No-one can be forced to supply capital so it is in the interests of staff to give fair play to shareholders.'

In January 1926 an article in the GWR staff magazine invited the employees to:

★ This sum was for *all* British railways. Some idea of its enormity can be attained from the fact that a 'Castle' Class locomotive cost £6,700 in 1926, while in 1992 a mainline express locomotive costs £2m, almost 300 times more.

'. . .assist by all means to increase the efficiency of the railway. Remember – road hauliers are not common carriers like the railway but can pick and choose traffic and devote themselves to that which is most remunerative.'

The cry was then, and for many years to come, 'GET TRAFFIC'!

The Great Western most certainly gave fair play to the population it served and kept open many loss-making lines and a lot more which barely paid their way. Some very minor lines lost their passenger service in the 1920s – Camerton to Limpley Stoke was reduced to a goods line on 21 September 1925 – but the Dinas Mawddy line, which in 1925 had an income of £4,357 against an expenditure of £4,653, kept its passenger service in spite of the Assistant Superintendent of the Line's 1925 recommendation to 'close it and save £4,653'. The Company kept it running until 1 January 1931 when, in the depths of the Depression, the passenger service was eventually withdrawn leaving one goods train a day, reduced to one every other day by 1937.

Another great loss-maker was the 7-mile-long 'branch off a branch' from Titley Junction in remotest Herefordshire to Eardisley Junction on the LMS, also in remotest Herefordshire. This line had an income of £2,500 and an expenditure of £4,000 in 1925. The Assistant Superintendent of the Line recommended closure but the line carried passenger and goods trains until 1 July 1940 when it closed for

ever. The branch from Abermule to Kerry retained its passenger service until 9 February 1931, and the Yealmpton branch, which lost its passenger service from 7 July 1930, is discussed in the chapter on road transport.

The greatest loss was made by the very inaptly named 'Golden Valley' line, nearly 19 miles long, from Pontrilas to Hay – this had an income of £7,805 in 1925 and an expenditure of £11,631. The line was recommended for closure but it retained a remarkably good passenger service until 15 December 1941 and retained its goods train until 2 February 1953.

The GWR had a legal duty to maintain services but it could, perhaps, have obtained permission to close these tiny branch lines suffering such large losses. However, that course was not pursued and in order to subsidise loss-makers the Company had to spare no effort in the struggle to raise revenue and reduce costs.

If it is remarkable that the GWR did not reduce its costs by obtaining Parliamentary sanction for closures, neither did it adopt ruthless attitudes towards old-established or fledging businesses which really did depend on rail transport and would thus have no power of opposition.

The men who directed the GWR, it seems to me, did not see the GWR as a thing apart, to make its profit without reference to those from whom the profit was being made. They saw the railway as part of the community – the financial health of the

A branch line survivor - the Lambourn branch train at the terminus in 1936. The locomotive is a Dubs 2-4-0 built for the Midland & South Western Junction Railway in 1894 and re-boilered by the GWR in 1924. The carriages date from about 1900. There appears to be a 'Siphon' truck at the rear. (C. R. L. Coles)

Heavy freight over long distances was the best paying traffic on the railway - heavy iron and minerals for instance. Unfortunately these industries were in decline between 1921 and 1939 and therefore so were the Company's takings. Operating costs rose while collieries and steelworks were reluctant to invest in larger-capacity wagons with better bearing lubrication.

Larger wagons meant fewer wagons, less shunting, less maintenance. The GWR set a fairly unheeded example by carrying much of its locomotive coal in 20-ton steel tubs. Here nearly new 'Grange' No 6820 hauls a long rake of 10-ton and 12-ton wooden coal tubs and GWR 20-tonners, empty, west of Patchway en route for South Wales in 1938. (G. H. Soole/Adrian Vaughan Collection)

GWR depended on the financial health of the nation's businesses, so, I think, the GWR Directors thought that it was better to be merciful towards customers in times of difficulty in order to assist everyone through to easier times when the increased custom could be, they hoped, retained.

A Development Officer was appointed to sell GWR services, and amongst his more unusual successes was turning the unprofitable rural charm of the Limpley Stoke-Camerton line to profitable use during 1931 when it was hired to a company who were making a film, *The Ghost Train*. The film company also filmed at Bramley, on the Reading-Basingstoke line, and on Barmouth swingbridge. The GWR earned £800.

Much more important was the Development Officer's work with industrialists in bringing factories to the lineside industrial estates that the GWR was creating in the vicinity of Slough - Citroen Cars, the St Martin's Preserving Co and the St Helens Cable & Rubber Co of Warrington came to new factories on the trading estate early in 1923. Firms moving into factory units here paid the GWR for the lease of the land but they did not necessarily have to send their produce out by rail. The GWR General Manager reported that 'it is not possible to say what traffic will pass by rail but we are watching the situation.' Ultimately, the St Martins jam concern and the St Helens Cable & Rubber Co were induced by the Development Officer to use 100 per cent rail transport instead of 100 per cent road as they had originally intended.

The British Sugar Corporation opened rail-connected beet-processing factories at Kidderminster and Yeovil. The Kidderminster factory, sited alongside the Bewdley line, was brought into use on 6 December 1925 and by the 31st the GWR had carried 22,844 tons of beet for £9,652.

During 1924 passenger traffic and general merchandise traffic increased; for instance, on the Didcot-Winchester and Lambourn branches the Sunday milk trains were reinstated in November 1924 after a petition from local farmers. However, heavy freight, the greatest revenue earner, went into a severe decline. This was due to many causes, some of them in far-away countries. The demand for iron and steel was drastically reduced at the end of the war, which reduced the demand for fuel. The Royal Navy, and other navies, once consumers of vast tonnages of best Welsh steam coal, were converting to oil-fired boilers.

The Central Electricity Generating Board, set up in 1923, began to build the 'National Grid' distribution network and began to close the many small generating stations, replacing them with far fewer, larger and more economical facilities. The National Grid distributed electricity to more and more people so that everyone, from the coal and steel industry to housewives, could use fuel-saving electrical appliances. The Grid was complete in 1933.

The resurgent European coal industry, its coal made cheaper by government subsidies, reduced the demand for unsubsidised Welsh coal. South Wales mine-owners, who had enjoyed a virtual monopoly of steam coal production before 1914 and who had been able to sell every ton their miners produced in those days, had not seen the need to improve their mining equipment below or above ground. Welsh miners laboriously hacked the coal out with pick and shovel without so much as a pit-head bath at the end of a shift. As was mentioned in the previous chapter, the mine-owners found it a revolutionary idea even to invest in 20-ton wagons to save their own costs and receive a rebate from the GWR. Welsh coal had become relatively expensive by 1924 and in October that year 50 South Wales collieries closed.

Whilst the GWR was trying to reduce its costs and increase it revenue, so was every other business in the land. In April 1923 all kinds of traders were badgering the Company for a reduction in carrying charges which, in relation to 1913 prices, seemed astronomically high. The Bank of England complained in July 1923 that the rates charged for gold bullion and specie carryings were too high – the GWR reduced them by 43 per cent to a figure which was still 80 per cent above that of 1913, but which lost the Company £3,200 per annum.

The Iron & Steel Federation received from the GWR a 12½ per cent reduction for coal, coke and limestone for chemical works and iron and steel-making, and demurrage charges were reduced in as much as the pre-war practise of a three-day free period was reverted to, making the railway wagon a sort of warehouse.

Newspaper owners also asked for a reduction and the GWR agreed to reduce the rate, losing the Company £2,750 per annum. On 11 October 1923 the coal-mining companies asked for their rates to be reduced to just one-third higher than they were in 1913, and Wiltshire and Berkshire farmers were looking for a reduction in milk charges. This traffic was very vulnerable to road competition and in order to retain it the GWR agreed to reduce the rate from 1.56d to 1.33d per gallon for those two counties, and in return all the Berkshire & Wiltshire Farmers Union agreed to do was to 'encourage' farmers to use the railway. Even the Sausage Manufacturers Association and the Cattle Cake lobby asked for and were given reductions.

The railways, the iron and coal industries and farming had been built for each other in the mid-19th century, and many GWR Directors were from those backgrounds, but there were now new indus-

tries with their lightweight products – electrical goods, gramophone records, ice-cream and cakes, or the emerging wholesale milk-processing industry – which did not need the railway. J. Lyons & Son and United Dairies (UD), for instance, held the threat of road haulage like a pistol at the GWR's corporate head. In 1926 the former company named its own rates and told the GWR that if it could not carry at those prices the traffic would go by road. The GWR bit the bullet and took the traffic - at the consignor's price.

Readers will not, I hope, be too greatly annoyed with me if I trespass briefly into the realm of wider economic history, for we have reached an event of the utmost importance to the fortunes of the Great Western Railway, and indeed the entire country.

There was financial and political instability in Europe and there existed in Britain a school of thought (a nostalgic hankering after the pre-war 'Golden Age') which believed that a return to the pre-war 'Gold Standard' would automatically bring back the supposed stability of that former era. Winston Churchill, as Chancellor of the Exchequer in Bonar Law's Government, advised by Montagu Norman, Governor of the Bank of England, had to make the decision. After much agonising about the amount of hardship the change would undoubtedly bring to the British population, Churchill took Norman's advice and in April 1925 attempted to produce stable rates of exchange by making a paper pound-note redeemable for gold, whilst setting the value of the pound sterling at $4.86.

Our former allies, the French and Belgians - who were already operating tariff barriers against British products - waited to see what the British rate would be, and with the rate fixed those wily governments then put themselves on the 'Gold Standard' at a much lower parity with the dollar, thus making their exports cheaper than the equivalent British product.

This monetary policy, combined with the British Government's continuing belief in Free Trade – there were to be no tariffs on cheap imports to protect British industry - was the major factor in the British decline up to 1929 when over-speculation in America and the collapse of the German economy in 1931 forced the devaluation of the pound by 'going off gold'. It is therefore against this background that the Great Western Railway struggled to survive.

4

Public service

In the 'Golden Age', pre-1914, traders requiring credit with the GWR had to provide a guarantee of their ability to pay, but after 1925 money became scarce and there arose a reluctance on the part of most traders to provide such guarantees, whilst they still asked the GWR for two months - and more than two months - credit.

The GWR had no choice but to comply with the wishes of its customers - credit had to be extended without the written guarantee as had been the pre-war practise. Large companies like the Ebbw Vale Iron & Steel Co and many much smaller firms were allowed to have a 'Ledger Account' whereby they got two months credit on their bills for railway haulage. Obviously the GWR did not like this, but there were competitors at the door, trade was not good and the Company was glad to get the tonnage and the potential revenue - and had to hope that the traders would pay. Needless to say, the GWR began to experience 'cash-flow' problems.

In 1928 the GWR carried 40,000 tons of steel between Guest, Keen & Baldwin's Landore works and the Earl of Dudley's works at Round Oak. In April 1929 Baldwin's informed the GWR that unless the Company could carry their Landore factory's output to Round Oak at a cheaper rate, they would be obliged to close the Landore works and buy the steel for Round Oak 'locally'.

Rather than lose the revenue on this tonnage the GWR agreed to give a 6d (2½p) per ton rebate provided that Baldwin's increased their rail cargoes to 50,000 tons a year; furthermore, the railway would grant an additional 2d a ton on any quantity over 50,000. Baldwin's sent 50,560 tons of steel by GWR and were duly granted a £1,268 rebate; but when, in 1931, Baldwin's South Wales rail-borne output of iron and steel fell below the qualifying minimum for a rate rebate, the GWR continued to give the discount 'in view of the exceptional difficulties through which the iron and steel industry is passing - it is not Baldwin's fault but due to the depression of trade'. The GWR Directors knew that for every ton of steel produced, 6 to 7 tons of coal and other materials had to be taken, by rail, to the steelworks, so it was a matter of concern to the GWR than 'their' iron and steel industry was prosperous.

In January 1930 three of the five blast furnaces at the Ebbw Vale ironworks were shut down, losing 200,000 tons of steel output in a full year - a terrific loss to the GWR. In October one of the four blast furnaces at the Earl of Dudley's Round Oak works was closed. Simultaneously, Midlands motor car and other engineering works were importing annually increasing tonnages of foreign iron and steel - because it was cheaper. In December 1930 14,500 tons of Belgian metal were carried by the GWR from Newport docks to Birmingham.

There were close personal friendships between Directors of the GWR and the owners of the big steelworks and collieries, but the GWR could be just as helpful to 'strangers', newcomers to the transport market. When in November 1932 the newly formed *Compagnie Nantaise de Navigation Vapeur* wanted to open a steamer service from Nantes and Brest to Weymouth for fruit, eggs, farm produce

Bulk traffic requiring little or no intermediate marshalling between point of origin and destination was profitable. This scene at Bodmin (GWR) shows china clay waiting to leave for the main line at Bodmin Road on 23 May 1935. The leading engine is No 4508. (H. C. Casserley)

and general merchandise, the Great Western agreed reduced rates for their traffic to enable the fledgling company to become established. In 1932 the Cornish and Scilly Isles flower-growers wanted to set up a bulb-growing research unit, similar to units already in use in Europe, and asked the GWR for a donation. The Company agreed to contribute a sum equivalent to 6d for every 112 lbs of flowers put on rail from West Cornish stations.

But what was really needed was not flowers but massive tonnages in bulk – that was what the railway did best, and contracts for bulk loads of all kinds were eagerly sought. Every month the General Manager reported the latest coup to his Directors, where the GWR had 'secured to rail' some contract for moving freight 'in spite of active road competition' – but this was done only by cutting the rail freight charge to the bone.

A couple of china clay bulk-load trains from Bodmin Moor to the docks at Fowey in St Blazey goods yard, circa 1925. The yard was built by the Cornwall Mineral Railway, and is liberally coated with the dust of its traffic. The route to Par and the main line diverges on the left, the Cornwall Mineral Railway wagon repair shops are in the centre and the old CMR engine shed is on right. (Clinker Collection/courtesy Brunel University)

The GWR would even undercut water transport costs to take a contract. In October 1929 a pair of 15-inch naval guns, 54 feet long and weighing 84 tons each, were made at Elswick, Newcastle-upon-Tyne, for a Chilean battleship being overhauled at Devonport dockyard, Plymouth. The LNER and GWR co-operated to quote a lower rate - and faster service - than by sea; the GWR's share of the revenue was £703.

In January 1930 the Oxford & Shipton Cement Co at their rail-connected works at Bletchington had to move 40,000 tons of cement powder to Lancashire. The GWR undercut road hauliers' and canal prices and took the contract. In 1931 cheap rates enabled the GWR to carry the entire 12,000-ton output of raw sugar from the Allscott sugar beet factory to Tate & Lyle's in Liverpool for £2,500.

The increasing demand for roadstone did put more traffic on to rail from quarries as far apart as Blaenau Ffestiniog and Cranmore, but the tonnage carried by rail was by no means what it ought to have been. In 1930 45 per cent of the output of the Somersetshire quarries went by road - even though the quarries were rail-connected. The problem was that the rail connections were not such that GWR trains could run over them, so the quarry owner had the extra cost of transferring loads from his rail system to the GWR and then from the GWR to the road at the end of the journey. The road lorry, puny though it then was, was a more convenient means of transport than rail for nearly half the output, and a large investment was needed if the GWR was to capture more of the traffic. The Company did not make the investment.

The GWR's search for bulk loads did much to assist the burgeoning motor manufacturing industry, not only by carrying its products cheaply but also by selling land for its factories and carrying its workers on cheap tickets. Cheap rates captured the contract for moving Morris cars from the Cowley factory to Scotland. A combined GWR/LMS team persuaded the Austin Car Company in Birmingham to put their London- and Scotland-bound products on rail. The railway also carried petrol in four-wheel tankers and supplied space on which the petrol company could build storage tanks; the petrol store at Reading Central Goods station was opened early in 1931.

Another 'growth' area for the GWR was the conveyance of motor cars through the Severn tunnel from Pilning to Severn Tunnel Junction. Motorists simply arrived at the station and drove on to a flat truck which was attached to the next down passenger train to stop at the station.

The Great Western saw that it had to compete with the road haulier's door-to-door service and so went into the motorised distribution business. The technique used was the 'bulking' system, which required the goodwill and co-operation of the factory. As early as 1924 the Company had made deals with McFarlane, Lang & Co, the biscuit manufacturers, and Hill, Evans & Co, the vinegar manufacturers, in Worcester. These firms agreed to make up their packages for a district; the GWR then collected them, loaded them into rail box vans and carried them to the designated railhead for that district. From there the GWR undertook to break up the bulk package and deliver individual packages by road to their multitudinous destinations. Many more 'bulking' agreements followed, and out of this came in January 1927 the first GWR removable containers on their flat trucks.

Any firm could have a container, load it with their multifarious packages and send it off to a distant railhead where the GWR would deliver the entire container to a single destination - or cart the container around a single town, dropping off the packages at the various retailers. More railhead distribution centres were established by the GWR, which erected a standard design of pre-fabricated concrete warehouse. This policy was assisted by the Local Government Act of 1929 whereby the railway obtained a rates reduction on buildings, provided that the money saved was spent on reducing freight rates.

Household removals by rail were also made easier by the use of the container. What was obviously required by the public, be they private individuals moving house or a firm making biscuits, was overnight door-to-door transport without breakages - a container carried by lorry and fast freight train was the answer to this need. In the year ended 30 June 1928 the Company had carried 4,500 tons by container for an income of £12,338, and this was secured in the teeth of fierce competition from the road hauliers. The only revenue which increased annually throughout the Depression years and beyond was that derived from container traffic and that other GWR invention, the 'Green Arrow' registered overnight wagon-load transit introduced in March 1928.

The number of factories using the road-rail container system increased from 43 in January 1930 to

Same-day delivery - loading parcels traffic and mails at Paddington in 1937. (C. R. L. Coles)

78 by April of that year, and the Company's entire stock of 828 containers was in constant and full employment in spite of the deepening depression of trade. During 1930 a total of 56,000 tons was carried by container for a revenue of £112,874, roughly a 25 per cent increase on 1929.

An interesting agreement was made in March 1931 between the Great Western and Imperial Airways whereby the GWR established 36 railway centres to which GWR road lorries could bring urgent parcels for rail-borne delivery via Paddington and Victoria to Imperial Airways at Croydon for destinations worldwide. Packages from abroad would be distributed by the GWR in the same way. The three-year agreement specifically forbade Imperial Airways from employing other than rail-way-owned road transport.

More of these profitable container services were required, but this demanded more vacuum-braked freight wagons running on oil-lubricated axleboxes (instead of the traditional slower-moving wagons lubricated with 'yellow fat') and greater numbers of more powerful locomotives. The investment required was considerable and the Company's income was declining, but the GWR did all it could and the number of express freight trains was increased until there were 75 such trains daily, or nightly, by 1935. Fresh vegetables and milk, 'door-to-door' container traffic, whether factory products or household removals, the carriage of motor cars

and petrol - the trains' speed and reliability was unsurpassed by any railway in the world.

Thus, with income declining and costs rising throughout the 1930s, the Great Western was forced to become more efficient through careful management and better methods - its locomotives were operated with greater economy than any railway in Britain. A great deal of money was indeed saved, but not enough to keep pace with rising costs; far too little was put by for 'Renewals', and the dividend to shareholders was roughly half, in the 1930s, of what it had been in the 1920s - and the dividends during 1930-34 were only kept up by raiding reserves and selling investments.

In January 1931 the miners struck and no coal at all was shipped at South Wales ports; with uncertain supplies, consumers had to look elsewhere. The Buenos Aires Electricity Company, which had bought 990,000 tons of Welsh coal annually, placed an order for only 330,000 tons in South Wales and bought the rest from Germany. The Brazilian State Railways' annual contract for 75,000 tons of Welsh coal went in 1933, for the first time, to the Ruhr in exchange for Brazilian coffee.

The economic situation in Britain became so bad in 1931 that loans had to be sought from French and American bankers, but these gentlemen would only help if the Labour Government of Ramsay MacDonald could reduce government spending - which meant reducing welfare payments to the unemployed. The Labour Government was split on this in August, there was an election, and a 'National' or coalition government of Conservatives and Labour was formed with MacDonald as Prime Minister.

Britain abandoned the 'Gold Standard' on 21 September, reducing by 10 per cent the value of the pound against the dollar, making credit in Britain cheaper and more freely available. British exports then became easier to sell while the 'cheap money' permitted an investment in new business. The change in policy took some time to improve the utterly dire situation, but the psychological effect was immediate - a feeling of enormous relief amongst businessmen.

In October the GWR's General Manager, Sir James Milne, reported happily that:

'As an indication of the developments which are taking place since the abandonment of the Gold Standard and in anticipation of the lowering of the bank lending rate to 2%, 44 applications have been received for factory sites attached to this Company. Eight of these are from continental firms.'

In November the ancient policy of Free Trade was abandoned and tariffs were imposed against imports, but that same month the General Manager reported to the Directors that a cargo of 2,341 tons of aluminium from Canada had been landed at Manchester, the largest such cargo ever to arrive in Britain. It was taken by rail to Cropredy, the GWR's share of the revenue being £1,425.

The newly formed multi-national company Unilever began to import cattle cake into Avonmouth and in November made an agreement with the GWR and LMS whereby the two railway companies took responsibility for the distribution within a radius of 70 miles of the docks for an average rate, irrespective of distance. The railways took cargoes out by rail to depots where their own lorries distributed to farms within a 10-mile radius. Some 34,000 tons of cattle cake were to be landed annually, for the distribution of which the companies were to receive £15,000.

On 17 December Milne was able to report a further 48 inquiries for sites on the Slough and Park Royal trading estates, and the recommencement of work at various factories, tin mines and coal mines. The list was very long and included the news that Baldwin's had re-lit blast furnaces at Cardiff and Port

Talbot, a knitting factory in Liskeard had re-started, the Gramophone Co at Hayes was working overtime, the Bowson Seam, the richest in the Forest of Dean coalfield, unworked for 20 years, had re-opened, and the Swiss firm Nestlé had begun to enlarge its Hayes factory. Welsh coal was more competitive in price against French and Belgian coal than it had been for six years.

But this list of improvements was given simply as a reason for feeling optimistic about the future - the Great Western's immediate financial position was still deteriorating. At the end of 1931 takings were £2,682,000 less than in 1930, but by selling investments and drawing on savings the Company paid 3½ per cent to holders of GWR Ordinary shares - the second-highest dividend to be paid until the final pay-out in 1948.

The year 1932 was the worst of the Depression, but at least it could only get better from that low point - all except the coal export trade. Milne reported on 17 March of that year that with a lower exchange rate between the pound and other currencies, and Welsh coal beginning once more to flow to France, the French Government had imposed a 15 per cent tariff on all imported coal along with a restriction on the tonnage which could be imported.

There was some small comfort in the unusual fact that Cuba had bought 50,000 tons of Welsh coal and Baldwins had re-lit four blast furnaces at Landore. Thirty-three coke ovens in Brymbo steel works were re-lit for the first time in four years, and in 1934 the Brymbo steel rolling-mills began work, giving the GWR 600 tons a week.

At the other end of the scale, a new carpet factory was opened in Kidderminster - and the Shakespeare Memorial theatre was opened in Stratford-on-Avon in April. Two more firms joined the GWR's 'bulking' scheme in April, making 159 firms in all, and the GWR's 'Country lorry' service was enlarged to a fleet of 142 vehicles. In October 1932 Morris Motors agreed to put the whole of its London docks export traffic on the GWR, traffic worth £3,500 per annum.

During 1933 the output of the iron and steel industry increased by 20 per cent, engineering and shipbuilding by 7 per cent, and the average increase throughout the economy was 5.8 per cent. In the first half of 1933 the GWR's income was £576,000 less than in the same period of 1932, but in the second half income rose dramatically so that for the whole year gross income was 'only' £38,687 less than the appallingly bad previous year. The Great

Western Chairman found this encouraging as the trend in the second half was upwards.

The net income for 1933 was £4,828,561, an *increase* of £369,158 over 1932. The result would have been better but for losses in the GWR's (non) coal-exporting docks on the South Wales coast; indeed, internal coal traffic was depressed - coal revenue in 1933 was £84,000 less than 1932.

The Great Western's method of increasing revenue was to see where they could cut fares and freight rates and thus encourage more traffic on to the line, but to do this they required the approval of the Railway Rates Tribunal (RRT). On 27 February 1934 the Great Western went to the RRT with requests to lower rates in order to secure contracts with certain traders and manufacturers. The Road Hauliers Association contested the reductions, but after hearing the evidence the Tribunal gave judgement in favour of the GWR on 23 March. The GWR General Manager rejoiced and reported that 'The new powers now enjoyed will be of the greatest assistance to the Company in meeting road competition.'

The greatest assistance was certainly needed. On 22 June 1934 the Railway Rates Tribunal held its 6th Annual Review in accordance with the 1921 Railways Act to assess the railway companies' financial situation, to see if they were managed efficiently, to see if they were over or undercharging, and to see if they had earned the 'Standard Revenue' to which they were entitled under the terms of the Act.

The Tribunal concluded that the railways were run most fairly and most efficiently, that they had not overcharged and that they had not earned the revenue to which they were entitled; the GWR's net earnings were found to be £3,638,000 less than they ought to have been. At the next review, in 1936, the deficiency was found to be £2,151.730.

The 1934 deficiency was not the result of inefficiency, said the Tribunal, but because of the railway companies' enormous 'overheads', the depression of trade and high unemployment, which reduced spending, and the Government's trade war with the Irish Republic. The most important of the factors, perhaps, was the intense competition from the road hauliers, who enjoyed the enormous advantage of running on public roads for which they did not pay their full share of the costs of maintenance. And, as has already been noted, a proportion of this maintenance was paid by the railway companies in the form of parochial rates.

5
Conservatism and innovation

In January 1935 the British Government agreed to relax its trade war with Ireland and to permit the exchange of British coal for Irish cattle. The GWR General Manager, noting this, warned his Officers to prepare to receive and transport 150,000 head of cattle annually from Fishguard and Milford Haven to English cities by cattle train 'specials'.

To attract freight traffic more 'overnight' deliveries were organised and more express freight trains were scheduled to run, and to run over longer distances: two vacuum-fitted goods trains from Acton to Llanelly were extended to Carmarthen and Neyland to improve the 'overnight' freight service into furthest Wales for cattle and other important perishable traffic.

In 1935 there were 75 express freights, most of them fully vacuum-braked ('C' headcode) running at average speeds of 40-45 mph, but also included in this total were some partly vacuum-braked ('D' headcode) and accelerated, non-fitted ('E' headcode) freights. More fast freights were put on in 1936.

Firms who could supply one or more full wagonloads each night were quoted specially low rates to secure their traffic to rail: Woolworths' traffic was captured by the GWR for a sum equal to 4.25 per cent of the retail value of the goods conveyed, and Crosse & Blackwell took all their produce off the road and on to rail after making a similar deal.

A similar policy directed passenger traffic. Main-line express passenger trains were accelerated, and their numbers increased. Cheap fares were issued at certain stations to encourage local 'commuter' travel and cheap excursion trains were run to all kinds of events. The Divisional Superintendents' officers kept a sharp eye on the calendar and supplied excursion trains for the seaside and to public entertainments of all kinds.

As the competition from the roads became tougher and the Company's net profit declined, so the operation became ever more efficient and its train services improved until the GWR was the most cost-effective railway in Britain, and the total of its express train services had the best average speed in Britain. This result required great care in management and great loyalty from the staff in carrying out the work effectively. It also took careful co-ordination and control from a central guiding body, and even then the financial results barely kept pace with the losses caused by a leakage of traffic to the roads.

The GWR innovation (March 1929) of the already mentioned 'Green Arrow' service - registered packages or wagons by freight train - carried, in the whole of 1935, 135,821 packages. In December 1935 the system was extended to carry registered parcels by passenger trains - the 'Blue Arrow' service. At the same time the GWR introduced its 'Cash on Delivery' (COD) service for mail-order firms and others who had put their goods on rail. This followed the successful introduction of COD by the Post Office. The GWR van driver collected the money due on the item and the GWR remitted the money to the sender less a small fee: for a value of up to 10 shillings, the fee was 6d; up to £1 it was 8d, and so on.

From mid-1935 the British Government decided

to re-arm in the face of the growing military threat from Nazi Germany. Re-armament required more steelmaking plants to be brought back into use – a new steel works was built at Ebbw Vale. Old collieries were re-opened and 49 new airfields were planned, eight of them in GWR territory. This activity brought an increased demand for coal, iron and steel – and workers – so GWR revenues received a welcome boost. In one month, December 1936, the GWR delivered 5,500 tons of fuel and construction materials to those eight airfields.

Also in 1935 Welsh steam coal and anthracite exports began to rise from their all-time lows. The trade in anthracite to Canada, which totalled 1,291,000 tons in 1934, was expected to increase in 1935 with the opening of an anthracite mine, 1,500 feet deep, near Llanelly. The GWR expected to receive 1,500 tons a day from this by 1937.

The number of people earning wages was increasing so there was an increase in demand for all kinds of goods; for example, more people could afford to burn coal fires at home, and it is recorded in GWR records that the demand for house coal rose. General freight carrying also increased, as did passenger travel. However, while revenue increased there was still a price to be paid through increased costs in wages and wear and tear, so some portion of the extra revenues earned were lost. Both income and expenditure continued to rise throughout 1936 as the GWR gained more traffic from improved industrial production, and enthusiastic Great Western traffic canvassers worked like bees to gather in extra work.

Some redundant staff were set to work as 'canvassers' and in March 1936 the Superintendents' meeting suggested that some canvassers ought to be supplied with motor cars! Selected men were put through a course of driving instruction and in October ten Ford Popular cars were purchased at £88 15s each and allocated to canvassers: Bristol and Birmingham, two each, Exeter, Penzance, Gloucester, Worcester, Newport and Swansea, one each.

The Superintendents' Meeting Minute 11711 of 22 October 1936 stated:

'As the majority of the representatives have only just passed their driving test . . . the Superintendents must impress upon the men that the cars are not insured for anything but GWR business and also that they are required to drive carefully and avoid endorsements to licence.'

The car-less canvassers got round their territory by pony and trap – or Shanks's pony – as they always had done, but still they secured large tonnages of traffic for their Company. But the GWR did not rely on its official canvassers – all GWR staff were expected to go out and get traffic. One official directive said:

'Many stations are lacking in energy in this respect. Competition with the road for race horse traffic, cattle, and general merchandise is keen and canvassers should report all traffic secured – or lost – to rail.'

The Great Western was in deadly earnest in its intent to beat the road hauliers. A GWR employee who was discovered secretly assisting road haulage interests in his district was dismissed for treachery. Everyone, from drayman to Director, was expected to bring business to the railway and, indeed, money prizes were given, to carters in particular, for initiative in getting traffic or zeal in reporting firms who were seen to be using road transport when hitherto the traffic had gone by rail.

An example of this was the Chinnor cement works which up to July 1936 had put most of its traffic on rail, but in that month GWR spies reported to Paddington that a road haulier had been seen 'in the office' – doubtless offering tempting terms. The GWR Goods Agent from High Wycombe was at the works next day and by dropping the rail rate from 4s 6d to 4 shillings per ton – provided that each wagon carried not less than 6 tons – he retained the traffic for rail.

The Great Western attempted to beat the opposition by developing to the greatest extent its tried and tested and very old-fashioned methods. As a Company it was magnificently old-fashioned and conservative – which was in part due to a lack of cash for modernisation but also due to the deeply ingrained 'gentlemanliness' of the huge organisation. It was perceived by a significant number of outside businessmen as being backward, expensive to operate and slow to act. Rightly or wrongly, many thought that rail transit was more expensive than road, that their goods were liable to be broken during shunting operations, and were vulnerable to theft by railway staff. They did not think that goods sent by road would be broken or stolen. This a class of men were known to the GWR Goods Manager as 'anti-rail'.

The Buckinghamshire furniture industry was in

this category. There were over 200 furniture factories in High Wycombe in 1936. The principal manufacturers owned their own lorries and for the rest there were 50 local trucking firms. Most of the stools, chairs, tables and wooden furniture was sent by road, owing to the likelihood of damage on rail due to rough shunting and the need, therefore, of much expensive packaging. Furniture was rated 'Class 20' under the 1921 Railways Act - the highest-rated freight - but even when the GWR had obtained permission to quote lower rates, the traffic was reluctant to come to rail. A single rail wagon of furniture from High Wycombe straight down the GWR main line to Birmingham took 1½ days to be delivered; longer distances, such as Bristol or Edinburgh, required two full days. The relatively slow delivery and the high risk of damage from shunting impacts prevented much of this traffic being diverted to rail - even at cut rates.

In 1936 these problems had not been attended to. The GWR Goods Department estimated that 105 tons of furniture left High Wycombe each day, and they knew for certain that only 35 tons - for very far-off destinations - went by rail; and even this tiny traffic was split between the LNER and the GWR.

Even some of the tree-trunks from which the fur-

niture was made came in by road - to the detriment of the Faringdon branch which had once done a good trade in 'round timber' to High Wycombe. The GWR rate was 8 shillings a ton from Faringdon to High Wycombe, and GWR investigators discovered that the road rate was 6s 8d a ton - at once the GWR began to work out competitive rates.

In December 1936 the GWR had 532 contracts for the carriage and distribution of newspapers and magazines, with 876 more being negotiated and 754 'under investigation'. One such contract was for *Radio Times* which was printed by Waterlow at their factory on the GWR's Park Royal trading estate. Each week 450 tons of this periodical was placed on the GWR, earning £31,000 a year. When in December 1936 the Newspaper Proprietors Association asked the GWR for a reduction in the rate for carrying newspapers - 'in view of the bulk and the regularity of the traffic' - the GWR granted reductions totalling £11,000 'in view of the importance to rail of this traffic'.

The GWR's Goods Department canvassed hard - especially visiting firms who had 'lapsed', so to speak. The feeling I get is that Paddington intended to so pester a factory that they would put traffic on rail just to get rid of the canvasser.

Conservatism and innovation. In the first photograph, the last shunting horse to be employed by the GWR at Paddington poses for posterity in the Goods Yard in 1921. A chain from each side of the horse-collar went to a hook at each end of the yoke suspended by straps at the horse's rear. A long chain was hooked to a separate hook on the yoke, and was carried around the wagon drawhook and back to a hook on the other end of the yoke. (British Rail)

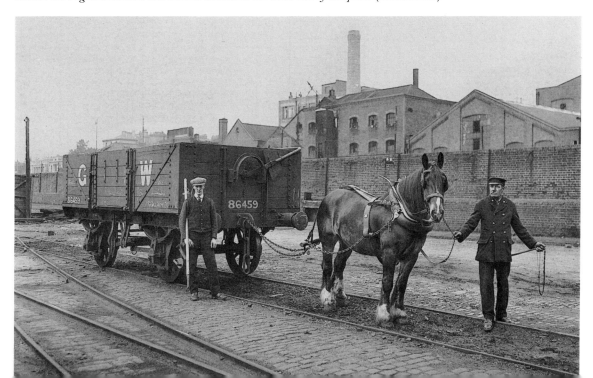

Above *Next we see GWR 'triple horsepower' and almost mediaeval cart, carrying a passenger carriage for the 'submarine railway' then under construction at White City, perhaps in connection with the British Empire Exhibition at Wembley in 1924. (British Rail)*

Below *Finally, the replacement for horses - a solid-tyred petrol-engined lorry 'For Efficient Rapid Transit of Parcels', circa 1925. (Clinker Collection/courtesy Brunel University)*

The Shrewsbury Goods District was fortunate in having David Blee for its Manager - later to become a Chief Officer on the newly formed Western Region of British Railways. Blee was really enthusiastic in his attack on the road hauliers. He undercut them fiercely wherever possible and left no approach untried. He was, in fact, an extremist railwayman whose undercutting price reductions were sometimes quite rash. Once he was trying to get basic slag on rail from Risca to Wooferton and was offering a 15 per cent reduction on the standard rate. Word of this reached Paddington, who wrote at once to tell him that the traffic had been secured in the past by a 7½ per cent reduction!

Sometimes he and his men seemed to be almost *begging* for traffic, as when he hit on the idea of asking all consignees to stipulate that their traffic *must* be delivered by rail; but even when a consignee did this there was no guarantee that the consignor would oblige. This had quite a lot to do with the ineptness of the GWR in not promptly paying claims for damage inflicted on goods during rail transit.

Johnson Bros of Horsehay made terracotta tiles and sewage pipes, and, said their General Manager, 'nothing in the world' would induce them to send their goods by rail, not just because of breakages but also because of GWR tight-fistedness in settling claims for damage. The Lightmoor Brick and Tile Co had the same complaint and added that 'loading to rail costs us 6d a ton more due to the extra packing and the extra time needed to load a railway wagon securely.'

It was not only the obviously fragile tiles which were liable to breakage on rail due to rough shunting - the GWR was quite capable of damaging tinplate and iron castings as well. There were several iron foundries in the Ketley area in the '30s, making small castings for the building industry; 9,600 tons a year was known to be sent away by road, but only 500 tons by rail because the consignees specified road transport.

The largest single recipient or consignee of Ketley castings was the Sinclair Iron Co. David Blee went to see them to ask if they would demand rail transport from Ketley, to which the reply was 'Yes, if you will carry at road rates, 18s 6d a ton, and at Company's (GWR) Risk'. Blee then went off to find an insurance company to indemnify the GWR against the inevitable claims from Sinclair, but without success.

Not all the staff of Blee's Shrewsbury office were 'ace' operators. Someone in the Goods Office in Shrewsbury, motivated perhaps by Blee's furious enthusiasm, wrote to the Lilleshall Iron Co of Shifnal and asked 'how the Works output by rail could be increased'. The letter was absurd and could only have been written by someone with no local knowledge - the firm wrote back with patient politeness:

'Whilst we would be interested in any proposition we fail to see how the present position could be improved since 100 per cent inwards and 95 per cent outwards traffic goes by rail, LMS and GWR, with the GWR getting the largest part.'

Blee and men like him could try to wheedle traffic on to rail by undercutting rates, but they could not remove the basic disadvantages of rail carriage as it was then practised. The railway as a carrier had several serious disadvantages to the manufacturers: the problem of packing, of loading and unloading several times between factory and consignee, and the slowness of transport owing to the system of local 'trip' working, marshalling yards and all the other ancient rituals beloved of railwaymen.

There was also a problem of decision-making when face to face with a prospective customer. Blee wrote of the latter problem in 1936 and contrasted the railway system, bureaucratic and slow, with the near instant decisions on price and delivery which could be given by the owner/manager of a road haulage firm who could see a job, jump in with an instant price and scoop up the work.

'There is an impression amongst traders that in business matters the railways move slowly compared to roads. This is due to the decision lying wholly within the discretion of the negotiating (road) haulier compared to the necessity of the GWR Agent having to refer back to District - and District to HQ - in many cases, involving Conferences, agreements, policies and repercussions.'

It is easy to feel Blee's impatience with the GWR system - and his enthusiasm to get traffic for his Company. Blee would have agreed with Pole's unheeded proposals for autonomous 'Divisions' handling everything locally in order to speed up decision making.

6

Fighting to the end

If Sir Felix Pole as General Manager had not been able to alter Company policy, then Blee, the District Goods Agent, certainly could not, aggressively enthusiastic for rail though he was. Instead, the Company continued to depend on maintaining traffic through keen staff members and a good personal relationship with the local businesses - good old-fashioned stuff and as cumbersome as ever.

The Company officially considered it vital to their business that its men had a good team spirit, and it enjoined its local Goods Managers to be humane to an employee should he fall short of what was required. An official directive said:

'At the best regulated station a man will occasionally misbehave or fail in his duty. The Agent will personally see the man and deal with him and only report him to the District Manager if the offence is serious. The Agent will take care to treat all his staff as men and encourage them to go right. Matters must not be left to settle themselves.'

This firm but respectful attitude towards the men was normal throughout the GWR - the Company depended on its men to work well and to use their initiative on behalf of the Company at every opportunity in order to beat the road hauliers.

In January 1930 the Great Western, the London, Midland & Scottish and the London & North Eastern companies concluded a tri-partite agreement. They would withdraw their goods agents for each other's territory, cease to 'canvass' competitively as between railways and place in a common 'pool' the revenue each earned from its freight traffic, except the 22½ per cent that each company could retain for working expenses. The revenue received from tolls over the North London line, which the GWR paid to the LMS for working between Acton Wells Junction and Poplar Docks was also put into the 'pool'.

Members of the GWR Goods Department seem to have had some difficulty with the concept of 'pooling' traffic. They sometimes did not try to get traffic from road hauliers by reducing rates if that traffic was to travel over the North London line and thus be subject to the toll, and if it was felt that the deduction of the toll, on top of the reduced rate quoted in order to get the traffic, made the traffic unprofitable.

In 1936 the Chief Goods Manager instructed his men not to subject individual streams of 'pool' traffic to a profit analysis because that would defeat the object of the 'pool'. Whilst the GWR might not get much out of certain traffics, the other companies would, and meanwhile the GWR was earning money, through the 'pool', from Birmingham, Yorkshire and Scottish traffic on the LMS and LNER that the GWR did not handle. It was of crucial importance to take the traffic away from the road hauliers - at all costs - and the 'pool' was there to support the companies in this endeavour.

But the predatory instincts of the GWR Goods Managers were not entirely put to sleep, as the Shepton Mallet bacon saga shows. The Co-operative Wholesale Society (CWS) bacon curing factory at Shepton Mallet sent between 10 and 20 tons of bacon to Cardiff every Monday morning by GWR, and the Company also distributed the meat at its destination.

In 1937 the CWS complained to the GWR that its service was no longer satisfactory - the CWS was unable to load the meat on to rail until the afternoon, by which time the only GWR freight service from Shepton to Bristol was via Westbury - a Great Way Round indeed. As a result, the consignment did not always arrive in Cardiff the following morning as required.

For 'next morning' delivery the bacon had to be at Temple Meads by teatime on the day of loading, and the only way to do this by rail was to send it via the Somerset & Dorset (S&D) - a concern jointly owned by the LMS and Southern Railway. Although the traffic was subject to the Pooling Agreement, the GWR share of the proceeds would have been less had it gone on the S&D, and in any case 'non-competition' had not sunk in so deeply that a GWR man would admit that the S&D ran a better service to Bristol - of all places - than the GWR.

The GWR's answer to the problem was to buy a road lorry and drive the bacon to Bristol so that it would make its connection for Cardiff, the GWR thus obtaining a larger share of the 'pool'. But there was more to it than this. The CWS was sending a lot of bacon to LMS and LNER destinations over the S&D and, to quote the Bristol Division Goods Manager, Mr Barefoot:

'Although under the Pooling Agreement we are prohibited from canvassing for this traffic, the institution of our road service to Bristol would probably cause the CWS to send its traffic by GWR without any intervention from us.'

The lorry was bought and the GWR captured the traffic as the wise - or crafty - Mr Barefoot had predicted.

A heavy, traditional traffic which was largely lost to rail in the later '30s was cattle, sheep and pigs - except in special cases such as the movement of pigs to Harris's pie factory at Calne. The Great Western and Southern companies co-operated in a survey of the problem in 1935, sending experienced Goods Department Officers to interview farmers and hauliers at cattle fairs at Swindon, Highbridge, Chippenham, Yeovil and Dorchester cattle marts or fairs.

The problem was that most farms were situated remote from railway stations, so the animals had to be walked 2 or more miles. This of course the farmers were unwilling to do as they had either bought their own lorry or were served by a road haulier, many of whom had new double-decker lorries for carrying sheep. The road haulier would charge a farmer 1 shilling per loaded mile and would visit three or four farms to pick up animals for market or to deliver from market.

Farmers generally preferred the farmyard-to-marketplace convenience of road haulage - even when the road haulier was more expensive than rail - and in the case of dairy animals going for sale as milking beasts rather than for slaughter, the road journey was kinder to them. Usually a town's market served farms within a radius of 12 to 20 miles, yet in spite of R. H. Nicholls's and Felix Pole's maxim that the railway could not compete with the roads on distances under 50 miles, the GWR persisted in its fight against the cattle lorry.

Conversely, cattle dealers tended to prefer rail transits because they were usually sending animals over relatively long distances and dealt in larger numbers of animals. Moreover, two lorry-loads of cows could be put into one railway truck, so there was a saving of money.

However, the location in a town of the weekly cattle fair could make the use of rail transport very difficult for the owner of the cattle. At Salisbury market the cattle pens were on the opposite side of the town from the GWR station, entailing a near-impossible cattle drive through Salisbury streets. Furthermore, the butchers who bought the animals had paid for them by weight, so they were very loth indeed to let them walk anywhere after purchase for fear of walking the weight off. The Southern Railway had a railhead closer to the pens at the old 'Milford' station, so the GWR sent empty cattle wagons round to Milford yard and brought the loaded wagons back, but this was still an awkward proceeding requiring two 'trip' workings between the GWR and SR station.

The Swindon cattle market was held near the 'Town' station of the former Midland & South Western Junction Railway, a GWR constituent, but it was unsuitable for any Bristol or London-bound destinations, which could only be reached from Swindon Junction goods yard. By road this was at least 2 miles away, down a steep hill and through the busy town. A special train service would have been required if cattle traffic for Bristol, London or South Wales was to be accepted.

A cattle dealer from Wokingham, Mr White, who bought six or seven cows weekly from Swindon market and took them home in his own lorry, said he would use the railway if it could deliver his beasts home by 7 pm the same day. The job would have brought in about £100 a year for the GWR, and the Goods Department thought this was worth having, so asked the Traffic people if they could provide a service. The answer was:

Special engine and brake-van to Swindon Town
Special 'trip' to Swindon Junction
Depart Swindon Junction 2.50 pm goods
Arrive Reading West 4.07 pm and detach wagon
Special engine and brake-van to Reading West
Special train Reading West to Southern Railway to connect with SR passenger train arriving Wokingham 7.8 pm.

The wonder of the above is that it must have been obvious to any experienced railwayman beforehand that something of the sort would be required, and that it was not worth bothering with. But the GWR men bothered - they wanted traffic.

The men in the Goods Manager's office had grown old in the service of the GWR. It was not merely a job to them - it was like fighting for your family or your regiment, capturing traffic from other companies and from the stripling road industry. The younger men learned from the example set by the old hands, so it was second nature to all of them to compete. Quite simply, to lose traffic to the road went against all their training and the habits of a lifetime - though, by modern ways of thinking, they would have been better off without it.

They saw no future for the railway in surrender. The old-hand railwaymen saw that once you begin to lose traffic your tracks and yards and all your equipment become less used and therefore more expensive to maintain. The road hauliers were the great enemy, and the feeling was that if they were 'given an inch, they'd take a mile'. Road hauliers had to be denied business even if it meant the railway carrying unprofitable traffic.

In March 1936 a GWR Goods Department report on cattle traffic stated:

'Whilst the competition we experience is at the moment limited, there is the real danger of considerable losses in the future when the road haulier can operate vehicles holding 10 or 12 fat beasts - and vehicles of this size are already on the road. The only reason we hold the carriage of cattle in full loads at present is that the beasts which can normally be loaded in one railway truck usually

Carriages or 'tail traffic' needed to change trains at junctions just as did the passengers, and shunting wagons between trains was a cumbersome and time-consuming part of the regular working of trains, especially unsuitable for livestock. 'Pilot' engines were booked to do this work - a small tank engine, or a mixed traffic or express engine which could double as a 'stand-by' engine to cover engine failures. The train engine itself would also be employed to shunt vehicles off or on to its train. Here in 1934 'Castle' No 5048 has a horse-box to attach. (G. H. Soole/Adrian Vaughan Collection)

take two lorries, but this advantage will disappear sooner or later and I recommend that the Company buys competing road hauliers at the earliest opportunity.

This advice was followed up to a point, and some small firms were purchased. One was that belonging to Mr Hubert Orchard of Roade, Trowbridge, who had three lorries, a 'Guy' and two 'Burfords', for a total capacity of 6 tons 17 cwt. He was paid £1,600 and continued to drive as a GWR employee, his lorries suitably re-painted, I suppose. It would seem that he had made a very good bargain, while the GWR looked forward to good business because 'Mr Orchard has good connections in the various markets'.

Whether it was a profitable idea for the GWR to buy off competitive hauliers and attempt to operate those lorries as feeders to the train is very much open to doubt. There is, in hindsight at any rate, a more than passing resemblance to the famous story of King Canute trying to hold back the tide. There were far too many farmers requiring transport, far more than the GWR could cater for, and there would always be a new haulier willing to fill the gap in the market - and there was still the problem of the interchange between (GWR) road and (GWR) rail.

In 1936, the Bristol Division's Goods Department representative, Mr Pottow, asked farmers at various markets whether they would support a GWR road-rail cattle transport system. The response was discouraging. Mr Carr of Yatesbury, 3½ miles from Calne, told him that he would not use the railway service even if the GWR came to his farm because of the additional time and inconvenience in unloading and re-loading at the station and unloading again at the town. He also had some uncomplimentary things to say about the inexperience of many of the men whom the GWR had employed in the past to load his cattle. The latter was an oft-repeated criticism.

Mr Vincent of Edington bought and sold all kinds of livestock at Salisbury, and although his farm was only 2 miles from Edington & Bratton station, he could not be tempted to use it - not even at 18 shillings for a half-loaded wagon. Mr Pike of Hilperton spent £800 a year with the road haulier Mansell & Gale of Melksham, upon which sum Mr Pottow cast covetous eyes, but Pike said he would not send by rail because the lorry was quicker and saved the intermediate unloading and loading.

However, against the majority picture of gloom

there were a few instances where Mr Pottow's investigations discovered farmers suffering under the impositions of a road haulier who presumed he had a monopoly of the traffic. He quoted them competitive rates and secured the traffic - but this was all relatively short-distance work and once the road haulier discovered he had been 'rumbled' I suppose he could easily have regained the traffic by virtue of his natural advantages of convenience, faster transits and a price to undercut the railway.

The only area of growth open to the GWR was, as Pole had warned 15 years before, in large consignments over distances greater than 50 miles. Road hauliers Austin Clarke & Co had captured from the GWR the Swindon cattle market-London CWS abattoir traffic to East London. The whole day's purchase of animals - pigs, cows and calves - was moved in one large double-decked lorry, delivering the sad animals to their gory fate that same evening. The London CWS said that the GWR could have the traffic if they could perform the same delivery time and do it for less money. An average load was 30 calves and 10 pigs, and the GWR quoted 62s 9d for the use of a 'Medium Mex' wagon, 7s 3d cheaper than the road haulier's rate.

So the GWR got this particular traffic back - for a while at any rate - but the record shows that throughout the 1930s there was a steady and at some places a spectacularly rapid decline in the number of trucks of cattle loaded at GWR stations. There were a few rare exceptions to this, Marlborough being one.

Carrying farmer-sized packets of cattle to and from farm and market was just too much handling - the distances involved being so short, a profitable charge could not be made. Rail was simply the wrong form of transport, and the farmers voted with their feet. The emphasis was shifting to road transport for speed, economy and, most of all, convenience - even in the 1930s, when tarmac roads were still a rarity in rural areas.

The GWR's own 'Country Lorry' service had 189 depots by 1938, adding the Dinmore, Moreton-on-Lugg and Fordbridge services in late 1938 or early 1939. These lorries could deliver to the railhead or take short-distance goods all the way by road.

In order to keep the dividend up, reductions were made in expenditure through more efficient day-to-day working and through co-operation with the other companies - which was good and legitimate - but also by reducing the amount put aside for renewing the fabric of the railway - which was bad and worrying. A report from Lord Plender*, head of the famous firm of Accountants, to the GWR Chairman, Viscount Horne, in 1938 (marked 'SECRET') threw light on the shoddy treatment meted out to the GWR by the 1921 Railways Act, whilst warning that the Company's Renewals Fund was too low.

Plender said that this was due to:

1 Inadequacy of the provisions accumulated by the Company prior to 1913 and to the small reserves taken over from the absorbed companies
2 Underfunding at Grouping relative to the large amount of rebuilding necessary
3 Raiding of the reserves to maintain the dividend when income was falling

The GWR was not keeping a sufficient fund of money to cover the depreciation of its rolling-stock. In this connection Plender stated that:

'you have no scientific basis for calculating the amount to be set aside. The individual percentages of the reserves to the expired-life proportion of original cost are: Loco, 22.5%; Carriage, 8.6%; Wagon, 37.5%. The apparently low figure relating to carriages, equal to £380,800, considered in the light of the Company's proposed carriage renewal programme - £550,000 during 1938 - appears to call for attention.'

The winter 1938-9 sugar beet season saw the GWR carrying 111,740 tons of beet to Kidderminster and Allscott by rail and 3,450 tons by GWR road lorry - an increase of 10,000 tons on 1937-8. In spite of such impressive tonnages, the trend in the first quarter of 1939 was downwards compared to the same period in 1938.

By August 1938 freight revenue was 8 per cent up on the first eight months of 1937, owing to the dramatic growth of the iron and steel industry in South Wales and the West Midlands, while passenger revenue was up by half a per cent. If only this had been, so to speak, a 'genuine' increase in pro-

duction - but it was only the prelude to another war, so the GWR, and everyone else, would have to pay heavily and in unexpected ways, for this small surge of prosperity.

Coal exports did not share this improvement; the Welsh coal industry continued to decline, although in the first four months of 1939 it fulfilled a few large contracts from overseas railways and power stations. A lot of coal contracts were bartered deals, the French and the Finns exchanging pit-props for coal in April 1939. In April there was a strike of Pennsylvanian miners which brought orders for Welsh coal from French, Egyptian, Palestinian and Tunisian Railways who purchased a total of 500,000 tons, and the USA bought 50,000 tons. In spite of this there was an 18.5 per cent decrease in coal exports in the first four months of 1939 compared with the same period in 1938.

Overall, shipments of coal from South Wales declined over the 45 weeks ending 2 November 1939, the total exported being 630,000 tons less than 1938. Sir James Milne, with unbelievable naivety, clutched at some Italian straws, and noted in his fortnightly report that

'. . .it is anticipated that the British coal trade will benefit from the recently concluded agreement with Italy to set up a standing committee to consider economic questions affecting us both. It is anticipated that Germany will not be able to maintain its coal supply to Italy - 6,000,000 tons in 1939 - and because of this Italy is thought to be purchasing 4,000,000 tons from South Wales.

Milne then went on to 'confidently expect' that as the sea routes for coast-wise coal were now dangerous owing to the wartime activity of German submarines, surface raiders and aircraft, the railways would carry an vastly increased tonnage. Gas coal was already going by rail from York to Dawlish, Torquay and Paignton. One wonders how he thought Welsh coal was going to arrive safely in Italy after a long sea-journey through the U-boat and Luftwaffe-infested waters.

As from 31 August 1939 the summer service and holiday excursion trains were abandoned and the following day, and for the next three days, a skeleton public service was run to clear the tracks for 163 special trains, starting from Paddington, Ealing and Maidenhead, carrying away the children of London and some adults to safe havens in the countryside, away from the bombing of London which was

---

* Plender had recommended 'a scientific basis' for calculating the amount to be set aside for carriage renewals in 1915. But no action was taken due to the war and, later, through lack of money.

Above On the declaration of war on 3 September 1939, the normal train service was suspended and the tracks were given over to Government traffic, trains of 'refugee' children from the cities, and a skeleton public passenger service. Young John Haywood, of Bristol Divisional Superintendent's Office, was sent to Savernake East box to act as a train regulator and he took this view of the 11.22 am Bristol to Reading (Emergency service) train as it left Savernake Low Level station behind No 5096 4-6-0 Bridgwater Castle on 4 September 1939.

Below Train-loads of children were sent away from London, Liverpool, Birmingham and other major cities for fear of devastating aerial bombardment, and also from East Anglian coastal districts for fear of invasion. London children were loaded at Paddington (seen here on 4 September 1939), Ealing and even Maidenhead stations to rural destinations. At the time that they left their homes, no parent or child knew where they were bound for - the children informed their parents where they were and who they were staying with once they had arrived at their billet. (British Rail)

expected to begin the moment war was declared. The GWR carried 112,944 children, and besides these there were train-loads of evacuees from East Anglia into GWR territory.

The estimated annual income for 1939 was £29,615,000, up £3,089,000 on 1938, an 11.6 per cent increase. The Great Western's Management continued to be optimistic - in spite of the frightening preparations for war - and the GWR tourist book *Holiday Haunts* was issued in 1940 as usual.

The late 1930s saw the Company's old-fashioned administration and old-fashioned systems at their most efficient and most admirable. The 1921 Act had recognised the need for a national rail transport network and had provided a framework within which the railways should work, and the companies had done their best to provide proper services - against all the odds and without much help from the Government.

Road competition had reduced profits and forced the four companies to integrate to a large degree. I refer to the schemes for 'pooling' wagons and freight revenue, and to the co-ordination of road and rail passenger and freight transport through railway part-ownership of motor bus and road haulage companies. But however well the GWR Directors ran their business, they only paid a 3 per cent dividend throughout the '30s, except for 4 per cent in 1937. They had reached the peak of efficiency using the equipment they had. Their expenses were too high and they did not have the money to replace their rolling-stock and other systems as they became life-expired.

Thus the GWR was finding it ever more difficult to handle the traffic of an increasingly mobile world. Large-scale modernisation was required, which the Company could not afford out of its own resources. It was not able to compete with road transport with its advantages of a more modern 'image', 'door-to-door' convenience, greater ability to adapt to the needs of the customer and to respond quickly to those needs - and of course, running on roads subsidised out of taxation.

For a Table of the GWR's financial performance see Appendix 1.

7

The Great Western v road haulage, 1921–27

Powered road vehicles were subject to a 4 mph speed limit until 1896, when the Locomotives and Highways Act raised the limit to 12 mph. The 1904 Heavy Motor Car Order permitted 20 mph for large passenger vehicles - the charabanc - and lorries. Thus the means became available for a firm to set up as a road haulier to operate powered haulage and thus to compete with the railway for freight and passenger traffic.

Lord Cawdor, Chairman of the GWR Board,

Steam railmotor No 85, its accommodation strengthened by an ancient clerestory coach, storming along on the down relief line between Pangbourne and Basildon (Berks) in about 1925.

The cars had vertical boilers feeding steam to cylinders 12 in x 16 in driving 3 ft 6 in wheels (early models), increased to 4 feet on later cars to reduce 'revs' and thus reduce wear on the machinery. The vehicle could be driven from either end, and the maximum speed was 50 mph, the average 35.

No 85 ran 369,060 miles as an independent power-car and entered Swindon Works on 5 May 1927 for conversion to a 'trailer', emerging in December as Trailer 154, allocated to Gloucester. (Clinker Collection/courtesy Brunel University)

announced at the 1903 Annual General Meeting that the Company would start to operate road motors as feeders to main-line stations. The first of these services began on 17 August that year with five Milnes-Daimler 'waggonettes', seating 22 people each, running between Helston railway station and Lizard Point, followed on 31 October by a service from the village of Marazion to Penzance. The Stonehouse-Chalford steam railmotors began service on 12 October 1904, stopping not just at stations but wherever a passenger required to be dropped; the cars had extending steps to the track in lieu of platforms. The popularity of this system was such that the crowds at level crossings wishing to use the cars caused long delays as they climbed aboard, and several wooden platforms or 'halts' were built at such locations.

The underlying lesson in all this was that the public wanted 'door-to-door' conveyances. The nearer the railway could come to this ideal, the more traffic they got. The railway-owned road-motor on the Helston-Lizard run avoided the expense of a 'light railway' between these places which the GWR had

been authorised to build, at an estimated cost of £85,000. The Company had also been authorised to build a light railway - at the probably underestimated cost of £75,000 - from Calne to Marlborough, and on this route too it later introduced a road-motor bus (Hungerford-Marlborough-Calne).

Meanwhile, major road hauliers - Pickfords, Carter Paterson and the Globe Parcels Express, for instance - expanded the sphere of their wholly road-borne parcels, freighting and household removals operations. As early as 1910 there were daily scheduled road freight services between Bristol and London. Other companies began daily road passenger services over medium distances such as between London and Luton, and Brighton and Margate. However, by 1910 too many operators brought about fierce competition and profits were reduced to uncommercial levels. Price-fixing agreements were tried but the instinct to compete was too strong. The only solution was amalgamation.

In 1912 Pickfords, Beans Express and the London Parcels Delivery Company were absorbed into Carter Paterson, which proceeded to rationalise

The steam railmotor was a good concept and it was successful up to a point, but they were difficult to work on for a number of reasons - shortage of steam was a common complaint. Even in good order they could not always cope with the varying loadings demanded by the passenger and freight traffic in those days. From 1915 they began to have their engines removed to become 'driving trailers' for haulage by 0-4-2 and 0-6-0 tank engines.

These trains were driven from the engine when that was leading, or from the leading end of the trailer when the engine was pushing at the rear. This arrangement was known as an 'auto-train' to the Company, and 'push-pull' to everyone else. In suburban areas it was a common sight to see a tank engine sandwiched between four trailers.

Here, purpose-built (1932) 'push-pull' tank engine No 5419 is hauling a purpose-built (1929) 'driving trailer' on a Banbury-Princes Risborough local near Brill on 22 June 1935. (H. C. Casserley)

their joint operations to produce lower costs and better profits. In the same year the London Traffic Combine came into being to reduce competition for road passenger traffic.

During the Great War the petrol engine and rubber tyres were intensively used and were developed into fairly reliable and economical units. After the war a large number of men and machines, surplus to Government requirements, were looking for work, and scores of one-man haulage businesses sprang up. A new crisis of over-competition was well on the way.

The 1921 Transport Act, establishing the 'Big Four' groups from the 120 former companies, reflected Parliament's concern that these huge combines should not coalesce into a monopoly, yet it was also aware that competition on rail was futile and fatal. The 1921 Act also implied a certain public service nature in rail transport. The waste of effort involved in competition was well known to the railway companies and the major road carriers long before 1914, and through the 1920s and 1930s the debate on competition v public service, individual initiative v planning, developed.

The need was to replace competition with opportunities for co-operation, whilst providing the nation with a co-ordinated transport system that could pay for itself as a privately owned venture. Under the Act one grouped railway company was not permitted to compete with another group, and could not buy a share in a road passenger or freight business if that would encroach into a neighbouring railway company's territory.

Immediately after the 1921 Act the newly grouped railway companies began a long-drawn-out negotiation with the Pickfords/Carter Paterson group with a view to the former buying a half-share in the latter, but this was illegal unless all four railway companies took a share, and even then there would be some doubt as to the legality of the railway companies working as road hauliers. These laudable negotiations were pursued, but until the law was clarified on that point, the final result could not be achieved.

Another intractable problem for the railways was that the roads were public property upon which the Government could and did spend huge sums of public money, whilst the railways - which came close to becoming national property in 1919 - were still, in fact, private property which had to fend for itself. During the year ended March 1924 the newly formed Ministry of Transport spent almost £51,000,000 of public money on road maintenance and improvement (in that year my friend Kenneth Leech road-tested his rebuilt motorcycle engine at 80 mph along the then unopened Watford bypass).

Better roads encouraged more vehicles. In 1918 there were 41,000 powered goods vehicles on the roads - in 1921 there were 128,000. Carter Paterson/Pickfords was able to extend its operation. House removals had become an important part of Pickfords work (furniture being so vulnerable to damage on rail) before 1914, and in 1921 the firm moved into the petrol haulage business with 1,000-gallon tankers - by 1935 they were running 3,600-gallon tankers.

Pneumatic tyres and refrigeration plant for lorries were introduced in 1924. These new vehicles at once made deep inroads into the GWR's meat haulage business from Liverpool to London over roads improved at public expense. The road hauliers' contribution to road improvements, through their road fund licenses, was a mere £4,245,000, the balance coming from taxes on light cars, local rates, general taxation and loans. As to the problem and expense of the deaths and injuries caused by road vehicles, there was, and is, apparently, no solution.

In 1925 the total expenditure by the four railway companies on maintenance of their tracks was £13,000,000, with a further £8,000,000 being spent to maintain the signalling in accordance with laws made to ensure the safety of persons using the railway. In addition to these outlays on their own roads, the railway companies were obliged to contribute £8,000,000 to local rates, a large proportion of which sum was spent, as has been pointed out before, on the upkeep and improvement of highways used by their competitors.

Long before the Great War the railways had actively encouraged housing developments which by the 1920s formed sprawling suburbs, many of whose inhabitants were some way from a railway station and who were glad of the more convenient services which trams and, later, buses could provide. This mass of 'commuters' attracted the attention of the London General Omnibus Co and other operators. The buses could go into the side streets and in the 1920s it was possible to see a bus or tram passing every 30 seconds along the main roads of West London and charging less than railway fares.

The GWR was prevented by law from entering the road transport business, but it was permitted to operate road motor services where it could show that these were acting merely as 'feeders' to its train services. In 1922 the Company purchased ten second-hand AEC chassis for £160 each and refurbished them at their Slough road motor works for local 'feeder' services. Cheap fares were introduced in heavily populated areas to compensate people for the inconvenience of their walk to the railway station; these were introduced between Reading and Paddington in December 1922, and that month an extra 3,286 passengers took advantage of the reduction, earning an additional £365, whereupon the GWR decided to continue the experiment for a further three months.

The return fare from Gloucester to Cheltenham was reduced to 10d in July 1921, to compete with the Corporation tramcars. This increased passenger carryings by 24.5 per cent and raised passenger revenue at Gloucester and Cheltenham by 11.2 per cent. On 1 February 1923 the fare was further reduced to 9d, and this, it was confidently anticipated, would further deplete road motor carryings, where the fare was 1 shilling.

In 1924 Cardiff and Newport (Mon) Corporations were buying buses to establish suburban and rural passenger services, forcing the GWR to issue cut-price passenger and parcel rates, cheaper season tickets for specific groups - such as commercial travellers and shoppers - and cheap tickets after the morning rush.

All these measures were carefully applied after studies of the needs of an area, and the Company's revenues were increased in those specific areas of dense population. But in the relatively sparsely populated rural areas, the GWR, with its high 'overheads' and low passenger journeys, had no answer to bus competition which much more closely met the demand for 'door-to-door' delivery for passengers and parcels.

In 1924 the GWR and the London General Omnibus Company made a secret - unwritten - agreement 'that there shall be mutual respect of each Company's existing and contemplated services in the Slough, Maidenhead and Beaconsfield areas.' Similar agreements were made with the London & Provincial Motor Bus Proprietors' Association when Oxfordshire and Gloucestershire, Devon and Cornwall were carved up into 'no competition' areas. Having arrived at this situation, the GWR did not charge exorbitant fares. The purpose was to avoid a price-cutting war, ruinous to both road and rail and which would leave the public without a proper service.

Forty bodyless Thorneycroft buses were purchased by the Great Western in 1924, after receiving a subsidy from the War Office on the condition that the vehicles could be used by the military in any national emergency. Bodies were fitted by the

Wantage Tramway Co No 5 with the two cars by Hurst, Nelson & Co of Motherwell, purchased in 1912. The leading car is No 4 which had been built as a conventional tramcar, double-decked and electrically driven. Locomotive No 5 was built in 1857 for the Sandy & Potton Railway and was purchased from the LNWR in 1878. The tram service connected the town of Wantage with all GWR trains calling at Wantage Road station, 2½ miles away. The tramway passenger service was withdrawn on 31 July 1925, two months after the GWR instituted a bus service between the town and the station. (Clinker Collection/courtesy Brunel University)

GWR and on 28 May 1925 some of them were used to increase the GWR bus service between Swindon station, Uffington, Wantage and Wantage Road station. This put the steam-hauled Wantage Tramway out of the passenger-carrying business from 1 August, although it continued to haul railway freight wagons between the station and the town until 18 December 1945.

In 1925 Totnes town council complained of the long interval between morning and evening trains to Newton Abbot on Sundays, and the GWR, loyal as ever to the public, used its Kingsbridge bus to provide connections all day between Totnes and Newton, the last one bringing Totnes passengers off the 2.40 pm from Paddington, due at Newton Abbot at 6.51 pm. The GWR's expenses in running this service was £260 per annum.

The bus passenger from Newton Abbot to Ashburton went along only one side of a triangle, whereas the train traveller had to traverse two sides; from Newton to Totnes, change trains, then to Ashburton. The GWR tried reducing rail fares - in some cases charging even less than the bus - but the passengers wanted the shorter journey time and the relatively 'door-to-door' element of bus travel, and were willing to put up with the relative discomfort of the bus for this convenience. The result of the railway's attempting the impossible was a total loss of money.

In 1925 the GWR Yealmpton branch, 6½ miles long from the Southern Railway at Cattewater Junction, Plymouth, had an income of £11,800, operating costs of £13,880 and a hostile road motor operator creaming off the passenger and parcels business. Superintendent of the Line R. H. Nicholls's advice to the Directors was 'close it and save £13,880 per annum', but the Directors ordered a GWR bus service to be run to drive the other man off the road. Yealmpton signalman Tommy Dodd took a Sunday turn of duty as bus conductor. In so doing the GWR competed against its own train service, but it finally broke the small operator. In spite of this, the branch could not be made to break even, and Nicholls informed his Directors of the general principle that: 'The only way we can compete with road transport for short-haul passenger and parcels traffic is on the road.'

Sir Felix Pole saw how vulnerable road and railway haulage was to 'small' road operators and in December 1926 he spelt out the disadvantages to his Directors with stark realism. The italics are mine.

A City of Oxford Motor Services bus, part-owned by the GWR since June 1930, forms the passenger service from Wantage Road station to Swindon via Wantage and Uffington. Wantage Road Station Master's house can be seen above the hedge on the left, while the Oxford road rises over the railway line in the centre distance, with the station office just visible to the left on the bridge. The tram tracks, for goods trains only, continued their useful role, carrying two trips a day, until 18 December 1945. The line closed on the 21st. (R. H. G. Simpson Collection)

'The economic position of road v rail will assume a new aspect with the elimination of *amateur* road hauliers and their *uncommercial* rates and the inevitable *increase in the road hauliers' share of road costs.* But even in fair competition *the railway is inferior to the lorry for hauling loads* short distances, particularly in the case of perishables, and *even the railway will move into road haulage* for these 30-50-mile hauls. Damage to goods en route, pilfering, the cost of packaging, loading and unloading make short-haul railway cartage expensive for the factory *even if the railway rate was less than the road rate.*'

But still the GWR entered the hopeless competition. In October 1928 the Company convened a meeting of business people from the town (of Yealmpton) and district and told them that if they did not make greater use of the branch it would have to be closed. Farmers and traders agreed to put at least £3,000-worth more traffic on the line annually.

The GWR continued to run the branch hoping for a break-even outcome, but on 7 July 1930 trade worsened and the Company was forced to withdraw the passenger train service leaving the field to the Plymouth-Modbury buses of the half-GWR-owned Western National. Tommy Dodd transferred to Hemerdon signal box where he remained until the early 1950s.

8

The Great Western v road haulage, 1928–39

To handle 'penny packet' perishable traffic by rail the GWR had a network of 'Station Trucks'. These ran daily attached to designated trains between specified places, carrying small consignments, often on a regular basis, between wholesaler and retailer, or producer and customer. The truck was methodically loaded so that each destination's packages were accessible when required, and it had to be shunted from train to train, main line to branch and back again, as it was worked around its appointed 'diagram' or rota. As the 'twenties wore on, the use of the Station Truck declined in favour of the system of parcels trains and local distribution by the GWR's 'Country Lorry' system.

Throughout the 1920s the GWR kept all its unprofitable branch lines running. This obviously had something to do with the 1921 Railways Act which laid upon the railway the duty to 'afford reasonable railway services'. But it is to the Company's great credit that it took its public service duty very seriously - there was no hanging back in the hope of

Ex-Cambrian Railways 0-6-0 No 849 and a typical mixed bag of freight to be broken up and remarshalled at Oswestry, and re-marshalled again somewhere else, as the wagons swap trains at junctions to reach their final destination. The cost of marshalling must have been collosal, but if the GWR ever 'costed' the operation I have never come across the results in 20 years of searching. The date is 28 May 1932. (H. C. Casserley)

A Leyland 'Tiger' carrying a Harrington body, in the service of the partly GWR/SR-owned Devon General, one of the 'Associated' road/rail bus companies. This arrangement ensured a reasonable profit in the absense of hurtful competition, and enabled the GWR to provide a co-ordinated local transport system between country towns more directly and more conveniently that could be done with trains alone. This handsome bus is on Devon General's route 46, the very useful Weymouth-Exeter run, seen here at Lyme Regis in May 1937. (G. H. F. Atkins)

being relieved by Parliament of a particularly unprofitable route.

The railway management also took the view that there was a financial benefit in keeping the marshalling yards, engines, men and machinery as busy as possible; thus every twig of the great GWR tree was important. Whether a certain traffic was remunerative seemed not to matter so much as to *get it* at all costs (as the staff were constantly urged) and '*keep the road haulier out*'.

The longest-distance road 'feeder' service was introduced on

20 October 1927 when the GWR inaugurated a service of express buses, four each way, from Oxford station to Cheltenham St James station via Witney and Burford. These buses ran in connection with the principal expresses and gave a fast service to places which previously had been poorly served, or not served at all by the existing trains.

These good intentions were, however, not well supported, and by 31 December 1928 the bus service had carried only 2,186 passengers for £364 19s 9d. The new General Manager of the GWR, Sir James Milne, reported to the Directors:

'Progress in the development of this traffic is slow but we are living in hope and plan other cross-country bus services.'

In 1932 the route was handed over to the 'Black &

White' motor bus company which was part-owned by the GWR.

In February 1928 the four railway companies put a Bill before Parliament which would enable then to own passenger and freight road haulage firms, and after 37 days of argument they won their case and the Bill became law that summer.

The GWR at once opened negotiations with bus and road freight hauliers to buy all or part of their business. The result was the Western Welsh and Western National motor bus companies, which were 50 per cent GWR-owned; the former was an amalgamation of Great Western bus routes with those of large operators in Cornwall, Devon and Somerset, while the latter was the amalgamation of GWR road services with those of South Wales Commercial Motors.

The Birmingham & Midland bus company, covering an area from Buckingham to Welshpool and Hereford, became Midland Red, 50 per cent of it owned by the original owners and 25 per cent each by the GWR and LMS. Crossville Motors was purchased by the LMS with GWR approval on condition that GWR interests were protected and that the Crosville routes in the Wrexham area would be sold to Wrexham Transport - which was 50 per cent GWR.

In October 1928 the 'Heavy Motor Car' Order of 1904 was amended to raise the national maximum speed limit for buses and lorries to 30 mph. It also ordered that all vehicles should be fitted with rear-view mirrors - GWR passenger vehicles already had them, but GWR goods vehicles had to be so fitted at a cost of £340.

On 1 December 1928 the Government relieved the railway companies of some of their local rates burden - provided that the money saved was spent in reducing their freight charges. This, it was hoped, would assist industry at a time of deep recession by reducing their costs and at the same time putting more traffic on rail. The Government's lost rating revenues were made up by increasing tax on petrol by 4d a gallon. This too was expected to put more traffic on rail. Unfortunately, the Depression of trade was deepening and GWR revenues did not increase.

In June 1930 the Company bought shares in the City of Oxford Motor Services (CoMS) and placed GWR employees in its office at 138 High Street, Oxford. On 31 October 1931 the Thames Valley Traction Co agreed to merge with the local railway companies and re-constituted its Board of Directors - two were nominated by the GWR, two came from the Southern Railway and there were three Thames Valley nominees.

This movement towards road/rail co-operation and a more regulated competition was continued with the Road Traffic Act of 1930, passed on 1 August. This was an attempt to control competition so as to produce a viable, national transport system whilst still leaving it in private hands. After defining numerous motoring offences, the Act instituted Traffic Commissioners for various areas of Britain. They had the duty of regulating every aspect of Public Service Vehicle (PSV) use: roadworthiness, the route over which a vehicle was to be used, and the wages and conditions of the men employed.

This was of vital importance if the unfair competition to which the railways were subjected by road hauliers was to be corrected. Without this law road hauliers could use badly maintained vehicles and cheap labour while the railways were bound by numerous laws to maintain a very high degree of safety, and were also bound by their agreements with trade unions to provide a reasonable level of wages and other benefits.

Section 93 of the Act laid down that the wages and conditions of bus crews 'must not be less favourable than wages and conditions which would have to be observed under a Government contract'. After the Act no-one was permitted to operate a bus without a license from the Commissioners for that specific route. An application to operate a route, and

objections against it from road or rail operators, were heard by the Commissioner, who took into account how many licenses had already been granted on that route, the *public necessity* of the service, whether it was already provided by rail, and the co-ordination of the proposed bus service with rail services.

The Act raised bus operators' costs, but also improved the safety of buses and reduced the number of competing services - which also helped established road operators. There was no room for more than a certain number of operators if anyone was to run successfully.

However, the Act did not go as far as the railway companies would have liked, and existing bus and lorry operators were able to 'cream off' the best traffic in their areas. The GWR's argument was that it was unfair that it should provide daily, regular passenger and freight services all year, running half empty trains (and worse) in the winter, and then have the special event (local cattle market, passenger excursion or holiday period traffic, for example, on which it had come ever more to depend to increase its income) exploited by opportunists who did not have to bear the loss on the same route at other times. A small firm with one or two lorries could take away enough rural traffic to make a whole branch line uneconomic, with the risk that the line would then have to close because its most profitable business - freight - which cross-subsidised the passenger and parcels services - was being lost.

A great problem for the GWR was the road haulier running a 'contract carriage' for some 'special occasion', which he was entitled to do under the 1930 Act. The crux of the matter was, what constituted a 'special occasion'? For instance, at Christmas 1931 in the Aldershot area, independent bus-owners put on services to take troops home on leave at fares not only undercutting the rail fare but actually below the legal minimum allowed by the Traffic Commissioners. The bus companies' case was that Christmas was 'a special occasion'. The railway companies took this case to law on the grounds that the Christmas holidays were not a 'special occasion' and therefore the special licences should not have been issued, but the Aldershot magistrates found entirely in favour of the small operators - the troops were a 'private party', Christmas was a 'special occasion' and the buses were 'contract carriages'.

The railway companies continued to push their case and in 1929-31 a Royal Commission on Transport under the chairmanship of Sir Arthur

Salter was set up. This consisted of eight men, four from the railways, four from the road haulage industry, who investigated the problem of how to 'place competition between road and rail on an equal footing and how to allocate to each form of transport the functions it can most usefully perform'. The report was issued in July and was unanimously approved by all members of the conference.

It is easy to see the disadvantages under which the railway competed from the recommendations made in the report. For instance, each class of commercial vehicle should pay its *fair share* (the railways wanted the wording to be 'full cost') of its use of the roads, and haulage operators should be controlled by license dependant in all cases on their *providing fair wages, hours of work and conditions of service*, and being tested on the necessity of their service to prevent wasteful competition.

The railway companies were pleased with the Salter Report – which recognised that the road haulier had a subsidised track to run on and still used cheap labour – and urged the Government to incorporate its recommendations in a new Road Traffic Act.

The subsequent 1933 Road Traffic Act, passed on 17 November, introduced the 'A', 'B' and 'C' system of licensing road vehicles. An 'A' licence applied to a vehicle carrying for hire or reward and restricted the use of that vehicle to a specified use and no other; a 'B' licence was for a vehicle carrying a specified traffic over a specified route for a short period; and a 'C' licence was for a tradesman's van or lorry carrying only in connection with his own business. All these licences were issued by the Commissioner after due consideration of each case, and any objections to it.

The Act did not give a definition of a 'contract carriage' nor of a 'special occasion' as the railway companies had requested, so they had to continue their fight against the opportunist road operator by fare-cutting and by exercising their right of opposing the issue of 'B' licences, those that were now required before a bus could be run for some 'special occasion'. The number of 'B' licences applied for by the coach operators and opposed by the GWR 1932-34 were:

Year	1932	1933	1934
Number of objections lodged by GWR	1,047	662	1,169
GWR objections sustained	25%	47%	81%

The mid-'thirties price war continued ferociously in spite of the Parliamentary attempts at control – station staff at some stations refused to buy groceries or any other goods from traders who did not send and receive their supplies by rail! When this became known to Sir James Milne he suggested to his Divisional Superintendents that 'the idea be laid before all Station Masters with a view to extending the action'.

In preparation for the summer of 1933, the independent bus operators wanted to introduce the following ruinously low fares:

Single fare	1d per mile
Period return	$\frac{3}{4}$d per mile
Day return	$\frac{5}{8}$d per mile

The GWR opposed this and was successful in persuading the Traffic Commissioners to retain the existing fare structure.

The independent bus companies could not sustain such a price war, and late in 1933 they were asking the railways, through the Commissioners, for a peace conference 'to obtain an understanding as to the railway companies' attitude to fares'. To this the GWR boldly replied that 'It would be inadvisable to make any statement which would lead the road operators to believe that the railway companies would increase certain of their fares in the event of new road fares being fixed on a higher level than rail fares.'

In December 1933 the railway companies were able to persuade the Traffic Commissioners to refuse 'B' licences to any bus operator who did not provide all-year-round services over the route for which the requested 'B' licence would apply.

On 1 July 1933 the four railway companies each paid 25 per cent of the price to purchase the largest road freight hauliers in Britain - Hays Wharf Cartage, Pickfords and Carter Paterson; Sir James Milne, General Manager of the GWR, became Chairman of Carter Paterson. The railway companies had hoped to divert the traffic on to rail and even restricted the amount of work their road division could take on, but this only resulted in a loss of revenue to the powerful groupings of independent road operators who were coming into the market.

Road haulage was more convenient for those wishing to have their meat, parcels, gramophone records, dried milk, household effects - or whatever - moved, and therefore increasingly by road it was moved, either by the railway-owned Pickfords or an independent such as the Bouts–Tillotson group. The Traffic Commissioner refused to listen to the railway companies' claim that they were supplying all necessary trunk haulage, and continued to issue 'A' licences to independent hauliers.

In 1938 the railway-owned 'A' licence road haulage fleet comprised only 18 per cent of the national total – the GWR and its allies could not buy every road firm in the Kingdom. It is significant that in 1938 the combined net profit made by the four railway companies from their own road haulage operations in 1936 was only £122,000, but the money earned by them from their holdings in the Pickfords group and the 'Associated' bus companies amounted to £967,000.

9
Locomotive economy, 1921–27

George Jackson Churchward was Chief Locomotive, Carriage & Wagon Superintendent from 1902 until 1916, then his title was shortened to Chief Mechanical Engineer (CME). He retired on 31 December 1921 and was succeeded by Charles Benjamin Collett on 1 January 1922.

Collett came to Swindon Drawing Office in 1893 after an engineering training at a general engineering company, Maudslays in London. His forte was seen to be as an organiser, rather than a locomotive engineer. He was a 'Technical Inspector' (what we should call a Manager) in the Works in 1900 and was later placed in charge of the maintenance of Buildings and Machinery of the Works. He became Assistant to the Locomotive Works Manager, H. C. King, in 1901, and took over as Works Manager in 1913, during the period of large-scale extensions to the Works. In addition to his post as Works Manager, Collett was given the additional task of

Steam locomotives were run more economically on the GWR than on any other railway. Even so they cost a great deal, not just in coal but also in the heavy 'fixed plant' required to service them. This is Westbury (Wilts) 'Running & Maintenance' depot, built to G. J. Churchward's standard plan and opened in 1915. On 23 May 1929 No 3388 stands under the massively strong walls of the coaling plant, on top of which rests a 45,000-gallon water tank. (H. C. Casserley)

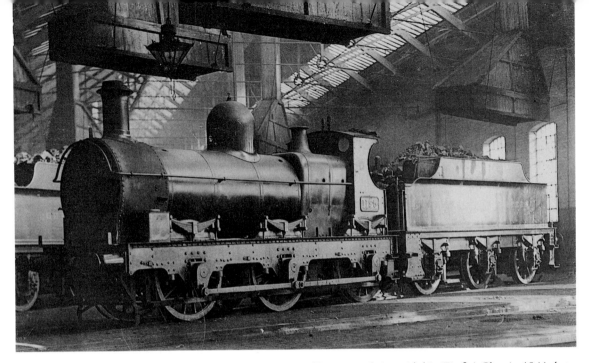

Daniel Gooch had begun the GWR's policy of standardisation of locomotive design with his 'Firefly' Class in 1841, but a rigorous adoption of this economic system of locomotive building did not begin until Churchward took over in 1902. This is No 1195, the last survivor of the 'Armstrong Standard Goods' of 1866, built at Swindon in 1876, and superceded by the Dean 'Standard Goods', at Oxley shed on 24 April 1932. Both classes were large, and small differences in construction occurred over the years. (H. C. Casserley)

Deputy CME on 9 May 1919, and formally relinquished the Works Managership to W. A. Stanier on 1 January 1920.

All GWR locomotive engineers were very capable men and each of them built on the achievements of his predecessor. Since the time of Daniel Gooch, in 1840, standardisation had been attempted, but the policy was never strictly implemented until the advent of Churchward. He devised a scheme of standardised locomotives in 1901; there were to be four boilers, three driving wheel diameters, two kinds of cylinder block and so on, and from this 'kit of parts' any type of locomotive could be produced.

Each component was very carefully designed, directed by Churchward using his own ideas, those of the brilliant team of engineers at Swindon, and drawing upon the best aspects of American, Belgian and French locomotive design. Each prototype was carefully tested before full production commenced. The resulting engines set the standards of excellence in Britain for many years and lasted until the end of steam operation on British Railways.

When Collett took over as CME on 1 January 1922, the GWR total locomotive situation was as follows:

No of locos in stock	3,160
No of locos under repair	962

No of locos available	2,198
Locos in use out of total stock	68.8%
Locos in use out of available stock	98.9%
Average hours in traffic per engine per week	85.5
Average hours in traffic per engine per 24 hrs	12.75

Standard Churchward engines numbered 793, and consisted of:

'22xx' 4-4-2T	29
'28xx' 2-8-0	84
'29xx' 4-6-0	86
'31xx'/'3150' 2-6-2T	100
'38xx' 4-4-0	28
'40xx' 4-6-0	61
'42xx' 2-8-0	95
'43xx'/'53xx'/'63xx' 2-6-0	242
'44xx' 2-6-2T	11
'45xx' 2-6-2T	55
'47xx' 2-8-0	2

More standard engines were needed, particularly of the heavy freight types, but building had been severely restricted by the Works' diversification into armaments and munitions – there was nothing at all in the way of skilled manufacture that the Swindon workforce could not accomplish – including rifling of large gun barrels.

Swindon Drawing Office had begun to scheme a

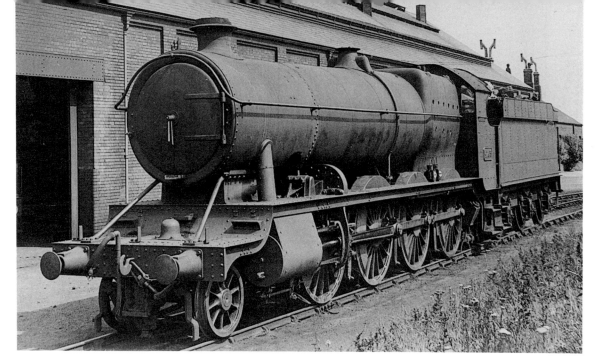

Churchward's ultimate power-house - the '47xx' 2-8-0 of 1919. No 4700 was built with 'standard mixed traffic' 5 ft 8 in driving wheels and a Standard No 1 boiler - the same as that fitted to the 'Star' Class 4-6-0s. However, this was not sufficiently powerful for the heavily loaded, fast freight trains, and a new Standard No 7 boiler was built and fitted to No 4700 in 1921; Nos 4701-8 came out with the No 7 boiler in 1922-3. The No 7 boiler carried 225 lbs per sq in pressure and had 30 sq ft of firegrate, equal to a 'Castle' but in overall dimensions larger, while in total heating surface it exceeded the 'King' Class boiler/firebox. The '47xxs' and their firemen did heavy work on the 'Night Vacuums' and on express passenger trains when occasion demanded. (Adrian Vaughan Collection)

new standard heavy freight locomotive in 1918. It was to be a 2-8-0 version of the 2-6-0 '43xx' Class and would have two 19-inch cylinders (instead of 18½ inches) and a very powerful boiler, the Standard No 7. The new locomotive was intended for very heavy, fast non-stop vacuum-braked freights from London to Plymouth and Wolverhampton. Problems with the weight of the boiler - to keep the engine within the Civil Engineer's weight restriction - delayed its production, and the first of the new engines, No 4700, appeared in January 1919 carrying the less powerful Standard No 1 boiler.

The need for more heavy freight engines was urgent and in 1918 the GWR, unable to build enough, purchased 20 brand new 2-8-0 locomotives of Great Central Railway/Robinson design, built by the North British Locomotive Co. These were numbered 3000-19, and two of them lasted until October 1958. In 1919 another 84 were hired from the Government; these had seen war service and were not in good condition, but were patched up, and on 9 March 1922 all of them were returned to the Government pool.

In 1925 the Ministry of Transport offered its fleet of Robinson 2-8-0s for sale at the gift price of £1,500 each. The GWR bought 80 and numbered

them 3020-99. After four months they were all taken out of traffic and assessed as to condition - a batch of 30 were worth rebuilding, but the rest were not. The lucky 30 were thoroughly reconditioned in the Works and went into traffic painted plain GWR green and numbered 3020-49, the last of them not being scrapped until October 1956. The remaining engines, numbered 3050-99, were merely tidied up in the Works, painted funeral black and then run into the ground - at £1,500 apiece the GWR could afford to do this. The last one was scrapped in 1931.

As a result of the Grouping, which became effective from 1 January 1922, the locomotive works, engine sheds and rolling-stock of 20 small companies was absorbed into GWR ownership and became Collett's responsibility. This included 925 engines, hardly two of them alike. A jumble of buildings, machinery, working conditions - wages, promotional systems, boundaries of supervision - and vast docks, with all their locks, cranes and other machinery, had to be reorganised. New 'Divisions' were formed for the South Wales railways and docks, several works were closed, and the engines and carriages were sorted out for scrapping or reboilering with Swindon standards.

'Star' Class No 4054 waits to leave Kingswear with a train for Manchester in 1931. The Collett-designed coach behind the engine has a Manchester destination board. (Adrian Vaughan Collection)

Cirencester Works of the former M&SWJR was closed, with some transfer of men to Swindon. The Cardiff Works of the Taff Vale Railway was closed and some of the men and machinery transferred to the ex-Rhymney Railway Works at Caerphilly, which was enlarged and modernised as the works for heavy repairs in South Wales. Extensions to Wolverhampton Stafford Road Works, to enable it to repair the largest engines, had been planned in 1900-02 and then shelved, but the plans were resurrected in 1927, the extensions built with some government aid and brought into use in 1932.

Meanwhile Swindon Works had to design and build new, standard engines and catch up with the backlog of repairs occasioned by wartime neglect. With such a workload in one department alone, it can be seen that the GWR's (approximately) £15 million compensation for its war work was merely 'chicken feed' relative to the cost of work which now had to be done.

A first-class organiser was needed at Swindon and it seems likely that it was for this reason that the Directors appointed Collett rather than Stanier to succeed Churchward as CME. Collett was a Production Engineer and knew best how to streamline production, improve working techniques and produce orderliness out of disarray. This was what was badly needed at that time - the brilliant team of locomotive engineers assembled by Churchward could cope with the details of locomotive design.

Under Collett and his team in the Works, the Churchward designs were developed to their highest pitch in terms of manufacture, maintenance on shed and operation, making them the most economical locomotives in Britain.

As passenger traffic increased from 1922, the standard express locomotives - the two-cylinder 'Saints' and four-cylinder 'Stars', each carrying the Churchward No 1 Standard boiler - were found to be overloaded on occasions. The intention, therefore, was to make a new standard express engine using the No 7 Standard boiler.

This boiler, planned by Churchward in 1918 to cope with the foreseen increase in loadings, was intended to be fitted on and increase the power of the '28xx', '29xx' and '40xx' Classes and to produce a new express freight locomotive, the abovementioned '47xx'.

The No 7 had the greatest heating surface of any GWR boiler before 1918 or afterwards, and would have produced all the necessary power, but on a four-cylinder engine it would exceed the 20-ton axle load limit for the under-line bridges. A compromise between the No 1 Standard boiler and the No 7 was therefore designed for express passenger work, to become the No 8, reduced slightly in size so as to keep the engine's weight within the Civil Engineer's maximum loading.

The first of this new class, No 4073 *Caerphilly Castle*, came into service in August 1923. This and subsequent 'Castles' were magnificent machines, but

One of the magnificent 'Castle' Class 4-6-0s being coaled from Churchward's standard coal stage/water tank at Old Oak Common, the largest such facility on the GWR, on 29 June 1934; the tanks held 290,000 gallons and there were five coal drops on each side. Opened in March 1906, millions of tons of coal were hand-shovelled from wagons to trams and tipped on to thousands of tenders before the stage was closed in 1965. (British Rail)

by the end 1925 major trains like the 10.30 am and 3.30 pm from Paddington were taking such heavy loads that a type along the lines of the original proposal was definitely essential.

The matter was raised with Collett during a meeting of the Directors' Locomotive Committee with J. C. Lloyd, Chief Civil Engineer, present. Collett pointed out that he could not build a more powerful engine than the 'Castles' because it would be too heavy for the under-line bridges over which there was the 20-ton axle-load limit. At this juncture Lloyd astonished everyone present by announcing that, except for four, all bridges between Paddington and Plymouth had been strengthened to carry 22½ tons before 1914.

This is *the* classic example of the effect of lack of liaison between GWR Departments, and also of the lack of control over the way Departments spent money. After making the vast outlay to strengthen the bridges, the Directors on the Civil Engineering Committee had not seen fit to inform anyone of this important development. It was as if the bridges had been strengthened merely for the sake of doing so. Had the fact been known, the expense of the interim design 'Castle' Class would have been saved, and neither would the 'King' Class, as we know it, with its special boiler, have been built. Two extra standards need not have come to life, and the original intention of a four-cylinder engine carrying the

already existing No 7 Standard boiler would easily have been sufficient.

Design of the 'Super Castles', what was to become the 'King' Class, began in February 1927. A new large No 12 Standard boiler was designed, the largest on the GWR, although with less heating surface than a No 7. The No 12 had a new working pressure of 250 lbs per sq in, a new cylinder size (for a GWR express passenger engine) of 16 in x 28 in, with the standard express locomotive wheel diameter of 6 ft 8½ in. This gave a nominal tractive effort of 39,000 lbs, and it would have done all that was required in the matter of hauling the heaviest expresses. However, the General Manager, Sir Felix Pole, wanted the figure of 40,000 lbs - it would look so much better in print.

To achieve this nominal figure, the cylinders were enlarged to a non-standard 16¼ inches and the driving wheel diameter was reduced to a non-standard 6 ft 6in - to produce a publicity-conscious figure of 40,300 lbs for the nominal tractive effort. This made the new engine the most powerful in Britain - and with its large Collett/Churchward boiler its actual performance was sure to live up to the mere figures.

In addition, an extra publicity opportunity was presented to the GWR. In September 1925 the President of the Baltimore & Ohio Railroad, Daniel Willard, and his friend Edward Hungerford, anticipating the centenary of their system in 1927, had come to view the Stockton & Darlington Centenary celebrations. There they had seen in the cavalcade the GWR's superb No 4082 *Windsor Castle*, and had invited Sir Felix Pole to send a 'Castle' to their own company's 'Fair of the Iron Horse' in September 1927 as the *sole* British exhibit.

Now that the 'Super Castle' was being planned, this was the engine to go to America - but Swindon would have to 'look sharp', for the Fair was only seven months away and the 'Super Castle' was still on the drawing-board.

The new engine, named *King George V* and numbered 6000, had its first official photograph taken on 16 June 1927. The rest of the class, a further 29 engines, entered service between July 1927 and August 1930. On 20 July No 6000

made a faultless maiden run on the 'Cornish Riviera' - no teething troubles, it simply *worked*.

Expenditure on the 'Super Castles', or 'Kings', was formally agreed by the Directors' Locomotive Committee on 28 July 1927, chaired by James Mason, with Sir Aubrey Brocklebank (Director) and C. B. Collett present, amongst others. Collett had reminded the meeting that Minute 8 of 17 December 1925 had agreed to the construction of 20 additional 'Castle' Class engines, but that these had not been built owing to the unsettled nature of 1926. The money for the construction of 20 engines was therefore still available, and Collett proposed that the funds be diverted to the construction of a small class of 'Super Castles'.

No 6000 and the broad gauge replica *North Star* set sail for America on 3 August 1927. On the 10th the 10.30 am from Paddington, hauled by No 6003 *King George IV*, suffered a derailed bogie running at 60 mph on a curve between Midgham and Thatcham. No-one was injured and No 6003 was not damaged, so returned to Swindon under its own steam.

The derailment was attributed to variations in the superelevation of the curve, to the spongy nature of the foundations after heavy rain - plus a design fault in the springing of the leading wheels of the bogie. Mr A. W. J. Dymond, a young ex-Taff Vale Railway draughtsman in Swindon Works Drawing Office (and who later became Mayor of Swindon), designed extra coil springs for these wheels, which cured the problem for all time.

The specifications for the new springs were telegraphed to Baltimore, with strict instructions that No 6000 was not to run until the new springs had been fitted. The work was carried out by Swindon fitters Williams and Dando travelling with the 'King' which, driven by Old Oak Driver Young, went on to amaze everyone with its performances. The engine returned to England on 3 November 1927, carrying an American locomotive bell on it buffer-beam as a token of American admiration.

Enthusiasm for GWR locomotives and No 6000 in particular was enormous, and regular 'specials' were run to Swindon Works from Paddington and Bristol by 'The King of Locomotives':

No 6000 special runs from Paddington, November 1927

Date	Passengers	Earnings (£)	Earnings per mile (£)
3rd	645	161	10s 5d
10th	451	113	14s 6d
16th	696	106	22s 3d

By 18 January 1928 29 trips, including tours around the Works, had been made, carrying 14,000 people.

A powerful standardised engine was also required for freight and passenger work on the steeply-graded South Wales 'Valley' lines. The intention was to reduce the wide variety of local types, to reduce the total size of the South Wales fleet and thus make the operation more economical to operate. Many of the ex-Taff Vale, Cardiff, Rhymney and Brecon & Merthyr railways' engines had the 0-6-2 wheel arrangement with inside cylinders, and in deference to local wishes this was adopted, rather than Swindon's outside-cylindered 2-6-2T.

The new engines had the No 2 Standard boiler, with 200 lbs per sq in working pressure, 4 ft 7½ in wheels, 18 in x 26 in cylinders with piston valves, and 1,900-gallon side tanks. The boiler and wheels were the same as the Churchward '45xx' 2-6-2T but the boiler pressure was higher. Between 1926 and 1928 Swindon built 150, Nos 5600-6649. Another 50, Nos 6650-99, were built by Armstrong Whitworth. The reason given in the GWR Minutes for this 'contracting out' was to allow the Works to catch up on arrears of repair work.

Churchward's 1901 plan for standard engines had envisaged a 4-6-0 with No 1 boiler and 5 ft 8 in wheels. No such engine had been built, and by 1924 the need was pressing for a 'mixed traffic' engine larger than the '43xx'. Collett's solution was to take a standard '29xx' 4-6-0, No 2925 *Saint Martin*, with its No 1 Standard boiler, 18½ in by 30 in cylinders and 10-inch diameter piston valves, and replace its 6 ft 8½ in driving wheels with wheels 6 feet in diameter.

This powerful machine entered service in December 1924, re-numbered No 4900, and was of course instantly successful, but it was not until 23 December 1927 that an order for 80 of the 'St Martin' Class was given to the Works. These cost £6,000 each and the Company's sensible policy was that their construction should be 'paid for' by the scrapping of 100 4-4-0, 2-6-0, 2-4-0, 2-8-0 (ROD) and 0-6-0 locomotives of an equal or greater replacement value.

The Great Western was fortunate – and for many years unique – in having the Automatic Train Control (ATC) system (see chapter 21 and Appendix 2). The system was first installed on the Henley branch in 1906 and in 1908 at some distant signals between Reading and Paddington. A handful of top-rank engines were fitted with the pick-up gear in that year – Nos 4000, 4003 and 4006 – but it was not until 1923 that ATC gear became standard equipment for all first-rank express engines. The 'Castles' were fitted with it as they were built, the older 'Star' and 'Saint' Classes received it between 1923 and 1927, and from 30 June 1927 the ATC gear was fitted as standard to all new and overhauled engines as they went through the Works. During the same period, 1923-27, the bogie brake gear fitted to the top-rank engines was removed without any appreciable reduction in their braking efficiency.

10

Locomotive economy, 1927–39

In 1927 the GWR locomotive running expenses compared with other railways were as follows:

	Loco miles	Running expenses	Cost per mile
GWR	96,324,425	£6,015,840	1s 3d
LMS	235,794,145	£15,314,834	1s 3.6d
LNER	168,913,409	£11,647,609	1s 4.5d
SR	68,761,717	£4,727,053	1s 4.65d

Great Western engines were and remained the most economical in Britain, thanks to Churchward's vision, to Collett's brilliant organisation of Swindon and the other Works – and also, it must never be forgotten, to skilled and conscientious railwaymen.

Nos 4901-5 of the 'St Martin' Class, or 'Hall' Class as it was to become, appeared in December 1928, and between 1 January and August Bank Holiday 1929 the class was increased up to No

In 1930 many locomotive depots were using servicing facilities which were inadequate when they were built in the 1850s, yet the GWR had not the money to rebuild them. However, as a result of the 1929 Loans Act several depots had their decrepit amenities replaced by a new 'standard' loco shed to a design typical of a 'light engineering' factory of the period, and a 'standard' coaling stage with coal tips rather than wicker baskets lifted from the ground by hand or buckets raised by hand-winch. This is the new 1932 Kidderminster coaling stage, seen on 9 March of that year. (British Rail)

4944. These fast and powerful machines were very useful on the multitude of relief trains and excursion trains run that year. In the week preceding August Bank Holiday the GWR ran a total of 657 extra passenger trains in addition to the busy summer service.

The 'Halls' took over from the small 4-4-0 classes and at once effected an economy - they could take longer trains and were less likely to require banking engines. Also, longer trains meant fewer trains, and fewer engines to haul them.

Between 1922 and 1929 the total number of engines in stock was reduced from 3,940 to 3,858, whilst the total engine-miles increased from 95,060,257 to 97,396,313.

The '43xx' Class 2-8-0s, working the slow freight, fast 'vacuum goods' and passenger trains in far-flung parts of the GWR, were subject to excessive tyre wear on the leading driving wheels when working regularly over the serpentine routes of Dorset, Devon, Cornwall or West Wales. In November/December 1927, four engines, Nos 4351/85/86/95, were given a 1-foot extension at the front and a 2-ton casting was attached behind the front buffer-beam. This brought more weight on the pony truck so that it would act more effectively to lead the forward driving wheels into curves, thus reducing flange wear on the latter.

These modified engines were renumbered from No 8351 onwards, but very shortly afterwards were 'de-modified' and returned to their original numbering. However, between January and March 1928 65 '43xx' Class engines were modified to become '83xxs'. In 1932, 20 'de-luxe' '83xx' engines were built, Nos 9300-19. These carried 'Castle' cabs and a screw reverser. So long as the '83xx' and '93xx' engines carried the weighted buffer-beam, they were 'Red route' engines, subject to the same route restrictions as the 'Hall' and 'Castle' Classes.

In October 1928 the engineering firm of William Beardmore & Co asked for and was granted permission to equip a '29xx' 'Saint' Class 4-6-0 engine with the company's special boiler and firebox designed to burn pulverised coal, all costs to be borne by Beardmore. Pulverised coal was startlingly filthy in use and after a brief trial on the '29xx' the idea was dropped, although a stationary boiler in the Works continued to burn the filthy stuff for a longer period.

Beardmore also asked permission to fit Caprotti valve gear to a '29'. The GWR did not allow this but they was sufficiently interested to purchase from Associated Locomotive Equipment for £860 a set of rotary cam poppet valve gear. This, together with new cylinders, was fitted by Swindon Works to No 2935 *Caynham Court* in May 1931. The experiment was successful but this engine remained the sole example, and was scrapped in December 1948.

There were in 1930 still a great many Victorian tank engines, in a variety of types and states of

A conventional Victorian branch train - semi-cabless tank engine dating from 1872 hauling four- and six-wheeled carriages from about 1878. Yet this is the Longbridge-Halesowen branch train on 29 May 1935, and it could equally well have been running on any of the GWR's short branch lines at this period. (H. C. Casserley)

Above and below Typical of the many Victorian tank engines still running by the dawn of the 1930s is No 1300, built at Swindon in December 1878, which worked in South Devon for all of its life and was, for many years, along with its sister engine No 1298, the Tiverton Junction-Hemyock branch engine. No 1300 was not withdrawn from service until May 1934, so the GWR got good service from it. It is seen here outside its shed at Hemyock and with its vintage train of mixed, passenger and freight vehicles on 25 May 1929 - not much competition here for the local bus company. (Both H. C. Casserley)

rebuilding, at work as shunters and even on main-line suburban passenger duties. The need was to reduce this expensive variety to a few standardised classes. Two basic designs were chosen, one based on the 1897-vintage '2721' Class of 0-6-0 saddle tank - part of a tradition of design going back to 1870 - and the other based on George Armstrong's '517' Class 0-4-2 tank which had a pedigree dating back to 1868, although improved somewhat in later years.

The '2721' 0-6-0 saddle tank weighed around 47 tons, had a boiler pressure of 150 lbs per sq in, two inside cylinders of $17\frac{1}{2}$ in x 24 in, slide valves, no superheating, driving wheels of 4 ft $7\frac{1}{2}$ in diameter, and a nominal tractive effort of 15,935 lbs. The new standard '57xx' differed only in its 'pannier' tanks,

the enclosed cab, leaf springs on the leading and central axles - instead of coiled springs - and a boiler pressure of 200 lbs per sq in, giving 30 per cent greater tractive effort. The first batch of 50, numbered 5700-49, came out of Swindon Works between January and April 1929. As a result of grant/loan money from the Government under the 1929 Development Act, a second batch of 50, Nos 5750-99, was built by the North British Locomotive Co between April 1929 and November 1930 in order to give some jobs in the depressed North East. Fifty more '56xx' 0-6-2Ts were also constructed 'outside', by Armstrong Whitworth.

The '57xx' became the most numerous class on the GWR - 863 were built, numbered in blocks between 36xx to 97xx. Numbers 6700-99 were freight engines, lacking both vacuum brake and steam heating connections. The '57s' and their variants were powerful machines, classed '4F' by British Railways.

To replace the ageing fleet of Dean and Armstrong 0-6-0 engines used as goods and light passenger engines, the Collett 0-6-0 was introduced from March 1930. The new engines were heavier than old Dean engines, so some of the latter were retained for working certain lines. The new engines, the '2251' Class, were to the standard scheme with 17½ in x 24 in cylinders, slide valves, the No 10 boiler pressed to 200 lbs per sq in, and 5 ft 2 in diameter wheels. Construction continued until 1948 and 120 machines were built.

Swindon was on short time from 1930 to 1933, sometimes working only a three-day week. In 1931 the Works was working well below its capacity and built only 93 new locomotives, including 10 'Kings', 295 carriages (including the 'Ocean' saloons), and 3,350 wagons, the latter being 45 per cent of full capacity. In 1932 2,700 men were laid off and 100 engines were stored due to lack of traffic. There was some irony in the fact that the Government paid to reduce unemployment in the North and Scotland by transferring work from Swindon and thus increasing unemployment there.

But there were also more long-term reasons for the lack of work in Swindon factory. Collett's continuation of Churchward's standardisation policy had reduced the size of the locomotive fleet and his reforms of production methods had reduced the amount of work required to maintain this reduced fleet. Collett and his Works Manager, R. A. G. Hannington, had developed a streamlined production system for standardised and very precisely made

parts which ensured a well-fitted and long-lasting machine. More miles were being run between 'shoppings' and the time spent in the shops was reduced.

To ensure that boilers lasted as long as possible - and that they fitted when lowered on to an engine - they were made with as much precision as a connecting rod. In the past the boilers had not always been exactly the right size when matched with an engine, so time-wasting modifications had to be made. To overcome this, Collett installed a *fitter* rather than a boilersmith as Manager of the Boiler Shop, the boilers were made more exactly to the drawings, and engines passed through the Works faster as a result. The mileage covered by boilers between major repairs increased throughout the 1930s so that it was known for a boiler to work 320,000 miles before being taken off the frames for rebuilding. The average mileage between heavy repairs for boilers was 165,000 in 1937-8.

Locomotive cylinders, frames and axle-box guides were aligned, conventionally, with taut wire and ruler, and a great deal depended on the efforts of the erector. A lot of time was consumed in setting-out the engine, and a badly aligned engine would not last long in service before it was 'knocking'.

In 1933 Collett introduced the Zeiss optical system of alignment and combined this absolutely precise system with a machine for grinding each pair of axle-box guides simultaneously to ensure that they were perfectly in line with each other across the frame. These improvements in construction, together with careful maintenance on the running shed, gave increased mileages to both engines and boilers. The GWR spent £6,500,000 annually on the construction, maintenance and repair of its engines, so even a 5 per cent saving represented a lot of money and was worth making.

In November 1931 the first of 25 '54xx' 0-6-0 pannier tanks appeared. This was No 5400 - simply No 2080, of the 19th-century '2021' Class, fitted with the 'push-and-pull' gear, 5 ft 2 in wheels and an enclosed cab, but still with the same 165 lbs per sq in boiler. A variation for hilly country, using 4 ft 7½ in wheels, was introduced in February 1932; there were 40 of them, numbered in the 64xx series. Starting in July 1936 another 50 were built, with increased (180 lbs per sq in) pressure and numbered in the 74xx series. These were not fitted for push-pull working.

Armstrong's '517' Class 0-4-2 saddle tank of 1868, with 5-foot wheels and 150 lbs per sq in pres-

'517' Class 0-4-2T No 3577, built at Wolverhampton in 1895, and a pair of clerestories of a design turned out of Swindon between 1894 and 1903, form the 1.50 pm Kidderminster- Wooferton Junction, leaving Cleobury Mortimer at 2.20 pm (if on time) in September 1938. The second vehicle is a brake-van/carriage incorrectly but unavoidably marshalled with the passenger accommodation at the rear of the train. (Clinker Collection/courtesy Brunel University)

sure, was well known for its simplicity and economy. The last ten were built in 1884/5 with side tanks, a longer wheelbase (15 ft 6 in), outside bearings to the trailing axle and 5 ft 1 in driving wheels. The greatest differences between the 1885 '517' and the Collett '48xx' was that the driving wheel diameter was increased to 5 ft 2 in, the boiler pressure was raised to 165 lbs per sq in, and 'push-pull' apparatus and an enclosed cab were fitted. No 4800 entered service in August 1932 and the class eventually numbered 75 machines. These were re-numbered in the 14xx series in 1946. A second batch, totalling 20 engines, was introduced from January 1933. These were the '58xxs', identical to the '48xxs' expect that they were not fitted for push-pull working.

Another up-dating of an old design began in January 1930 when the boiler of 'Duke of Cornwall' Class 4-4-0 No 3265 (built in July 1896) was placed on the engine and frames of 'Bulldog' Class 4-4-0 No 3365 (built in February 1902). This was the prototype of the '32xx' 'Earl' Class, 29 of which were introduced between May 1936 and November 1939. They were, strictly speaking, rebuilds of the 'Bulldog' Class, since the engine, wheels and frames of the latter were used, married to a 'Duke of Cornwall' Class boiler. The first 13, built between May 1936 and May 1937, carried the names of Earls but the names were removed during June 1937. The first 19 had reconditioned 'Duke' boilers, all with pressure increased from 160 to 180

lbs per sq in, and all but three of them had a one-row superheater.

A type of 4-6-0 locomotive envisaged by Churchward in 1901 was introduced in August 1936. This was the '68xx' or 'Grange' Class, a pure Churchward standardisation - '"Halls" with small wheels' (of 5 ft 8 in diameter). They were replacements for the 300 or so standard 2-6-0s, but only 80 of the new class were built. The wheels and valve gear of scrapped '43xx' engines were used, otherwise these were new engines.

The 5ft 8in driving wheels of the 'Granges' gave them a higher nominal tractive effort than the 'Halls', useful for starting heavy loads and hill-climbing, so they were used a lot for heavy, fast goods work between Penzance and Paddington. They were also capable of cruising at 75 mph with 10-coach trains on level track. They were, however, 'Red route' engines, and something lighter was required.

Continuing along the Churchward tradition of standardisation, the gap was filled with a 'Grange' carrying a smaller (lighter) boiler. This became the '78xx' or 'Manor' Class, weighing 6 tons less than the 'Granges' but with a nominal tractive effort only 1,500 lbs less. Thus a very powerful 4-6-0 was available for all GWR secondary main lines and cross-country routes in England and Wales. Twenty were built under GWR auspices between January 1938 and February 1939 - and another ten by British Railways.

A statistical survey in the *Great Western Railway Magazine* compared average costs of 1935 with those of the three years 1923-25. It showed that there was a decrease in the weight carried, per journey, by each wagon. Why this should have been is not at all clear, but was possibly because, as traffic leaked away to road and the Company went after any traffic it could get, smaller consignments were going to more diverse locations, so more wagons were needed to convey smaller loads. In 1935 the average wagon carried 3.77 tons less than in 1925.

The effect of this was that there were 430,000 more wagon journeys in 1935 to carry the same tonnage as in 1925, the average weight of freight per train being 131.77 tons, 2.6 per cent less than in 1925. The railway in 1935 was therefore busier than in 1925, with more shunting in the yards, more wagons on the move, more trains, and a greater use of the track - but those extra wagon journeys were earning less revenue than in 1925. The average miles per wagon per engine-hour was, in 1935, 119.29, the highest recorded up to that time and a 10 per cent improvement on 1925. At 1925 standards of efficiency, this mileage would have required an additional 700,000 freight engine-hours.

Freight trains were travelling faster. In 1925 the average train miles per engine-hour was 8.2; ten years later the figure was 9.75, while the average of train miles per engine-hour of coaching trains - passenger, parcels, milk - increased from 13.53 in 1925 to 14.08 in 1935. These figures include the entire time the engine was associated with its train, whether standing, running or shunting off wagons or carriages.

These small increases, mathematically speaking, represented a large saving in money. In the freight operation, 450,000 more train-hours would have been required, at 1925 levels of efficiency, to run the 1935 service, while on the coaching side 120,000 more engine-hours would have been required. In 1935 there was a 5.19 per cent improvement in the availability of the total locomotive fleet for duty (this including even those engines stored out of use but serviceable) compared to 1925, and those engines ran a greater daily mileage - an average of 108 miles per engine against 103 in 1925. These improvements continued until at least the end of 1939.

The GWR spent £1,637,000 on coal in 1935. That year the coaching trains' engines burned 5.3 per cent less coal - per engine-mile - than in 1925, but this gain was halved by the freight engines which used, on a 'per engine-mile' basis, 3.27 per cent more coal than in 1925. In the train running costs, overall, there was a saving of 4.76 per cent compared to 1925.

From 1933 to 1937 the Company's gross income increased from the all-time low of 1932, and the margin between income and expenditure gradually widened in favour of income up to a peak in 1937 - which actually exceeded the 1930 performance - and which was also the peak year of the decade for 'miles run per loco'. This improvement was in large measure due to the efficiency of Swindon Works, and the Locomotive Running & Maintenance Department.

Between 1927 and 1937 there was a *decrease* of 11 per cent in the total stock of GWR locomotives, yet an *increase* in the miles worked by each locomotive and a *decrease* in the coal burnt.

Each week in 1927 not less than 74.6 per cent of serviceable engines were actually available for duty. In the years 1936-39, this figure was never less than 82 per cent, and in most weeks it was around the 90 per cent mark.

	Locos in stock	Total annual loco miles	Miles per loco
1927	4,088	95,953,179	23,472
1929	3,945	97,396,313	24,689
1933	3,779	89,369,677	23,649
1937	3,621	100,421,983	27,718
1939	3,701	97,611,406	26,374

These 'miles per loco' averages include such characters as the '1101' Class of 0-6-0 dock tanks which made a very low mileage, as well as the 'Castles' running from Paddington to Plymouth. In the autumn of 1937 the average working time for each engine was 13.73 hours per day, which was fairly typical of the 1936-39 period.

Greater savings could have been made by investing in diesel or electric motive power, but this would have required a vast initial outlay which the struggling Company could not afford. Thus the old-fashioned but tried and trusted system was made to run as efficiently as possible and, indeed, was the best-run steam railway in Britain.

In 1938 the cost of repairs to GWR engines was £484 per locomotive - the best figure in the Grouping companies, and due in large measure to the highly standardised fleet. The LNER, at the bottom of the league, was spending £568 per loco. LNER wages costs for footplate crews and shed staff were, in 1938, the highest amongst the four companies, with the GWR in second place.

On 11 October 1938 the price of locomotive coal was 32 per cent higher than in 1934, and the GWR Chairman, Viscount Horne, noted 'an increasingly serious situation owing to the decline in the Company's receipts. It is imperative to curtail expenses.' The feasibility of electrifying the Taunton-Penzance section, where coal costs were heaviest, was discussed in 1938 and theoretical costings were circulated amongst the GWR's top men, but with a war obviously imminent there was no future for the proposals.

1938 was the first year that fewer engines were built or re-built than in the preceding year - 122 locos, 28 less than 1937 - and 117 were scrapped. But in 1938 the Works also carried out 1,000 heavy and 1,000 light repairs to locomotives, 4,000 heavy repairs to carriages and 11,000 to wagons, with a total workshop staff of around 8,000.

It is easy to see how financial savings could have been made if fewer wagons could have carried more traffic - and if the GWR had not been forced to maintain more carriages than was strictly necessary for its scheduled service. The extra stock was required to cater for seasonal peaks in an attempt to earn extra revenue and make up for a declining regular traffic.

The Great Western arrived at the start of another war financially poorer yet mechanically richer than it had been at any time in its long history. The Works, the Locomotive Department and the locomotives themselves were the most efficiently run of any in Britain, and this was to stand the Company and the country in good stead during the next six years of war, when the gigantic efforts of railways and railwaymen and women was, according to Winston Churchill, speaking in the House of Commons in 1945, of the most vital importance to the successful outcome of the Allied war effort.

11
Modern motive power

The GWR Board had been interested in cheaper forms of rail traction since 1903. Between 1904 and 1908 99 steam railmotors were put into service in relatively heavily populated rural or suburban areas; they were successful in developing traffic, but for technical reasons they were not powerful enough to service the increased loads. Whilst the last 10 were not withdrawn until 1935, the rest of them were turned into 'driving trailers' for locomotive 'push-pull' haulage, commencing in 1915.

In 1911 the Company had purchased a four-wheeled, 40 hp petrol-electric railcar, each axle being driven by an electric motor. It could seat 46 passengers and run at 35 mph. It was used on the Windsor branch, but overheating problems forced its withdrawal in 1919. In 1924 the GWR considered buying four of the newly designed 'Sentinel' steam railmotors, but nothing came of this.

A steam railmotor at Himley on the Kingswinford-Oxley branch. This branch and the 64-chain Stourbridge Junction-Stourbridge Town branch were the last places to be worked by these machines, the last being withdrawn in 1935.

The driver and fireman are standing by the cab door, the very smart Station Master by the wall, a porter and guard in the shadows - four staff and not a passenger in sight. Perhaps they have already boarded the car; if so, the crew seem in no hurry to move on. (Lens of Sutton)

In 1927 the GWR considered electrifying the London-Birmingham 'New Line' with overhead catenary, but as this route was joint property with the LNER from Ashendon Junction south to Northolt Junction, the idea was dropped and instead the possibility was studied of converting to electric haulage with overhead catenary the route between Taunton and Penzance. The plan did not get beyond the discussion stage, because of a lack of business confidence as well as a lack of cash, but I have found some pencil sketches of proposed layouts for Taunton station, where steam and electric engines would have been changed. The existing steam engine shed was to have been retained on the down side, while a second shed for the electrics was proposed alongside with an Engine Line in a tunnel under the running lines to the east end of the up side of the station.

In October 1938, with coal costs 32 per cent higher than in 1934, there was another discussion of the feasibility of electrifying the Taunton-Penzance section, but as mentioned in the previous chapter, nothing came of it.

In March 1929 the Directors told Collett to look into the possibility of using diesel traction, and he investigated - with a closed mind - the potential for diesel multiple units and diesel locos on main-line, branch, suburban and shunting work. In his report he referred to the difficulty of obtaining a diesel engine to meet the specifications, and of the prohibitive expense of the diesel-electric system. He also said that oil firing was 'too expensive', and went on:

'Steam locos using coal are very economical. The Cornish Riviera went out of Paddington [recently] with 16 on for 550 tons and after slipping two at Westbury, Taunton and Exeter, arrived at Plymouth with 10 for 350 tons, in 4 hours, having used 4½ tons of coal'.

The fireman therefore shovelled an average of 42 lbs of coal every minute for 4 hours; Collett assumed that his top-link firemen had trained themselves to standards of Olympic fitness and strength. But it was the engines that were tuned to be economical.

'This,' Collett's report continued, 'is the main reason why our steam locomotives are still holding their own against electrification. Electrification needs cheap electricity from the National 'Super' power stations and it also needs business confidence before embarking on such expensive plans.

'Diesel and diesel-electric types are being consid-

ered but their very high first cost prevents their general introduction on the railway. A small diesel-electric car on the LNER will be successful only if it can be single manned. We employ a small petrol shunter. One diesel-electric is at work on Canadian National Railways supplied by Wm Beardmore & Co. It cost £57,000 and the experiment continues.'

William Beardmore Ltd proposed for the GWR two three-car 500 hp diesel-electric sets with a power car at each end, but Collett squashed this idea by pointing out that the six-car train would cost £34,000 to build against £17,700 for two push-pull fitted '517' Class locomotives and six 'push-pull' suburban carriages - and the steam-hauled train had 384 seats against the 336 of the diesel-electric.

Collett estimated that separate diesel-electric locomotives big enough to haul suburban trains would cost £60,000 against £22,000 for a '31xx' 2-6-2 tank engine. A small diesel locomotive of 500 hp for branch-line work would cost anything from £11,800 to £14,300 from Beardmore against a steam locomotive costing £3,000. The investment ought to have been made, but the GWR had no money for it and no-one was likely to invest in a concern which paid such a small dividend.

Coal for GWR engines was found by coal-brokers Gueret, Llewellyn & Morrett. On 25 July 1929 they supplied 31,000 tons of Llynhelig large screened coal at 17 shillings per ton, and 52,000 tons of Abercynon large screened at 17s 6d. But there was far more to the expense of running a steam engine than the price of coal. Water supply was also a heavy expense. The GWR had to maintain dozens of steam pumping engines (replaced through the 1930s by electric motors) and their pump-houses, lineside water trough installations, water softeners, hundreds of storage tanks, pipelines and water columns.

Water was pumped from wells, rivers and canals. But well water might be full of lime, and river and canal water full of mud, which made boiler washing not only more difficult but more frequent. Locomotive water at Old Oak Common came from the Grand Union Canal at the back of the shed, and was somewhat muddy - and not lacking in wildlife. This was probably why, on 26 July 1934, this supply was discontinued in favour of taking water from the Metropolitan Water Board. The MWB charged 8d per 1,000 gallons daily if not more than ½ million gallons were consumed, and 1 shilling per 1,000 gallons for any daily quantity in excess of that.

In his report Collett made no reference, as far as

can be seen from the Locomotive Committee's Minutes, to the substantial savings to be made from reduced running, maintenance and labour costs, increased availability for work, faster running times and the abolition of an enormous estate of fixed plant like engine sheds, workshops and water-supply works if diesel or electric traction was adopted. Neither did the report inform his Directors of the advantages of a more rapid acceleration from rest and a virtually instant turnround time. He even went so far as to claim that his steam express engines were an economic match for electric locos!

This lack of enthusiasm for modern traction and the lack of questions from the experienced members of the Locomotive Committee prompts the question whether Collett and his Directors were so in love with their beautiful steam engines they could not bear to get rid of them? The most sensible answer must be that in 1930 the diesel was too new. During their first ten years on British Railways, 1958 to 1968, when the technology had been tried and tested after years of war, diesel locomotives were still remarkably unreliable, so in 1930 Collett was perhaps right to be cautious, especially given the very difficult financial position of the GWR.

The Company's steam engines were tried, tested and, by steam engine standards, very cheap to run. With Britain deep in recession it was no time to be buying an entirely new and untried form of motive power - but then, when is the right time? The potential savings, increases in revenue and profits which dieselisation or, better still, electrification would have brought were badly needed. But the final decision rested with the Directors, and probably because of a lack of money for the investment and a lack of confidence, they decided to proceed no further with the business at that stage.

Savings continued to be made by reducing the size of the locomotive fleet, replacing smaller, older designs with a smaller number of more powerful standardised machines, relatively cheap to build and maintain and capable of hauling a greater tonnage. The locomotive building plan authorised on 25 July 1929 was as follows:

To replace	No	Replacement cost
'38xx' 4-4-0s	20	£101,000
'ROD' 2-8-0s & '39xx' 2-6-2Ts	-	-
'22xx' 4-4-2Ts	30	£110,000

0-6-2Ts, 0-4-2Ts, 2-4-0Ts, ex-TVR etc, all 50/60 years old	20	£64,000
0-6-0Ts	30	£90,000
Total	100	£365,000

Build new	No	Cost
'60xx'	10	£75,000
'49xx'	20	£112,000
'51xx'	30	£123,000
New autos	30	£90,000
Total	100	£446,000

£81,000 from 'Betterment' fund. Expenditure approved.

The firm of Hardy Motors, which had been working on internal combustion engined railcars since 1923 and which by 1932 was a subsidiary of AEC of Southall, produced in 1933 a diesel railcar cheap enough to attract the Great Western. The 'AEC' railcar, as it came to be known, was given its preliminary trials on the Southall-Brentford branch, without a body, in July; it was then fitted with a beautifully streamlined body designed by Swindon Drawing Office and built by Park Royal Coachworks Ltd after wind tunnel experiments at the Chiswick Works of the London Passenger Transport Board. The finished vehicle was shown at the Motor Show in October and then went out and about around the London-Didcot area, for, I suppose, crew training.

On 1 December 1933 it gave a press run from Paddington to Reading, covering the 36 miles in 40 minutes, start to stop. The car weighed 20 tons, was 62 feet long and had seats for 69 people. It had a single 130 bhp engine (at 2,260 rpm) driving through an epicyclic (pre-selector) gearbox and cardan shaft to one bogie, giving a top speed of 60 mph. It did not have conventional draw-gear and could not haul any tail-load. It could be driven from either end and had a public address system to enable to guard to speak to the passengers.

Its single engine made it rather slow in getting away, but it cruised up to and maintained 61 mph and at that speed it ran steadily and 'silently'. The car cost a mere £3,000 and was a revolutionary step for the technology of diesels as well as for railway operating.

On 4 December 1933 diesel railcar No 1 was put into daily revenue-earning use. It was stabled at Southall and ran 218 miles a day in 16 trips between Southall, Windsor, Henley and Reading at a fuel consumption of 7½ mpg. It was withdrawn after two weeks for modifications to its braking system

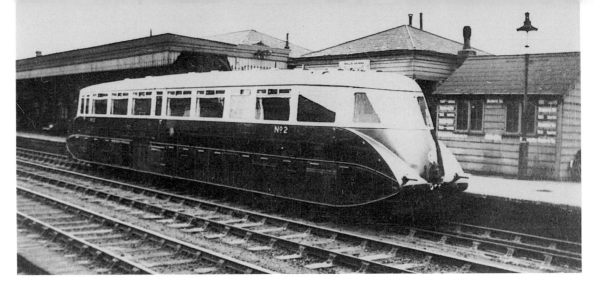

While lack of funds prevented thoroughgoing modernisation of GWR rolling-stock, the Company did what they could. This is diesel railcar No 2, a beautiful vehicle introduced in December 1933 and seen here at the up platform of the shabby Oxford station forming a service to Princes Risborough via Thame on 20 July 1935. In total the Company managed to build 36 diesel railcars. (Dr Jack Hollick/Adrian Vaughan Collection)

and to have the ATC gear fitted and returned to traffic in February 1934.

Passengers and the GWR were delighted with the new vehicle and an order was placed with AEC for three further cars, more powerful and with better accommodation. Nos 2, 3 and 4 cost £3,500 each, and were intended for long-distance express travel with an engine on each bogie, giving 80 mph on level track. They had two small lavatories, a bar and tiny kitchen, and seats for 44 people with tables between the seats. Nos 2 and 3 came into use in July 1934, No 4 in September.

The original idea had been that these cars, with limited seating, would provide cheaply a sort of 'mopping up' service where there were some passengers but not enough to justify the expense of a locomotive and coaches. But when used on certain main lines they generated more traffic than they could handle!

On 6 July 1934, a year after the Company had inaugurated its Plymouth-Birmingham air service, one of these larger cars made a successful trial run from Birmingham to Cardiff. The distance of 105½ miles was covered in 115½ minutes, 7¾ minutes less than the schedule. A regular passenger service with the cars was inaugurated immediately and, being a bright, fast and modern innovation, they attracted a lot of passengers whilst at the same time reducing the operating costs to a fraction of that of running steam locomotives and coaches.

This service was a complete success and in December 1934 the General Manager asked the Directors to buy an additional 13 streamlined twin-engined cars, some with buffet facilities, one each to work the following routes:

> Didcot-Worcester-Hereford
> Kidderminster-Malvern local
> Swindon-Oxford-Leamington
> Malvern-Worcester-Birmingham-Stratford
> Bristol-Salisbury
> Bristol-Weymouth
> Swansea-Tenby
> Stourbridge Town
> Uxbridge-Denham-Gerrard's Cross
> Spare cars at Oxford, Worcester, Birmingham and Swansea

This request was granted, and between July 1935 and April 1936 13 new railcars, numbered 5-17, were put into service (No 17 was not a passenger vehicle but a high-speed streamlined parcels delivery van working between Paddington and Reading). They worked more or less as shown above except that the proposed Swindon-Leamington service seems to have been to Banbury only. The cars at Oxford worked to Worcester, Hereford, Leamington, Didcot, Princes Risborough and Fairford.

In June 1935 the GWR received a petition from the villagers of Charlbury for the crack 8.55 am Worcester-Paddington and the return 4.45 pm Paddington-Wolverhampton via Worcester to stop at Charlbury. The villagers were accommodated with a diesel railcar originating from Oxford at 8.15 am and running 'all stations', calling at Charlbury at 8.36 and arriving at Kingham at 8.55 to connect with the 9.00 am to Chipping Norton. Leaving

Castle Cary station seen from the front cab of the first diesel railcar in public service between Weymouth and Bristol on 17 February 1936. Signs of industry are the smoking chimney of the milk factory, the 'Siphon' on the right and the box van on the 'goods shed road'.

The hip-gabled signal box and adjacent goods shed were destroyed and the signalman was killed by a direct hit from a German bomb on 3 September 1942. (John Haywood/Adrian Vaughan Collection)

Kingham at 9.10 am, the railcar ran 'all stations' back to Oxford, calling at Charlbury at 9.25 and terminating at Oxford at 9.50 am. The 8.55 am from Worcester left Oxford at 10.10 am. The evening service to Charlbury off the 4.45 pm Paddington express was the 6.08 pm from Oxford, a locomotive and coaches running 'all stations' to Worcester, calling at Charlbury at 6.35 pm.

The first revenue-earning service by diesel railcar on the Bristol-Weymouth route began on 17 February 1936.

In the same year the GWR purchased an 0-6-0 diesel-electric shunter for work in Acton yard. It had a six-cylinder engine, each cylinder being 10 inches in diameter by 12 inches stroke, developing 350 hp at 680 rpm, with traction motors on the leading and trailing axles. It could haul 1,000 tons at 9.5 mph on level track. There were also six *Simplex* petrol-engined shunters, Nos 15, 23-27, one of which worked the Provender Stores sidings at Didcot, and at least two more were stationed at Reading, working in the Low Level yard. There

A 70 hp diesel-mechanical shunter built by Fowler of Leeds and owned by the GWR from about 1934 until 1940. It had a six-cylinder engine driving the 3-foot diameter wheels - and of course a whistle and a brass-capped exhaust pipe. The GWR also owned one large diesel-electric shunter and five small petrol-engined Simplex *shunters, some of which were used in the S&T Works and Low Level Goods Yard at Reading. 16 August 1936.* (H. C. Casserley)

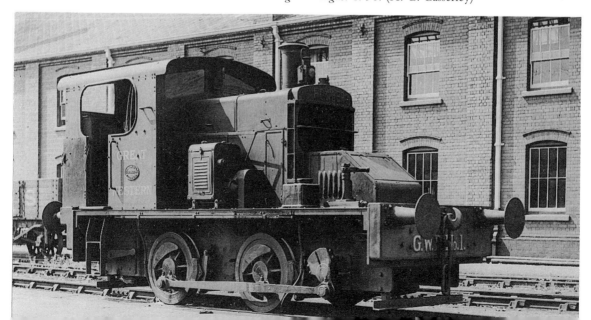

was also a pair of 70 hp diesel-mechanical shunters, Nos 1 and 2, built for the GWR by Fowler of Leeds. They were 0-4-0s with 3-foot wheels - and each carried a copper capped chimney!

With hindsight such timidity in not doing more to modernise shunting power seems quite remarkable - especially considering the rocketing cost of running steam engines. Dozens of small tank engines could have been scrapped, bringing large financial benefits and reductions in costs. The GWR Directors must have had their reasons - and a sheer lack of cash may have been the greatest of these. But still one wonders how they could have afforded *not* to dieselise their vast shunting operation in order to save large sums of money.

In 1936 the Traffic Department asked for 13 more diesel railcars to operate services on the following routes:

	No of cars	Daily mileage	To Displace
Banbury-Kingham	1	188	Auto-trains
Banbury-P. Risboro'	1	395	Auto-trains
K'minster-B'north	1	580	Auto-trains
Leam'ton-Stratford-Honeybourne	2	280	Locos & coaches
Newport-P'pool Rd, Chepstow-Monmouth	1	228	Auto-trains
Weymouth-Abbotsbury-Yeovil	2	540	Locos & coaches
Chippenham-Devizes-Westbury	2	241	Auto-trains
Frome-Taunton	1	205	Auto-trains
Teign Valley	2	252	Auto-trains

The estimated annual saving of this scheme, if implemented, was £11,700.

The request was not immediately granted, and one gets the impression that the Directors were weighing the pros and cons of the case. The diesel railcars had been very successful in developing new traffic, they were not too expensive to build, they were cheap to run and they were fast - but they were new technology, they were not as reliable as steam engines, and they were unable to haul any tail traffic or shunt sidings.

It is significant that, simultaneously with the building of diesel cars Nos 5 to 17, Swindon was also building 0-6-0 pannier tanks fitted for 'push-pull' working - the 5 ft 2 in '54xx' Class and their 4 ft 7 in variants the '64xxs' to work many of the services on which the Traffic Department wanted to employ the railcars.

Diesel car No 18 came into traffic in April 1937. This had conventional drawgear and buffers, so could haul an extra coach or some tail traffic, or shunt a siding to pick up or detach such traffic. Yet even then No 18 was the sole addition to the railcar fleet that year. The Company was, supposedly, still waiting to see how the cars worked in service and allowing the engineers a chance to modify the machines so that they were more reliable.

When management felt that they had got on top of the problem they ordered more railcars. In December 1938 the General Manager reported the following (the italics are mine):

'The diesel cars are becoming *more reliable* and the 18 have made a combined total of 97,000 in 1937, 5,388 miles each, and 97,600 miles in 1938. *Twenty more have been authorised.* Chassis, engines, gearboxes from AEC bodies, bogies and underframes by Swindon. Twin engines. Of the 20, 4 will be in 2-car sets. In the pairings one of the cars will have a buffet and 44 seats, the other car will have 60 seats. Max 70 mph. 14 cars will seat 48 passengers and do 40 mph. Another one will have a dual range gearbox, 48 seats and 60 mph in the second gear box (sic). There will be 1 parcels car with dual gear for 40/60mph.'

Cars 18-38 had Swindon-built chassis and body, the latter having a sharply angular styling, powered by an AEC standard bus engine and epicyclic (preselector) gearbox. Although No 18 had started work in April 1937, No 19 did not appear until July 1940.

The two-car sets, Nos 35/36 and Nos 37/38, which could have an ordinary coach sandwiched between them, came out in November 1941 and 1942. The chassis and bodies for these twin-car sets were ready in Swindon in 1939, but the fitting of the AEC engines and gearboxes was delayed because they were standard equipment in heavy-duty military vehicles, and had been diverted to that use; the railcars had a low priority.

12
Passenger trains, 1921–32

After the outbreak of war in August 1914 there was an increased demand for passenger travel, especially at holiday times. But the civilian passenger traffic got in the way of war effort traffic, so as from 1 January 1917 the Government ordered a drastic curtailment of services. Many of the most important express services, including the 'Cornish Riviera', were suspended, and those that remained were subject to a speed restriction of 60 mph. All slip coaches and restaurant cars were withdrawn. Then more cuts were made and in April 1918 passenger train mileage was only 44 per cent of the 1914 figure. However, from 5 May 1919 some expresses were restored together with some restaurant cars and slip coaches, and by the end of 1921 the train service was back to its 1914 frequency.

Trains left Paddington made up of coaches for two or even half a dozen destinations hundreds of miles apart. These would be detached at various junctions and worked on by other trains until they finally arrived back at Paddington the next day, the day after or, in some cases, four days later. Obviously there was an enormous amount of sorting and shunting to be done in breaking up and re-

In 1906 a new coach was introduced employing the great size of the 'Dreadnought' with the old idea of giving each compartment a door to the platform. This was the oddly shaped and aptly named 'Concertina' coach. In 1907 the first of the 'Toplight' designs were introduced.

This train, posed on 4 June 1922 at Rushey Platt west of the M&SW overbridge near the Works to record the first cream and brown coaches to be turned out of the Works since 1909, consists of 11 of the latest 'Toplights' with a 'Dreadnought' restaurant car fourth in line. The engine is 'Star' Class No 4019. (British Rail)

A close-coupled four-coach set for the Birmingham local services, with No 3151 (April 1907) at the head, poses for the photographer on 12 October 1924, again at Rushey Platt. (British Rail)

forming these trains. The situation had simply grown out of decades of cobbling additions on to the timetable. It was magnificent in its complication - but it was not good management.

On 28 October 1922 the Superintendent of the Line laid before the Directors his scheme to tidy up this chaotic system. He planned to use 61 coach sets with a straightforward 'consist' on an 'out and back' basis. This would improve the turnround time and get more work from fewer carriages. A reorganisation along these lines would, he estimated, save £1,000,000 in capital stock and reduce enormously the amount of carriage shunting required.

He also proposed an 'interval' departure time system so that the staff and passengers would become used to departure times whilst a route like Paddington-Swindon, carrying traffic for Plymouth, Swansea, Bristol and Cheltenham, would have the expresses coming down 'bunched', so that signalmen could get each batch of 'fasts' out of the way in a matter of 15 or 20 minutes in each hour and then have a decent 'margin' in which to run their freight trains. This 'interval' departure system was introduced from 1924, but the system was not strictly adhered to.

The carriage working was tidied up but it was still complicated by the need to run trains made up of coaches for two or more destinations. There were, in 1926, in a normal 24 hours, 190 loaded and 190 empty trains to be worked to and from Old Oak Common and Paddington together with 100 light engines for the departing trains. Besides this there were the usual quota of 'relief' trains catering for overloading on the 'main' trains, together with advertised excursions and 'specials' catering for sea-

sonal traffic or the 'one off' event such as an International rugby football match.

Through the 1920s regular daily passenger travelling on the GWR declined, whilst the holiday travel peak periods grew more frantic. The General Strike meant that 1926 was obviously going to be a bad year, but the figures for 1927 were worse than 1925.

	Number of Passengers	
	1925	1927
West of England	47,094,383	46,600,373
Midlands & North West	26,199,402	24,082,344
South Wales	36,647,644	40,562,104
Total	113,855,889	107,329,671
Receipts	£13,838,900	£12,529,901

A comparison of 1927 and 1925 passenger receipts on the GWR and the other three companies shows that they were all in decline:

SR	GWR	LNER	LMS
-2.7%	-4.9%	-7.1%	-7.2%

The Aberdeen-Penzance service, with GWR, LMS and LNER through carriages, made particularly heavy losses, and as early as 1924 the LMS and GWR wanted to discontinue it, but the LNER was keen to continue. The GWR withdrew its restaurant car between Swindon and York after 31 December 1925, and the LNER thereafter supplied two cars to cover the working in each direction. By the summer of 1929 the train started at noon from Truro, arriving at York at 11.13 pm, with through coaches from Penzance to Aberdeen. The GWR census of passengers on this train at Oxford shows these averages:

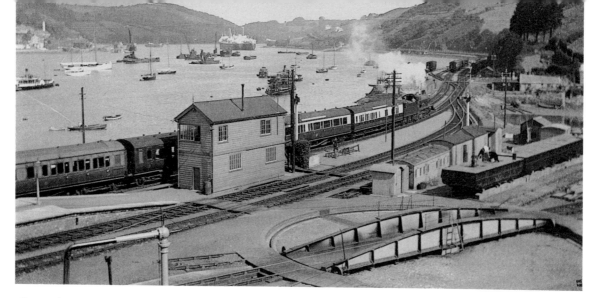

'Star' Class No 4054 'sets sail' out of Kingswear in 1931. The LMS coaches demonstrate the inter-company nature of the working to Crewe and Manchester. (Adrian Vaughan Collection)

	1929	1933	1937
Northbound	50	45	49
Southbound	14	24	16

Another pre-Great War survival in the summer of 1929 was the 7.20 am Southampton, which stopped 'all stations' over the Didcot, Newbury and Winchester route, hauling in addition to the local coaches a Van-3rd and Composite Class coach for Scarborough and a similar pair for Glasgow. At Oxford the local coaches were detached, a restaurant car and Van-3rd for Newcastle was attached, and it set off as an express train.

The back-working was the 1.2 pm Newcastle express, losing its restaurant car at Oxford and becoming a stopping train between Didcot and Southampton, on which section these Betjemanesque trains were very lightly loaded.

The decline in regular daily passenger travel was due in part to competing road transport and also, to quote the GWR General Manager, 'the large and growing number of unemployed people who have no money to spend on train journeys'. Yet despite the deepening recession the purchases of the mass-produced motor car continued. In 1928 2,500 new cars came on the road each week, with a total of 1,909,000 on the roads in July of that year, plus 662,000 motor cycles, 290,000 goods vehicles and 87,000 taxis. Milne also noted some instances where coal-miners were going to work by taxi, clubbing together to pay the fare instead of going by exceptionally bad four-wheeled railway carriages.

The Company tried to economise by reducing train costs. From 24 September 1928, 'due to the severe depression in trade', the 'Cornish Riviera'

lost both its Taunton and Exeter slip coaches but retained the Weymouth slip dropped at Westbury. The train ran non-stop through Taunton and stopped at Exeter. The Taunton slip was re-established before 1936.

The Company also abolished, from 24 September 1928, the following trains:

3.30 pm Paddington-Falmouth
5.00 pm Paddington-Cheltenham
9.20 am Birmingham-Cardiff
3.30 pm Cardiff-Birmingham
6.20 pm Plymouth-Taunton
6.28 pm Taunton-Paddington
2.30 pm Cheltenham-Paddington

These were some of the best expresses on the line and their abolition looks fairly panicky – the sort of measures British Rail might take – and not what one would expect from the GWR. In particular the removal of the 2.30 pm Cheltenham-Paddington, the 'Cheltenham Flyer', was particularly ill-considered since this was the fastest train in Britain (between Swindon and Paddington) and was, with the 'Cornish Riviera Limited', the standard-bearer of GWR honour.

The Company saved wages and the costs of 2,250 train-miles per day, but such was the outcry from the travelling public that the services were restored from 1 March 1929.

During the summer of 1929 the demand both for 'relief' trains to booked services and for excursion trains was so great that the Company had no choice at times but to turn parties away because at that moment there were no spare coaches to make up a train; the existing stock was used so heavily that it was not always serviced or cleaned properly.

In October 1930, at the end of the summer 'rush', Sir James Milne reported the paradoxical situation that

'. . .passenger train receipts continue to decline whilst the requirements for coaches at busy periods have remained as heavy as ever. The Company's stock was fully occupied on every Saturday from the middle of June to the middle of September and the *usual extreme* difficulty [author's italics] was experienced in meeting the demands of "peak" days.'

Overcrowded trains, and the expense of the fare for a family, made the primitive cars on the poorish roads of the period seem worth the effort. Perhaps it was as well for the railways that at least some people found their own way to Devon and Cornwall - since the GWR had not the stock to handle the traffic. Steady, regular traffic was what was required, not peaks and troughs, but Sir James Milne noted glumly that

'Groups of holiday-making workers from the Austin car factory in Birmingham are hiring large Austin cars for their journey rather than using rail. It is suspected that these cars are being made available at non-commercial rates by the Austin Car Company.'

To make up for the loss of regular passenger traffic the GWR actively pursued a policy of running 'Day' and 'Half-day' excursions. The Company also did its utmost to encourage excursion and long-stay holiday travel - with advertising posters, books, brochures, cheap excursion tickets and 'Holiday Returns'. The latter allowed people to travel outwards on Saturday, the idea being, one supposes, to attract more working class travellers who would normally be at work on a Friday.

This well-intentioned plan exacerbated the terrible Saturday rush on the railways because people who would normally have begun their holiday on Friday night, on the normally priced ticket, bought the cheap, Saturday, holiday fare at Paddington and all GWR major stations, hence the rush was ever more focused on the single day. The stations were swamped - and not just with people but also with their luggage - for in those days holidaymakers carried a week or fortnight's supply of clothing in great square wooden trunks. So much baggage was carried by this sort of passenger that the trains were delayed whilst it was being loaded into the brake van and delayed again at the detraining points as literally tons of boxes and suitcases were dragged out of the vans.

When the line was crowded with trains, the lengthy occupation of a platform by an unloading train stopped other trains further back along the line, thus intensifying the delay and frustrations of the journey. This was always the case on the Torquay line where the trains normally queued 'block and block', waiting to enter stations occupied by trains loading and unloading - and this was in spite of the running of separate 'Passengers Luggage in Advance' (PLA) trains on the night before the great rush. Looe, Brixham and all those small coastal resort stations, as well as the larger stations like Torquay and Kingswear, would be jammed with boxes of luggage, and extra porters would be drafted in to help sort out the bedlam.

The discomfort on summer peak trains made passengers vow never to go by train again. Regular daily trains had room to spare, but the GWR had to build more stock to reduce overcrowding on its seasonal trains, just because that was the only expanding traffic - and then those coaches had to be found employment, if possible, out of season. Moreover, these carriages had to be very high quality because of the need to provide such fine accommodation that no-one would want to use their cars! Amongst the stock which was constructed in 1930-5 were ten three-car sets comprising a Kitchen Car sandwiched between a Composite Class and a 3rd Class dining car.

As the GWR lost regular passenger revenue and came to depend more on seasonal trade, so, significantly, its empty stock mileage increased as the extra stock was moved, empty, into position before the 'rush' and back to the depot afterwards.

Empty Coaching Stock trains

Year	No of trains	Miles run	
1927		693	74,726
1928		709	72,920
1929		792	90,500

On 21 March 1929 the GWR Board authorised the introduction of Pullman car services between Paddington and Paignton and in the 'Ocean Liner' specials. The Pullman Car Company agreed to supply and overhaul cars for a three-year period, whilst the GWR would carry out running repairs. A sup-

The quality of passenger trains had to keep pace with passengers' expectations. Here, No 4172, an 'Armstrong' Class 4-4-0 with 7-foot driving wheels, entering Warminster from Westbury on 29 April 1928; the journey included the ascent of Upton Scudamore bank, 2½ miles at 1 in 70/75.

The train is an inter-company Bristol to Portsmouth working consisting of some very dingy clerestory coaches. No 4172 was scrapped a year later. (H. C. Casserley)

plementary fare in addition to the usual fare was charged: 7s 6d 1st Class, 5 shillings 3rd on the Torquay service; 10 shillings and 5s 6d on the 'Ocean Liner' trains. The GWR retained 1 shilling from the Torquay supplementaries and 2 shillings and 1 shilling respectively from the 'Ocean Liner'

supplementary fares. The 11 am Paddington to Paignton and the returning 4.30 pm Paignton-Paddington was formed with eight Pullman cars running on Mondays and Fridays only during the summer of 1929, and also on Saturdays during the winter 1929-30. The scheduled formation of the

A Bristol to Portsmouth seven years on. 'Bulldog' Class No 3412 clatters over the North junction at Westbury, signalled to the down Salisbury line, on 27 May 1935. The carriages are all high quality and relatively new; the last vehicle is a 60-foot passenger brake-van, one of several built at Swindon in 1930 especially for the cross-country service. It was 9 ft 5 in wide over the door handles and 61 ft 4 in long, the extreme width and length acceptable to the Southern Railway. (H. C. Casserley)

train in the summer of 1929 was: Brake-3rd, 3rd Class kitchen car, 3rd Class parlour car, 1st Class kitchen car, 1st Class parlour car, 3rd Class parlour car, 3rd Class kitchen car, Brake-3rd.

The 'Torbay Pullman', consisting of eight cars weighing about 345 tons tare, was the slowest of the West of England expresses out of Paddington; it was booked to cover the 95½ miles from Paddington to passing Westbury station in 99½ minutes, 5½ minutes slower than the 'Cornish Riviera', which was 150 tons heavier - and it was 10 minutes slower than the 'Riviera' to Taunton.

The 'Torbay Pullman' was a financial disaster. The total number of seats available in the eight cars was less than the capacity of five cars since there were *three* kitchen cars in the formation, and two of the passenger cars were also partly brake vans. The average number of passengers carried per trip over the 18 months from April 1929 to September 1930 was stated by the GWR General Manager to be 'less than 18'. If this figure is correct and not a misprint in his typed report to the Directors, it suggests that on occasions during the winter the Pullman ran completely empty in order for the overall average to be so low, since it is recorded in the GWR Minutes

that on Whit Friday, May 1929, the down 'Cornish Riviera' and 'Torbay Pullman' between them moved 1,500 passengers.

The Pullman cars were useful on occasions when a really good impression had to be made. On 17 January 1930 150 American VIPs, including the American Ambassador, Senators and Congressmen, going to the London Naval Conference were landed at Plymouth off the SS *George Washington* and were conveyed to Paddington in an 'Ocean' special made up entirely of the Pullman cars. The run was so fast and comfortable that the American Ambassador sent a letter of appreciation to the GWR.

But as a regular service the 'Torbay Pullman' was a dead loss and in April the GWR and the Pullman Car Company mutually agreed that the three-year agreement would terminate at the end of that summer's timetable.

At this point the French Lines shipping company advised the GWR that its transatlantic passengers would not transfer to the GWR at Plymouth unless Pullman accommodation was provided. As French Lines landed more passengers at

Plymouth than any other shipping company, its warning was taken seriously and in October the

Without ceremony, without any differentiating mark - and with a motley collection of none too clean carriages - the fastest train in Britain, the 2.30 pm Cheltenham-Paddington, leaves Swindon, coming off the branch platform and past the East signal box. At this date, 8 July 1929, the train had 70 minutes to cover the 77¼ miles to London. The engine is No 5000 Launceston Castle *with driver Jim Street and fireman Sherer. (British Rail)*

GWR Directors authorised expenditure on the construction of eight 'Super Saloons', the GWR's answer to Pullman cars. The bogies, underframes and body shells were constructed at Swindon but fitted out, furnished and decorated by Trollope & Sons. The total cost of the eight vehicles was estimated at £29,416, and to cover the cost the GWR scrapped several life-expired vehicles - two Royal saloons, 12 six-wheel saloons, and ten four-wheelers - the replacement cost of which was quoted as the necessary £29,416.

The first two 'Super Saloons', Nos 9111 'King George' and 9112 'Queen Mary', were completed in November 1931. They were superb vehicles, in my opinion, even more elegant and opulent than the Pullman cars they replaced. Their maiden run was to convey to Paddington VIPs off French Lines' SS *Colombie* on her maiden voyage from New York.

When the 2.30 pm from Cheltenham was restored in March 1929, the train's schedule was cut to 70 minutes and 'Castle' haulage became the norm. On the inaugural run No 5000 *Launceston Castle* with 280 tons (carrying a 'Cheltenham Flyer - World's Fastest Train' headboard) made the 77¼-mile journey in 68 minutes. Driver Jim Street and Fireman Frank Sherer, 'top link' Old Oak men, worked the engine. From 14 September 1931 the timing was cut to 67 minutes. Again No 5000 made

the inaugural run - with a mere six coaches for 190 tons - in 59½ minutes. Street and Sherer were again in charge. *Launceston Castle* was 'regular' on the working in 1931, day after day, reliably taking down the heavy 10.45 am Paddington-Gloucester, then back up with the 2.40 pm Cheltenham (as the timing had by then become).

In May 1932 there were nine British trains scheduled to average 60 mph or more over the whole length of their journey. Five of these were Great Western, and of these the 'Cheltenham Flyer' was the fastest. People, especially children, living near the route would go especially to see the 'Flyer' go through, and even the newspapers recognised the 'Flyer' as a bright spot in the otherwise dismal commercial world of the early 1930s.

From 18 July 1932 seven more GWR trains were accelerated to run at a start-to-stop average of 60 mph, and in September the 'Cheltenham Flyer' had another 2 minutes cut from its schedule between Swindon and Paddington, giving it 65 minutes for the 77¼ miles and requiring a start-to-stop average of 71.4 mph. Only three other trains in Britain had schedules requiring an average in excess of 70 mph. The 'Flyer' was a glorious advertisement for the perfect engineering embodied in GWR locomotives, the skill of the locomotive crews and the condition of the track. It was also a great morale raiser in those difficult times.

13
Passenger trains, 1932–39

While the GWR was running its prestigious high-speed 'Ocean Specials' to Plymouth, its 'Cornish Riviera', its 'Cheltenham Flyer' and, from 1935, its 'Bristolian', it was also running its standard expresses at respectable speeds. The 6.30 pm Paddington to Plymouth had 82 minutes for the 77¼ miles to Swindon, which was passed non-stop. This was a realistic schedule requiring the engine to cruise well within its capabilities at around 60-65 mph, and leaving a margin to permit punctual running with an extra heavy load, temporary speed restrictions or signal delays. The 4.30 pm Paddington was allowed only 79 minutes to the stop at Swindon.

The 4.45 pm Paddington-Worcester had its first stop at Oxford, 63½ miles in 70 minutes. This was

Branch line services were necessarily slow affairs, sometimes especially so. Here, No 4403 is seen at Princetown on 15 June 1926, running round its train after its 10½-mile slog on gradients varying between 1 in 40 and 1 in 47 for which 55 minutes were allowed with four stops. After an hour's wait, during which the engine crew would probably undertake some shunting, fill the loco water tanks, attend to its fire, brew tea, and maybe watch convicts being loaded into the carriages, the train will leave for Yelverton with a 38-minute schedule. (H. C. Casserley)

more difficult than it might at first glance appear because there a 40 mph restriction over the junction at Didcot, so the train began to brake from about 70 mph at Moreton Cutting, 1¼ miles away.

The local and branch-line services were, however, slow. This could not be otherwise, given the nature of the traffic - the several starts and stops in a few miles, and the time required to attach trucks or unload parcels. These trains were often run with the most antique locomotives and carriages, distasteful to the public - but at least they ran to time (see Appendix 3).

The Company did the best it could with limited resources. One advantage of retaining tried and trusted methods and machinery was that everyone became so thoroughly conversant with the job that they performed it with great efficiency - only the passengers got bored with ancient equipment as the rest of the world marched on into cleaner, faster, more convenient systems.

Above and below Another leisurely branch line, that to Looe. No 4405 stands at the platform on 25 May 1935 with its well groomed 'B set' coaches - neatly designed to have the brake-vans against the engine in either direction of travel. This set was built in 1929 and specially fitted with short (7-foot) wheel-base bogies to cope with the sharp curves on the branch.

Later No 4405 runs round its train and backs on to the stock, the shunter riding on the footstep, ready for the run back to Liskeard. (Both H. C. Casserley)

Kingham East Junction looking westwards to the flyover across the Oxford-Worcester line, with the tracks diverging to Kingham station on the left. The signal box was opened on 8 January 1906 and contained a 23-lever frame. It can be seen that the junction was constructed to the GWR's highest standards in 1905-6 in anticipation of important 'coast to coast' traffic with the Great Central Railway and North Eastern Railway, which never developed as expected. (Clinker Collection/courtesy Brunel University)

Throughout the period 1921-39 the GWR and LNER ran a train, which, whilst not of 'Ocean' prestige, would none the less have been of use to ships' crews, between Swansea, Barry, Cardiff and Newcastle - coast to coast. This was a remarkable express service that traversed the rural Vale of Glamorgan line between Bridgend and Cardiff and the utterly remote King's Sutton to Gloucester line via the Kingham flyover - perhaps the most 'forgotten' 42 miles of second-class cross-country railway on the GWR. From 1921 until 1939 one through train a day, complete with a restaurant car, ran over this route in each direction between Newcastle and Barry. One set of coaches was supplied by the GWR, the other by the LNER.

These 'A' class trains - the 7.40 am Swansea-Newcastle and the 9.30 am Newcastle-Swansea, as they were in 1929 - were formed with seven coaches including a restaurant car and were worked by medium-sized GWR 4-4-0 of the 'Bulldog' Class or a 2-6-0 of the '43xx' Class. Gradients were mountainous - 1 in 80 and 1 in 60 was commonplace - and frequent slowings had to be made to pick up and set down the various single-line tokens, yet the average speed between these pick-up points was 43-45 mph. It was not in the same league as a 'Plym A', but a great deal of very skilful 'hell-for-leather, hammer-and-tongs' driving and firing was called for.

The GWR and LNER evidently considered this 'one off' service across a lonely, hilly single track to be important and worth the upkeep of the Hook Norton viaduct and three tunnels, Hook Norton (418 yards), Chipping Norton (714 yards) and Andoversford (384 yards), so much so that during the first half of 1938 clearances along platforms were improved 'to admit larger engines' - the new 'Manor' Class 4-6-0s.

The Easter holiday traffic of April 1932, in the deepest part of the Depression, was 'disappointing' to the GWR General Manager, with passenger receipts over the two weeks of the holiday down by £68,000 over 1931 - which itself had been a record low. The Cup Final in April produced only enough extra passengers to fill 10 extra GWR trains, but the Company consoled itself with the thought that this was not so bad since the teams involved were from London and Newcastle; therefore most of the supporters had no need of the GWR and the Company had done well to fill even 10 trains.

On the bright side there was the opening that April of the Shakespeare Memorial Theatre in Stratford-upon-Avon; on the 27th the GWR ran 27 Specials to carry 5,910 passengers to Stratford and back.

There was also the enlivening sight of 1,500 booted and knapsacked 'hikers' who arrived at Paddington on Good Friday in response to the GWR's advertisement of a 'Hikers Mystery Tour'.

The Company underestimated the response and a second train was at once assembled and brought to the platform to clear the rest of the crowd. The destination remains a mystery to this day.

As the Depression eased, holiday passenger traffic increased and once more the Company found itself barely able to cope with the enormous peak demands made upon it. On the April Thursday before Easter of 1933, the 'Cornish Riviera' ran down in four parts without slip coaches, carrying a total of 1,416 passengers. The first and second parts ran non-stop through Plymouth, called at Devonport to change engines and men, and made their first passenger stop in Cornwall. According to the General Manager this was the first time that this had happened. The third and fourth parts were full-length trains for Minehead/Ilfracombe and Weymouth respectively.

On the same day the 'Torbay Express' (12 noon from Paddington) and the 3.30 pm each went down in three parts conveying 1,445 and 1,806 passengers respectively. The first part of the 3.30 normally terminated at Plymouth North Road after running there non-stop. On this day it was extended to Penzance, forming yet another 'part' to the 'Cornish Riviera'.

It was the usual practise for the long-distance express trains out of Paddington to have a dining-car in their formation. Hot meals were cooked from the raw ingredients - purchased daily from Covent Garden and Smithfield markets - on a gas-fired stove in the tiny kitchen, or galley. The chef was not only an expert cook but also something of an acrobat as he balanced himself against the rocking of the train, surrounded at very close quarters with hot metal, boiling water and flaming gas rings; the kitchen staff were probably more at risk of injury than the men on the engine.

The Great Western's policy regarding traffic regulation along the open track and through congested junctions was to leave it to 'the man on the spot' rather than tell the man faced with the problem to waste time asking for instructions from a 'Controller' sitting in an office miles away. The GWR, of course, did have a system of 'Control' and these men would phone the signalmen with requests for trains to be held back or given precedence if they knew of some outstanding reason for this to be done. However, in general the Great Western felt that 'It is *undesirable*, in regulating trains, to take away the responsibility and authority of the signalman'.

Because of this policy there was always a very well worked-out routine of sending train-running information between the signal boxes. The load and 'consist' of each train, its engine number, number of coaches and tonnage had to be 'wired' ahead from the main station whence it began to main centres - junction and other key signal boxes - and its destination. The only difficulty was the relative lack of telephone circuits between boxes and the dependence on the 'single-needle' telegraph. Of course the Company was doing its best to improve the situation but it cost a lot of money, and as late as 1935 the GWR was still considering a large expenditure to improve communications on the vital trunk routes between Bristol and Torquay/Plymouth; Swindon, Westbury and Weymouth; and Birmingham and Leamington.

Passenger trains carried one tail lamp and two side lights on the rear of the last vehicle (see also chapter 15 on slip coaches). At large stations a lamp porter cleaned these lamps' burners and trimmed their wicks, filled their paraffin fuel tanks, and supplied them to the trains. A considerable saving in lamps, maintenance and fuel was made as from 1 June 1933 by abolishing the side lamps on passenger trains.

It was in July 1934 that the GWR introduced route identification codes, white numbers on a black plate - like a cricket scoreboard - mounted in a frame on the locomotive's smokebox. The numbers were repeated in the signalmen's train notices so that they could easily identify which train was approaching, a very important point indeed when trains began to run out of their booked 'paths' as they sometimes did at these peak times. The 1934 scheme was applied only to Weymouth and West of England trains and their 'reliefs' - cross-country trains and their 'reliefs' carried these numbers only when running between Taunton and Newton Abbot.

Each route was numbered in a specific series. Thus the first down train to Weymouth - the 8.30 am from Paddington - might be numbered '100', a 'Relief' to this train would then be 101 and a second 'relief' would be 102. Trains for Devon and beyond might be numbered in the '200' series. 'Ocean Specials' were numbered according to their code - a 'Plym A' carried '001', a 'Plym B' 002, and so on (see chapter 16 on 'Ocean Liner' trains).

In July 1935 the scheme was extended to cover all GWR main-line and cross-country expresses, and also cross-country services between the Southern and the GWR, for which 75 additional frames and

In the mid-1930s the relative lack of telephone circuits between signal boxes was a problem. Here in 1952 we have a history of railway telephone instruments in Friars Junction, the next box 31 chains west of Old Oak Common West. Nearest the camera are two 'Ericson-type' phones from the mid-1930s with 'all-in-one' handsets, here in use as closed circuit 'box-to-box' phones communicating only with the signal box on each side. They would be used for the transmission of important messages between signalmen which would be open to interruption on the open circuit 'bus' lines ('omnibus', open to use by all on the circuit simultaneously).

The 'Control Phone' (fifth along) has twin bells in its polished mahogany front with a small round selector knob (1 to 4) above, and beyond that is a pair of ''bus'' line phones with 12 lines each, the telephone mouthpiece projecting above the selector knob.

Turning to purely signalling equipment, beyond that are four 1905/8 pattern 'Absolute block' instruments for the passenger lines, and three Tyers 'Permissive block' instruments for the goods lines. Above the instruments is a GWR illuminated track diagram dating from about 1927, a primitive non-fail-safe device where the clear track sections are represented by an illuminated electric lamp and an occupied section by a non-illuminated hole in the plan. The signal box and lever frame dates from March 1902. The frame is a 'double twist' with levers spaced at 5¼-inch centres (see chapter 20). The short-handled levers operate colour-light signals. (British Rail)

275 number plates were constructed at a cost of £220.

In 1923-4 'break section' signal boxes were installed at Cotfield, Powderham and Bishopsteignton, and in 1934-5 several more were constructed along the West of England main line via Newbury, at Wootton Rivers, Crookwood, Pinkwood, Wyke, Westcott and Rewe. These boxes were switched in only on summer Saturdays and other peak holiday times when otherwise lengthy block sections had to be shortened to keep traffic moving. Others were installed in Cornwall - Boldue in 1938 and Treverrin, for instance.

Whether it would have been cheaper for the GWR to have installed electrically operated sema-phores to be worked remotely from an existing box is a difficult question. Although these little boxes were only required for certain peak times, it is recorded that sometimes spare signalmen could not be found to work them and they remained shut when they were needed. Thus the GWR lost the use of their investment. An electrical installation would have cost more to instal but would certainly have been in action all the year round, shortening the section, irrespective of staff shortages.

Lack of investment cash also resulted in a grave shortage of coaches. In June 1935 the General Manager reported that 'every available corridor coach was in use during the week, and at weekends non-corridor and even branch 'B sets' were incor-

An example of one of the train identification boards applied to locomotive smokebox doors from 1934, photographed in that year at Bristol Temple Meads west end.

The station is in the midst of rebuilding (see chapter 21), with a new gantry on the platform which has not yet received its colour-light signals. The semaphore signals are part of the temporary system which required signal boxes to be installed as dismantled almost weekly as the layout was gradually enlarged - not for the GWR the luxury of closing down a large station for 6 months! (John Haywood/Adrian Vaughan Collection)

The mid-1930s saw an acute shortage of carriages. On 22 June 1935 a Paddington-Birmingham '2-hour' express behind No 6017 heads northwards towards the Brill or Rushwood tunnel, (193 yards). The train's seating capacity has been augmented by a 48-foot clerestory coach - obviously Swindon Works was still refurbishing Victorian carriages for top-class express work! The next vehicle is a 70-foot long, 9 ft 6 in wide 'Dreadnought', introduced for the 'Cornish Riviera' in 1904 and seating 72 passengers against the leading clerestory's 48.

The 'Dreadnought', magnificent though it was, had a severe design fault in that the compartments had no doors to the platform; passengers had to struggle along the corridor to get out, carrying their luggage, and meeting other passengers getting on! (H. C. Casserley)

porated into main-line express formations. Passengers who had reserved seats in corridor coaches from Paddington or other main stations travelled to Torbay and other long-distance destinations in lavatory-less non-corridor accommodation without access to the restaurant car. This resulted in bitter criticism of the Company.'

The GWR was in a 'vicious circle'. It was constantly looking for more traffic to increase revenue to keep up with rising costs, but having gained the extra traffic it had the utmost difficulty in handling it since it did not have sufficient equipment owing to lack of funds. Furthermore, although extra traffic brought increased revenue - total receipts for 1936 were £27,166,000, an increase of £750,000 on 1935 - there was then an increase in 'wear and tear' and in operating costs and wages due to the need to run trains of empty coaches over long distances, together with extra marshalling.

The GWR celebrated 100 years of corporate existence in August 1935 with the introduction of a 'Cheltenham Flyer'-type express each way between Paddington and Bristol called the 'Bristolian'. There was also a poster campaign demanding fairer treatment of the railways in the face of apparent government partiality towards road hauliers.

The down 'Bristolian', 10.00 am from Paddington, ran 118¼ miles via Bath and the up train, 4.30 pm from Bristol, ran just over 117½ miles to Paddington via Badminton in 105 minutes, an start-to-stop average speed of about 67½ mph. The train normally consisted of eight coaches for 218 tons tare, and was worked in both directions by one set of Old Oak men with a 'King'; after a while an Old Oak 'Castle' became the usual power for the train.

Throughout 1935 and up until July 1937 there was a small but continuous improvement in revenue and a reduction in costs, but then - in spite of the re-armament programme - came an unexpected depression of trade with the inevitable loss of revenue to the Company. Their steam-hauled operation had been honed to the keenest possible edge and it was not possible to improve it further, so in 1938 working costs began to rise. Unemployment was also rising. Between July 1937 and 1938 unemployment rose by 22 per cent to over 1.7 million.

An example of the way in which this affected railway revenues is that in a large West Midlands factory in 1935, the workforce accumulated £10,000 in their 'holiday clubs' - money to be spent, in part, on train fares. In 1938 the same factory had only created a 'kitty' of £2,000 - the cheapest transport was therefore needed by the hard-up holidaymakers. Note this comparison of train and motor-coach return fares out of London:

	Coach	Train (3rd Class)
Aberystwyth	28s 9d	41s 3d
Barnstaple	31s 6d	33s 1d
Penzance	48s 3d	53s 3d
Torquay	31s 6d	34s 8d

The following table shows the numbers of long-distance passengers carried on Saturdays 30 July 1937 and 1938, the weekend before the August Bank Holiday weekend, on London Coastal Coaches from its Victoria coach station and by the GWR from Paddington:

	30 July 1937	30 July 1938
London Coastal	40,000	46,000
Great Western	34,313	29,454

The coach company used 1,500 coaches to move its passengers - 30.66 people per coach - and Sir James Milne believed that 'in the eyes of the modern traveller' the 'luxury' (road motor) coach is 'equal or superior in comfort to 1st Class railway accommodation at considerably less than 3rd Class railway fares.'

This seems to be a most astonishing statement, but because of overcrowding, long-distance railway travel was undoubtedly becoming less comfortable and less popular as passengers crammed the suitcase-laden corridors. But then, what could the journey from London to Torquay have been like in a fully seated motor-coach of that time - and over the narrow, twisting West Country roads of the period? Was it really more comfortable on that bus than seated in a GWR 1st Class compartment? If Milne was right, and the public did think this, then the motor-coaches of the 1930s must have been either a great deal more comfortable than they looked, or else people *felt* more comfortable in an very inferior vehicle, in which case the GWR was faced with an 'image problem'. Hence, perhaps, its enthusiasm for running it 'show' trains, the 'Bristolian' and the 'Cheltenham Flyer'.

In July 1937 the GWR was allowed to make a 5 per cent increase in its rail passenger and parcels fares in a desperate attempt to regain revenue, but over the year to July 1938 this produced a *drop* of 4.4 per cent in passenger revenue and widened still further the gap between road and rail fares. Significantly, of the seven motor bus companies associated with the GWR, five recorded an increase in income of about 4 per cent, and Western Welsh had a 12.4 per cent increase. The part-railway-owned Devon General experienced a 6.6 per cent decrease and the Royal Blue company, which had no connection with the GWR, recorded a drop of 2.9per cent.

Overall, passenger revenues for 1938 were down only by 1 per cent on 1937, but wages and materials costs were rising, so any reduction in income was a very serious matter, since there was in any case insufficient money to re-invest in desperately needed extra rolling-stock, modern signalling and modern motive power. The Company's Officers decided that the 5 per cent fare increase had had a marginally negative effect on long-distance passengers, but they were certain that it had driven away passengers from short-distance travel. Where rail fares were less than 1 shilling, the 5% per cent increase could not be precisely applied - a threepenny rail fare became 3½d, which was a 16 per cent increase. The public were duly incensed and turned to using the cheaper and more convenient buses. On this the GWR Superintendents commented:

'The improvement in regularity and frequency in road services, coupled with modern vehicles and "door to door" facilities has no doubt been a factor in turning users to road transport.'

Between October 1937 and January 1938 both Birmingham Corporation Tramways & Buses and the 'Midland Red' increased their revenue by £60,000 and £55,000 respectively. Moreover, in 1937 there was a 10 per cent increase in the number of new cars registered compared with 1936, and of course there was a large market in second-hand cars which allowed 'individuals of quite modest means' to purchase their own transport. The GWR noted this in a delightfully prim paragraph with the additional comment:

'. . .and the question of *depreciation* does not seem to be taken into account - so long as the vehicle can be kept in service for a year or two.'

Such improvidence - not to 'cost out' one's purchases correctly!

By 1938 there was a chronic shortage of carriages for long-distance express trains. On two (unspeci-fied) Saturdays during that summer, the total number of non-corridor coaches used in main-line expresses was, respectively, 110 and 80. These trains were packed when they left London, so the chaos can be imagined at intermediate stations along the route as more people tried to board the train.

To provide more seats at major stopping places along the way, desperate Station Masters attached to the overloaded holiday trains workmen's four-wheeled coaches with wooden slatted seats. In a Report to the Directors dated 19 August 1938, Sir James Milne described these vehicles and stated that they had been used 'on several occasions'. He went on:

'. . .these circumstances are deplorable and must inevitably result in passengers abandoning rail travel for the motor-coach or private car. Railway travel has got to be made more attractive if it is to hold its own against the roads.'

There was very little that the railway could do but try to work as economically as possible and to attract more traffic. One proposal was that the Company should move into the 'motor-rail' business and carry holidaymakers and their cars from the cities to their rural or seaside destination.

From January to March 1939 the railway recaptured some traffic owing to heavy snow and rain which prevented lorries from working. But in spite of the Company's efforts to retain the traffic with the cheapest rates it dared to quote, it melted away with the snow. A severe frost in December 1938 and January 1939 destroyed the Devon and Cornwall broccoli crop. The farmers lost 22,500 tons and the GWR reckoned it lost £44,000 as a result.

The summer of 1939 was glorious - as regards weather - but fearsome as Europe descended once more into war. The GWR now ran special trains to evacuate art treasures from London to North Wales. It also put on extra trains to carry voluntary evacuees and their household effects from London to the country ahead of the heavy aerial bombardment which was expected the moment the war began. On 3 September, as the long-awaited war against Nazi Germany began, the normal train service was suspended, and a 'skeleton' service substituted so that the tracks could be cleared for the trains which were to carry many thousands of London children to the safety of rural Wales and the West Country.

14
Extra passenger trains

The Great Western took on any sort of passenger traffic, from a one-coach private special to a 14-coach excursion to the seaside, the management always confident that they could find the engines, rolling-stock and men to do the job.

A wealthy person could arrive at any station of respectable size and ask for a special train to run him or her home. At the GWR's Windsor station, serving the Royal castle, there were often requests from famous entertainers or from political people, British and foreign, for a private train to act as a taxi home. Adelina Patti is known to have asked for and received a one-coach special as a taxi service to her home near Aylesbury. The Station Master simply asked the nearest driver if he and his engine were able to make the trip; if they were, the job was done. There would be a guinea for the driver at the end of it - or more - depending on the mood of the 'toff' in the train.

The 1920 General Appendix to the Rule Book devoted two pages to the method by which a Station Master was to calculate the mileage for private specials. If it was to or from a political meeting, or from an evening concert/theatre, the rate was 10 shillings per mile, with a minimum charge of £6. If the request was for a railcar, rates were cheaper. Private specials for the fox-hunting fraternity with horses and hounds in vehicles attached behind were 4s 6d per mile, minimum charge £3. The practice of 'hunting specials' in the remote and relatively transport-less countryside lasted into the 1930s, but the private hire of a train - at a moment's notice - does not seem to have survived after the mid-1920s,

as millionaires and similar persons had by then purchased motor cars.

A section of each Divisional Traffic Superintendent's staff kept watch on traffic trends and a number of extra trains, based on past experience and present likelihoods, were planned to cater for the locality at the Easter weekend or some special 'one off' event such as a race meeting. It was the GWR which created Newbury racecourse and thereby developed a tremendous traffic in passengers and horses.

The GWR maintained stocks of spare coaches to meet the demands of peak traffic. Wells, Yatton, Chippenham, Frome, Castle Cary, Bridport and Maiden Newton all had a 3rd Class coach, the cleanliness of which was the responsibility of the Station Master. Salisbury had two coaches, Weymouth, Swindon, Westbury and Trowbridge had four, Weston-super-Mare had six and Bristol Temple Meads nine. These were intended to meet an unexpected demand for seating - foreseen peaks of travel were catered for by the Station Master ordering in advance an extra coach or coaches.

All major events - and many that were relatively small scale - were covered by the Company, eager for traffic. Over the weekend of 17-20 April 1924 there were two internationals at Twickenham, the annual Motor Show at Earls Court and the FA Cup Final. The GWR covered all these events with long-distance extra trains from the provinces into Paddington. On Cup Final Saturday, 28 extras, carrying 9,700 passengers, came up to Paddington or Ealing. The following month the enormous British

A 'Castle' entering Reading station on the down main line with an 'A' headcode express on 13 April 1933. The make-up of the train suggests a hastily marshalled 'relief' to some scheduled train, possibly using coaches kept available for the purpose. It is formed from eight assorted clerestories, one Churchward 'Toplight' and two Collett coaches.

The train is signalled down the Bristol road; the directing distant for the Westbury road is to the right. A train is also signalled on the up main. Note that the up signal arm suspended directly over the track is thickly coated with soot. These up line signals form the 'repeaters' for the actual directing signals at East Main box, seen at the far end of the train. This system of 'repeating' homes was an ancient extravagance which the GWR was trying to abolish at the date of this picture, along with side lamps on passenger trains, which are carried by this train. These were abolished on passenger trains from 1 July 1933. (D. S. Ffoulkes-Roberts/courtesy Bill Rear)

Empire Exhibition opened at Wembley, and this brought 374 extra trains into Paddington from 1 May to 30 June 1924. From Maundy Thursday to Easter Saturday 26,000 passengers left Paddington by the principal expresses, with 1st Class ticket sales up 6½ per cent on the previous year; by 31 October earnings from all kinds of passenger traffic were £53,000 higher than for the same period in 1923, a fact attributed largely to the Wembley exhibition.

On 1 May 1925 'Half-day' excursions were re-introduced, and from 1 May to 30 September 1925 1,040 such excursions were run to a variety of events or beauty spots, carrying in total 490,224 passengers and earning on average £112 per train. The same year also saw the re-introduction (albeit short-lived) of the remarkable 'Day Excursions' to Killarney, a well-known feature of the pre-1914 GWR.

For a fare of around 25 shillings the excursionists were taken from Paddington to Killarney and back in 24 hours, the trains being fast enough to allow time for the tourists to have a ride to the lakes by

jaunting car and tea in the Great Southern Hotel in Killarney as part of the day out. Sleeping cars were available for the trip back from Fishguard to Paddington. Ten of these trains were run from London during the season, each with connecting services from Birmingham (joining at Newport or Cardiff) and carrying a total of 3,235 passengers for £3,559.

Half-day and all-day excursions were run every summer weekday. From Swindon to Paignton, Bedminster to Paddington, Yeovil to Weymouth, Weston-super-Mare to Weymouth, Weston to Paignton – and some of these were 'fed' from the short branch lines along the way. For instance, on one occasion the 12.5 pm Swindon-Paignton half-day excursion, formed with nine 3rd Class corridor coaches with a Brake-3rd at each end, called at Dauntsey to pick up any venturesome inhabitant of Malmesbury who, having seen the posters exhibited in the town, had the time and money to afford a trip to the seaside for the afternoon. Such persons came

The seaside terminus at Weymouth, seen here in September 1931, was the destination of many GWR and SR/GWR excursions. With its Brunellian overall roof, it opened on 20 January 1857 - note that the glass windscreen is perfectly clean.

The Southern 'T9' 4-4-0 No E730 with its SR coaches on the right demonstrate that the Southern Railway had running powers into Weymouth dating from the opening of the line.

GWR 4-4-0 No 3324 Glastonbury *is Station Pilot, coupled to a clerestory coach and a 'cell' (battery) truck. Steam railmotor No 103 is on the left, working the Abbotsbury branch and/or the Dorchester shuttle. (British Rail)*

to the main line on a regular branch train, but were taken home from Dauntsey at 12.36 am the following morning by a special trip of the branch train.

In the 1920s the GWR ran seaside excursions for Sunday School parties almost every day of the week during the season. On Tuesday 13 July 1926, to give a typical example, empty coaches off a Horfield-Temple Meads local, booked to the carriage sidings, were instead sent to Stapleton Road to pick up 60 adults and 150 children from All Hallows Sunday School. The engine ran round its train and left at 8.45 am for Lawrence Hill and the 100 adults and 300 children of St Luke's Sunday School. A very optimistic *3 minutes* was allowed for loading 300 excited children before the train left for Weston-super-Mare via the Bristol Avoiding line, calling at Bedminster to pick up a further 20 adults and 150 children from the Bristol City Mission Sunday School.

On the 14th the Southern Railway ran a Sunday School special from Sherborne to Weymouth involving a *triple* reversal of the train. The Southern engine ran round its train at Yeovil Junction and took it down the bank to Yeovil Town station. Here the engine was uncoupled and a GWR engine attached to the rear to draw the train round to Yeovil Pen Mill, where the engine ran round to

take the train to Weymouth, passing under the SR main line at Yeovil Junction 1½ miles to the south.

Throughout the 1920s the GWR carried heavy extra traffic for all the main agricultural shows on its territory. The Devon County Show at Newton Abbot on 20-22 May 1924 brought an additional 176 wagons of livestock and 266 wagon-loads of buildings and machinery to this very busy junction station, which was already bursting at the seams and ripe for enlargement.

The Bath & West Show at Taunton on 27-31 May brought 366 wagons of livestock, 950 wagon-loads of other traffic and an additional 18,000 passengers. Bearing in mind the very limited platform and siding accommodation at Bath, and the need to handle the regular traffic, these figures assume gigantic proportions, and the men that handled the traffic become heroes - at least, they do to this ex-railwayman author.

The Royal Agricultural Show was held at Reading on 6-10 July 1926. The GWR carried the timber and metal for the stands, and brought in the prefabricated sheds, the show machinery and other freight amounting to 3,000 tons. The Company ran 44 special trains of horses and livestock, while no fewer than 1,258 horse-boxes and cattle trucks, also carrying show animals, came into Reading on scheduled passenger trains. Using their own motor buses the Company ran a shuttle from the station to the showground at a 6d single fare. Some 21,548 passengers were carried for £563, making a surplus, after all expenses had been paid, including an allowance for 'depreciation', of £378.

When one stops to consider the extra everything that all this work entailed - locating the wagons and locos, the crews, collecting the rolling-stock from yards and from outlying stations, arranging for them to be picked up by a certain train, the unloading and shunting of empty vehicles at Reading, the timetabling and general organisation of the trains - one is, or ought to be, lost in admiration of the organisation that achieved all this without a computer, without two-way radios - and without any 'organised for quality' 'consumer services representative' in sight. The GWR simply had a conscientious staff of experienced 'railwaymen'.

Nor did the Company confine its search for extra passenger traffic to within the shores of Britain. It also eagerly sought traffic from around the world and, apart from permanent offices in Paris and New York, it had a roving representative with the pleasant job of touring through Egypt, India, Ceylon, Australia and New Zealand, drumming up tourist trade and anything else that might be carried on the Great Western. The Company subscribed £900 a year to the 'Come to Britain' movement devoted to increasing the tourist trade.

The American tourist trade was considered to be very important to the GWR and every effort was made to welcome and cosset deputations and individuals. Annually the GWR invited large groups of American hoteliers and tour operators to Britain and gave them a 'slap up' time. In April 1926 300 American hotel-owners were invited to Britain as the guests of the GWR. They crossed the Atlantic in the SS *France*, disembarked at Plymouth and were most extravagantly conveyed to Paddington in two special trains. They were lodged in the GWR's Royal Hotel at Paddington where they were joined by European hoteliers. From there they were taken out daily by train to see the standard GWR beauty spots, starting with, of course, Swindon Locomotive Works (what could be more beautiful or more dramatic than this castle of skills?), then other places like Oxford and Stratford-upon-Avon.

The guests were suitably impressed and American tour companies began sending over 'package tours'. On 1 August 1926 an American tour company landed 600 tourists at Liverpool. They were ferried to Birkenhead and sent up from there to Paddington in two special trains - doubtless they could have been packed into one train, which would have been more 'cost effective' for the GWR, but the two trains provided the passengers with more comfortable accommodation and thereby ensured a repeat performance with a fresh batch of tourists. After a week in London the 600 returned to America via

Wolfhall Junction on the GWR 'Berks & Hants Extension Railway' in the heart of racehorse country, looking east towards Newbury in about 1925. The ex-M&SWJR route from Cheltenham through Marlborough Low Level and Savernake High Level to Southampton bridges the GWR on the left of the view, with the Kennet & Avon canal at the centre. The M&SW connection to the GWR snakes down on the right. (Clinker Collection/courtesy Brunel University)

Stratford-upon-Avon and Crewe in two GWR specials from Paddington. The GWR earned £1,602 from this.

The Great Western's two westbound main lines ran on each side of the high chalk downs of Berkshire, where the springy turf makes the best racehorse training grounds in England. Trains of horse-boxes were run from main-line stations between Swindon and Didcot and on the remote Midland & South Western Junction section, the Didcot-Newbury line and, of course, the Lambourn branch. Train-loads of GWR horse boxes went to places as far apart as Ayr, Newton Abbot, Newmarket and Chepstow.

For one such trip to Ayr, for example, on 14 and 15 July 1926, an engine and Brake-3rd coach left Trowbridge at 3.43 pm to collect horse-boxes along the route at Devizes, Newbury, Compton and Didcot before 'setting sail' with a will for Oxford, passed non-stop at 7.20 pm, Leamington, where the engine was changed in 5 minutes (8.20-8.25), Birmingham Snow Hill, passed non-stop, and Wolverhampton, standing from 9.30 to 9.40, presumably to allow the attendants to attend to the horses. From there they were non-stop to Crewe via Market Drayton and arrived in Ayr at 6.30 am next day, well in time to recover from the long journey and to be ready for the races.

The City of Bath is squeezed into the deep, steep valley of the river Avon and the race-course was most inconveniently situated for rail-borne horses on the level hilltop 780 feet above the city and 3¼ miles from the GWR station. However, this did not prevent the GWR from making elaborate and, one supposes, expensive preparations to cater for additional traffic on Bath race days.

There was a race meeting from 13 to 16 July 1926. Passenger traffic to it was catered for by strengthening regular trains and, on Thursday 15th, with an excursion train of 1st Class carriages from Paddington. A GWR official, Mr Beacham, was on duty at the race-course each day, acting as canvasser for horse traffic and to answer and sort out any problems that might arise. Four extra porters were drafted in to Bath station each day to assist with passengers and their luggage, while another porter and a man from the permanent way department were posted to Westmoreland sidings to clean and disinfect the incoming horse-boxes - or 'Pacos' as GWR men called them, using the single-needle telegraphic code word.

Each day a locomotive was sent up from Bristol to shunt the horse-boxes between Bath station, where they came in on regular trains, and Westmoreland sidings. These engines might have been 'Metro' Class 2-4-0 tanks, or 0-6-0 'Dean Goods' - whatever the type, it had to be capable of working a special train of horse-boxes if the single scheduled train was insufficient for the traffic.

Unfortunately for the railway, the racehorse trainer recognised the inconvenience of taking his horses to the railway station where they might be upset by (to an honest horse) the noise and the strange sights, followed by a long shaking journey in a four-wheeled box. All this must have had a detrimental effect on the performance of thoroughbred horses,

Oxford's 'North End Pilot', 0-6-0 No 1051, shunts a 'Paco', or horse-box, on 29 November 1929. The signal box on the extreme left belongs to the LMS's Rewley Road station. (Dr Jack Hollick/Adrian Vaughan Collection)

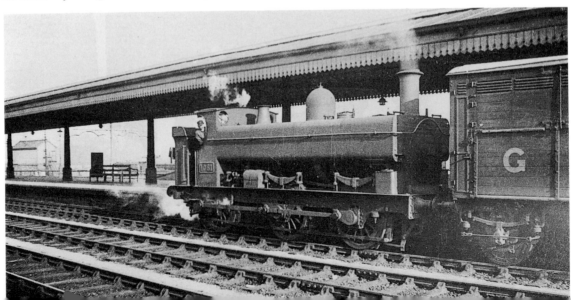

but that was the way of it then, and most horses would have been under the same handicap.

In the later 'twenties road lorries built especially for racehorses began to appear. Some were owned by racehorse trainers, while others were for hire. The Southern Railway had bought such vehicles by 1929 for use within its own area and also to transfer racehorses across London, but the GWR held back at first because it felt that they were not a commercial proposition 'owing to the long periods that the vehicles would stand idle and the difficulties which arise when road vehicles of one company penetrate the territory of another'.

It is interesting to note that at this time the GWR was having the same difficulty in swallowing its pride over buying road tankers to collect milk from the farms - even though that traffic was being captured by independently owned road tankers.

In spite of the deepening recession and 'severe competition' from the road, racehorse traffic increased and the GWR carried 18,778 animals in 1929 and 20,657 in 1930. The Company was particularly vulnerable to this competition when race meetings were at Newbury, Windsor or Ascot, since these places were relatively close to the Berkshire and Wiltshire training areas. The GWR was obliged to buy specialised road vehicles by which racehorses were collected from the racing stables and taken either direct to the meeting or to the railhead. Two articulated road horse-boxes were stationed at Swindon for use in the Berkshire and Wiltshire racehorse training area. Even so, I was fortunate enough to experience the job of loading racehorses into rail boxes and coupling them to the rear of 'King'-hauled passenger trains at Challow in 1961.

Special trains for theatregoers were long a feature of the GWR's service, but of course they became less well patronised and less frequent as the Depression of the later 'twenties deepened. The Birmingham-Paddington evening theatre specials ran with dining cars in each direction. There was also a useful revenue derived from London theatre companies - actors, staff and scenery - travelling by special train to the provinces for tours of local theatres. In 1926 the total receipts for all theatrical traffic on the GWR amounted to £30,812, and 53,265 actors and theatre staff were carried.

On 10 October 1927 the GWR laid on nothing less than Royal saloons for a Special to take the Australian cricket team from Paddington to Birkenhead. The engine from Paddington was No

4082 *Windsor Castle*, with Driver Roberts. The load must have been very light and the 210 miles to Birkenhead was covered in 235 minutes with one stop at Shrewsbury. The train left Paddington to resounding cheers, passed Haddenham at 92 mph and Birmingham Snow Hill, 110½ miles from Paddington, rather more sedately, in 106 minutes. The 33 miles to Shrewsbury were taken leisurely in 54 minutes. At Shrewsbury No 4082 came off and Driver Jones with No 3811 *County of Bucks* came on. Jones was keen to impress the Aussies and ran the train at an average of 60 mph all the way to Chester, bringing them into Birkenhead at exactly 1 o'clock.

On Saturday 31 July 1927, the start of the Bank Holiday weekend, the weather was hot and sunny and *all* main-line express trains out of Paddington and *all* principal cross-country services were run in two parts, many in three. The 'Torbay Limited' went down in three parts and the 'Cornish Riviera' ran in five parts, a record which was occasionally equalled in later years but never beaten; it meant that each of the three 'slip' portions had become separate trains, together with an extra train for Penzance.

The following day, apart from all the regular trains out of Paddington there were the inevitable excursions to Weston-super-Mare and seven 'Half-day' excursions, four to the Wye Valley and three to the Severn Valley line. The latter was popular for walking or fishing and was a regular destination for local excursions from Birmingham, which city of course also sent excursion to West Country resorts, Weston-super-Mare being the closest and most popular.

The Great Western served Weston in the holiday season with as many trains as could be got in and out of its two stations - the 'through' station and the ancient Bristol & Exeter Railway terminus at Locking Road. Paddington to Taunton expresses which called at Weston *en route* were run in three parts, and to back these up, Swindon-Bristol local trains would be strengthened with extra carriages at Bristol and extended to Weston. Although the Great Western had a monopoly in Weston-super-Mare, as they had at many resorts - Newbury Racecourse also springs to mind - the Company lavished services on these places as if they were in dire competition with the Southern or the LMS. Inter-company competition was unnecessary - the GWR was desperate for work.

On 10 July 1926 33 regular trains, running through Bristol, were duplicated or triplicated. On

Sunday 1 August, two 10-coach excursion trains were worked 'empty stock' from Didcot to Wantage Road for a journey to Bournemouth, via Swindon (Town) and Andover. The train reversed at Southampton, then headed westwards to its destination.

In June 1927 the Company ran 3,651 long-distance passenger trains - reliefs, excursions and boat trains - in addition to the month's 2,296 scheduled top-rank expresses and 106,000 local and branch trains; these were typical figures for the time. One can only wonder where the Company found the resources - in rolling-stock, men and sheer mental energy - to keep this work organised and rolling, week after week.

The International Boy Scouts Jamboree was held in Birkenhead from 31 July to 13 August 1929 - right through the most intensive period of holiday travel - and thither went, by GWR, no fewer than 6,500 eager-beaver teenagers in 14 special trains, whilst another 3,500 travelled to the show by scheduled GWR services.

May 1937 was a month of incredible activity owing largely to the Coronation celebrations. Between 8 and 22 May (the Coronation was on the 12th) the decorations and illuminations in London attracted 148 day, half-day and evening excursions carrying 80,000 passengers, and of course regular trains were heavily loaded. The GWR not only ran these extra trains, but they also organised sight-seeing tours around London by motor bus and provided meals for those who travelled on them.

On the 15th HM The King reviewed ex-servicemen in Hyde Park and the GWR ran 26 specials into Paddington, each carrying 2,000 passengers, to see the parade. Between 16 and 20 May 13 specials were run from London, Bristol and Birmingham to Weymouth to see the Fleet lying in Review Order at Spithead. Some GWR trains ran via Basingstoke to Weymouth with the GWR engines working

through to Bournemouth. On arrival at Weymouth the GWR Irish ferry SS *St Patrick*, sent from Fishguard, took hundreds of sight-seers on a cruise through the lines of warships. On the 22nd over 9,000 passengers from Rochdale were brought up to Windsor in 20 dining car specials, 13 of which ran over the GWR branch from Slough.

Also during May there were:

Wales v Scotland: 45 extra trains from London/Midlands to Cardiff, 27,000 passengers
Wales v England: 19 extras to Paddington, 9,000 passengers
Football in Cardiff, Birmingham, Wolverhampton and Chelsea: 22 other specials
Whitsun bank holiday: 277 holiday specials for 136,919 passengers, 52 more trains and 63,144 more passengers than in 1938
The Aldershot Tattoo, 10 to 17 June: 30 specials for 9,957 people, 1,727 more passengers than 1938

The GWR management's attitude towards extra traffic was that it kept the railway fully employed. Instead of burning coaches because they would stand idle at certain times during the winter months, and rather than talk accountants' jargon to show that to run fewer trains - or none at all - was wise and clever, they did their damnedest to find work for all their stock and tolerated the few slack periods as a necessary evil if they were to profit from the heavy traffic offering for nine months of the year.

They had a sense of duty to the public, as well as a certain desperation in the face of the threat of road transport - the road had to be opposed at all costs and therefore 'any traffic is better than no traffic'. This fighting, well-organised, 'no surrender' attitude, and the hard work which went with it, kept the railway workforce in a high state of training - and morale.

15
Slip coach working

The GWR slipped 74 carriages a day in 1910. They were withdrawn as an economy measure from 1 January 1917 and restored on 5 May 1919, but they never achieved their pre-war usage, when they were slipped at wayside stations like Tilehurst and Wantage Road. The most slip coach workings between 1921 and 1939 was 29 per day, in 1929. Slip coaches were expensive to operate, requiring extra guards and extra handling at stations, and usually worked complicated 'diagrams'.

The slip coach was a likely source of danger to level crossing keepers, who were warned in the General Appendix to the Rule Book to be aware of which trains carried slip coaches and never to open their gates to road traffic behind such a train until they were quite certain that the slip coach had also gone by. One must suppose that 'thereby hangs a tale'.

The coach was also a source of danger to permanent way men who, having stood aside for the passage of the train, might go back on to the track when the slip coach was perhaps 30 seconds away behind the main train. The coach was fitted with a warning gong, operated by the guard.

For as long as possible on the journey the slip coach was coupled to the main train by placing its screw-link coupling over the conventional draw-hook on the last coach of the main train and connecting the vacuum brake pipes without the self-sealing valves being interposed between them. In this condition there was, practically speaking, no slip coach on the train and no special lamps were required, merely the usual side lamps and tail lamp on the rear of the slip coach.

At the last station stop before the slipping point the coupling on the last coach of the main train was slung over the slip coach's special draw-hook and the self-sealing adaptors were introduced between the vacuum brake pipes of the slip coach and main train. Having done this there was then a need to place the special 'slip' tail-lamp at the rear of the slip coach in addition to the side lamps, and also the special 'double red' tail lamp on the main train.

There were three categories of slip tail-lamp: a red and white light side by side, indicating 'first slip'; red above white indicating 'second slip'; and two red and a white in a compact triangle for 'third slip'. A headlamp on the slip coach was carried at all times.

Once the slip coach had been made operational, a special 'slip gone' tail-lamp, taking the form of two red lights arranged vertically, was placed on the rear of the last vehicle of the main train. For recognition in daylight, all the lamps concerned with slip working had a broad red or white metal ring around the glass lens, according to the colour of the light.

For example, the 8.30 am Weston-super-Mare slipped a coach at Didcot, so the vertical 'double red' tail lamp at the rear of the main train was the correct tail signal eastwards from Didcot, but it was an emergency signal if it was showing west of Didcot. The signalmen therefore had to be alert to which trains conveyed slips and where those slips were supposed to be dropped.

It was rare but not unknown for the slip to be made in open country. In any event the guard could not make the slip unless the main train was signalled clear through the station ahead; therefore it was essential that he got a clear view of the distant signal to see whether it was lowered to 'All Clear' or horizontal at 'Caution'. Special 'slipping distant' signals were placed low down on the post of the main distant signal and worked by the same wire that moved the main arm; there are known to have been examples at Reading and Bicester, and the Regulations stated that these special signals were provided 'where the distant signal cannot easily be seen by the slip guard'.

The slip guard had a prescribed landmark at which he pulled his slipping lever, but he had to exercise good judgement in this and have regard for the wind and the slipperiness of the rails so that he gave himself plenty of braking distance. If there was thick fog or falling snow, it was the slip guard's decision whether to slip or not. If he decided it was too dangerous he would, some way before the slipping place, open a cock in the vacuum brake pipe to allow a small amount of air into the system which began a gentle brake application. Therefore, if 2 or 3 miles before the slipping place the driver felt the brakes going on and saw his vacuum gauge needle falling slowly, he understood that this was the slip guard's signal that he was not going to slip and that therefore the train must be stopped at the slipping station. The driver acknowledged this understanding by giving three short blasts on the engine's whistle.

Prior to a slip being made it was essential that all brakes were fully released and that at least 23 inches (out of a possible 25) of vacuum had been created in order that the slip coach should have its full brake-power. If this was not the case, if for example there had been a signal check just before the slipping point which had made the driver brake hard, then once again the whole train had to stop to detach the slip.

Otherwise, all being well, the slip guard removed the slip lever padlock and pulled the lever fully backwards (towards himself). This removed the wedge holding the hinged draw-hook in place so that it fell and slipped off the coupling. The lever's movement also opened the air valve in the vacuum brake pipe to apply the brake on the coach.

As the slip coach dropped back from the train, the vacuum brake pipes parted and were sealed to atmosphere by the special valves. This was the most critical moment of the operation, because if the main train's vacuum pipe did not seal while the slip coach pipe did, the brakes would be applied to the main train and there was the danger of a collision between the two parts.

Some air entered the main train's vacuum pipe before the self-sealing valve operated, so the driver, alert on his engine, watched his vacuum gauge for the brief tell-tale nod of the train-pipe vacuum gauge needle which proved that the slip had been made.

He now had a coach running loose behind his train, and the slip guard now became a driver. Once the coach had dropped back from the main train the guard pushed the lever forward to a 'stop' in its travel. This altered a port in the brake valve allowing the air at atmospheric pressure which had entered the brake cylinders to exhaust into the ample capacity of the vacuum chamber (reservoir) carried on the coach. These reservoirs were large enough to swallow the air from several brake applications.

At Princes Risborough, the official slipping point was '200 yards before reaching South box down distant signal', the coach being brought to a stand at South box's down home. Once it was at a stand the signalman allowed the engine of the 'Risborough-Banbury 'all stations' to collect it and attach it to its train.

At Didcot, on the down road, the slipping point was opposite the allotments, 800 yards east the platform, while on the up road the coach was slipped approaching Foxhall Junction signal box. It was indeed an odd sight to see an up 'fast' go speeding through the station at perhaps 75 mph and then, a minute later, to see this solitary coach come coasting under the Foxhall road bridge, towards the platform.

Coaches could be slipped at Reading on either the Up Relief or Up Main lines. The Up Relief ran alongside its own platform, but the Up Main platform was served by a loop from the Up Main, the entrance points for which were worked from Reading West Main signal box. Slip coach working here was, in the early 1920s, complicated by the practise of allowing some slip trains to go through the station at full speed and sending others through the platform loop.

The slip coach could only enter the platform loop non-stop if the whole train was routed that way - the facing points for the loop could *not* be switched between the rear of the main train travelling along the Up Main and the approaching coach, bound for the loop. If the whole train went through the loop, it had to reduce speed to 20 mph in order to negotiate the points, yet a full vacuum had to be re-created before the slip was made - a skilful piece of driving. If the main train was to continue up the main at full speed, the slip coach had to be stopped at West Main's inner home signal before reaching the platform loop facing points, after which these points would be turned for the loop.

In order that the slip guard should know what was going to happen, there were three slipping distants on the Up Main line. The first was below Reading West Junction's Up Main starting signal, and a *pair* of 'splitting' distants below Reading West Main's Up Main home signal, the left-hand or right-hand arm being lowered according to how the road was set ahead. If the first slipping distant was lowered, the guard slipped at once and brought his coach to a stand at Reading West Main's home signal, to await the switching of the platform line facing points.

If the first slipping distant was at 'Caution' he did not slip but waited until he could see the 'splitting' distants to learn whether the train was routed through the platform loop or Up Main. If the left-hand signal was lowered he was routed via the platform and slipped at once, understanding that the train would proceed through the platform. If the right-hand arm was lowered the train was routed 'up the main', so he slipped at once but brought his coach to a stand at the home signal.

This fascinatingly complicated working was simplified, made safer and savings in signalling made merely by laying it down that all trains on the Up Main line with a slip coach for Reading must pass through the up platform loop.

For an example of the complications of the rostering of slip coach working I will take the rota of workings on two trains, the 6.45 am Weston-super-Mare to Paddington and the 4.30 pm Paddington to Plymouth in the summer of 1929.

The 6.45 am Weston was a 'stopper' as far as Bristol and express thereafter, calling at Bath, Chippenham and Didcot with slips for Swindon and Reading. The train left Weston with nine coaches, including a dining car. The coaches were conventionally coupled, the special tail-lamps were in the guard's van of the main train and an ordinary single tail-lamp was on the rear of the last coach. The train guard as far as Bristol was a Weston man who thereafter worked local trains. From Bristol the guard was a Bristol man starting out on a 'double home' job - up to Paddington and down to Kingswear that day, returning to Bristol via Westbury and Paddington next day.

The slip draw-hook and the self-sealing adaptors for the Swindon slip were brought into use at Chippenham, together with the 'double red' tail-lamp at the rear of the Reading slip - which was still attached as an ordinary coach. The Swindon slip was manned by a Swindon guard who joined the coach at Chippenham after working down with a stopping train.

After the first slip coach had come to a stand at Swindon and unloaded, the station pilot took it away to the carriage shed at the west end of the up platform where it rested until being attached as an

'Dean Goods' No 2568 running into Flax Bourton station with what is thought to be the 11.2 am Stoke Gifford-Weston-super-Mare 'all stations' in 1939. There is a 1910 'Toplight' carriage next the engine and what might be the two coaches slipped at Stoke Gifford from the 8.55 am Paddington-Pembroke Dock. (C. R. L. Coles)

ordinary coach to the 1.50 pm to Paddington. From there the empty coach was taken back to Old Oak Common and marshalled at the rear of the coaches for the 7.55 pm to Fishguard to be slipped at Stoke Gifford for Weston-super-Mare.

The second slip, for Reading, was prepared for slipping at Didcot and was manned by a Reading guard who worked down to Didcot on a stopping train. After slipping and stopping at Reading, the coach was shunted to the 10.30 am 'stopper' to Paddington, attached as an ordinary coach with the ex-slip guard now in charge of the whole train. This slip coach was also taken back to Old Oak Common where it was re-marshalled into the stock for the 4.30 pm to Plymouth (via Bristol) as the Bridgwater slip.

We next return to the first slip, now part of the 7.55 pm Paddington to Fishguard. During the train's stop at Reading the slip guard, a Weston-super-Mare man, joined the coach, attended to the couplings and saw that the special tail-lamps were put in place. He slipped the coach at Stoke Gifford at 9.57 pm, whence he worked it home as an ordinary coach on the 10 pm 'A' headcode express from Stoke Gifford to Stapleton Road and Bristol Temple Meads, arriving at 10.16 pm. An hour later he took it through to Weston where it was re-marshalled in the stock for the following day's 6.45 am 'up' working.

At Newport a specially designated porter removed the 'double red' tail-lamp from the main train and personally saw that it was put inside the guard's brake-van of the 11.4 pm up express which was non-stop to Paddington. At Paddington another porter/lampman met the train, removed the lamp, cleaned it, trimmed it and made sure it was placed on the rear of the main part of the 8.55 am non-stop to Newport, which slipped a coach at Stoke Gifford. At Newport the lamp was once more promptly returned to Paddington where it was placed in the guard's van of the 7.55 pm for use again that same day between Reading and Newport. On the steam railway even the tail-lamps had a life of their own requiring detailed knowledge on some-one's part!

The 4.30 pm Paddington-Plymouth was formed with five 70-foot coaches, including a dining car, for Plymouth, three 70-foot coaches for Kingswear, the Bridgwater slip (returning home having been slipped at Reading from the 6.45 am from Weston that morning) and behind that a slip for Chippenham. This Chippenham slip was also part of the 6.30 pm Paddington's train-set whose perambulations of the system we had better not follow – those of the Bridgwater slip are complicated enough to stand as typical of the magnificent complications of the job!

The Head Guard of the 4.30 pm was a Bristol man, who was on the homeward leg of a 'double home' job – the day before he had worked the 7.45 am Bristol to Paddington and the noon express to Kingswear, and had returned to 'Padd' with the 11.20 ex-Kingswear. From Bristol to Newton Abbot the Head Guard of the 4.30 pm was a Newton Abbot man who had earlier worked as slip guard on the 5.15 pm Bristol-Weston (12.31 pm from Portsmouth) and had slipped at Yatton (for Clevedon) at 5.31. He returned on the next up stopper from Yatton and arrived at Bristol at 5.50 pm in time to take over as Head Guard on the 4.30 pm, which left Bristol at 6.55.

The Bridgwater coach was slipped there at 7.25 pm and went on to Taunton in a local train at 8.23 pm. At 3.35 am the next day it left, empty, in a parcels train to Newton Abbot and was marshalled into the 11.5 am passenger train to Paignton, this stock returning from Paignton to Newton at 12.10 pm. Here it was attached to the rear of the 9.15 am from Falmouth, the 12.52 pm departure from Newton Abbot, to be slipped at Reading. At Reading it was shunted on to the 5.8 pm local to Paddington.

Next day it went down on the 1.15 pm, slipping at Bath at 3 pm and working 'all stations' to Bristol, arriving at 4.45 pm. At Bristol it was stabled for an hour then attached to the rear of 12.31 pm Portsmouth to Weston, to be slipped at Yatton for Clevedon. It returned from Clevedon to Yatton at 5.50 pm and formed the 7.57 Yatton-Weston. At last the coach had got home, and was marshalled into the stock of next day's 6.45 am Weston, to begin the circuit again.

By 1939, in spite of their expense and complication, there were still 13 slips made every weekday, and the unlikely location of Taplow was still honoured by a slip off the 5.15 pm Paddington-Bristol.

Slip coach working was remarkable not only because it was a survival and development from the earliest days of railways but also because it survived under British Railways - indeed, BR's Western Region actually converted at least one ordinary coach to slip operation, and did not cease the practise until the end of the summer service of 1960, the last slip being off the 5.10 pm from Paddington at Bicester.

16

The 'Ocean Liner' trains

The first railway to Plymouth was the South Devon Railway, incorporated by Act of Parliament in 1844 and opened by stages from the Bristol & Exeter Railway at Exeter, reaching the Plymouth Millbay terminus on 2 April 1849. The Plymouth Great Western Dock Co was incorporated in 1846 to construct about a mile of railway southwards from the Millbay terminus to new docks on Plymouth Sound. This line was opened in June 1857, becoming the property of the 'Associated Companies' - GWR, B&ER and SDR - in July 1874, and the sole property of the GWR on 22 July 1878 when the two smaller companies were formally amalgamated with the Great Western.*

Millbay docks faced directly on to the sheltered deep-water Plymouth Sound, which was undoubtedly the most conveniently placed first landfall for eastbound liners. Passengers and mail could be disembarked into small ferries, or 'tenders', to be taken back to the waiting train on the quayside, thus reaching London and elsewhere a day or more sooner than by remaining on the Southampton-bound or London-bound liner.

The London & South Western Railway opened their branch off the Cornwall Railway† to Devonport King's Road on 17 May 1876, their branch off this line to the quay at Stonehouse Pool opening later that year. Stonehouse Pool was close to Millbay but had a tortuous access to and from the Sound, while the LSWR trains had a very poor route to Exeter - they used the GWR main line to Laira Junction where they turned north on the single-track steeply graded Launceston branch and passed through Yelverton and Tavistock to Lydford Junction where the LSWR diverged for Crediton and Exeter. In spite of these disadvantages the LSWR was able to compete with the GWR for Plymouth-London traffic due to the penny-pinching nature of the GWR management at that time.

Plymouth North Road station, on the London side of Millbay and Devonport King's Road, was built by the SDR at the cost of the LSWR as a Joint station, and opened on 28 March 1877 as an GWR/LSWR Joint station.

On 2 June 1890 the LSWR opened its own double-track railway from Lydford through Tavistock, at a higher level than the GWR, to Bere Alston, Devonport and Plymouth North Road. Thirteen months later it opened its own station at Plymouth Friary. The new double-track line placed the LSWR in a very strong competitive position with the GWR - the distance from Stonehouse Pool to Waterloo was 230 miles against nearly 247 miles from Millbay Quay to Paddington.

---

* The GWR leased the B&ER and the SDR from January and February 1876. The Great Western and South Devon Railway Companies Amalgamation Act was passed on 22 July 1878.

† Leased to the GWR on 3 May 1859, and opened to Truro on 1 August 1861 - Cornwall Railway (Consolidation and Amendment) Act - and amalgamated with the GWR by Act of Parliament of 24 June 1889.

Shaugh Bridge platform on the line from Plymouth (Laira Junction) to Tavistock via Yelverton, on 15 June 1926. The view is towards Bickleigh whose distant signal can be seen. The tortuous nature of this route as it contours up the river valley, used by LSWR boat trains until that company opened its own double-track route in 1890, is apparent. Less obvious is the 1 in 58 gradient rising towards the bridge. (H. C. Casserley)

This event coincided with the change of Great Western management referred to by the Company's historian, E. T. McDermott, as 'The Great Awakening'. Fast trains and modern rolling-stock were now the priority and the 'Ocean Mail' trains made an excellent shop window. Throughout the '90s some very fast running was done carrying passengers, mails and gold bullion.

In April 1903 the North German Lloyd and Hamburg-Amerika shipping companies decided to make all their eastbound liners call at Plymouth to put off the New York-London mails and passengers, and in April of the following year the LSWR opened a new 'Ocean Terminal' at Stonehouse Pool. There was now a regular traffic which the two companies agreed to share, the GWR taking the mails and the LSWR the passengers. From this there arose a racing mania between the railwaymen of the

A '44xx' 2-6-2T runs into Yelverton, crossing the junction with the Princetown branch, with a passenger train from Plymouth to Tavistock on the same day. The train has just emerged from the 641-yard Yelverton tunnel - a cloud of steam at the rear of the train marks the spot. In the cutting there was a fine spring of bright water that provided the station staff with drinking water at least until 1947. (H. C. Casserley)

two companies as intense as anything experienced 9 years earlier on the East Coast and West Coast main lines.

The GWR had the better engines and, in spite of their route being nearly 17 miles longer than the 'South Western, they made the best times to London. In trying to beat the GWR, the LSWR came to grief disastrously with a crash at Salisbury on 1 July 1906, killing 24 of the 42 passengers and injuring seven seriously. Four railwaymen were also killed.

Around 1907 the major railway companies of Britain began to see the wastefulness of cut-throat competition. The GWR and LSWR maintained duplicate facilities in Plymouth and ran competing services between Plymouth, Exeter and London. In 1908 the General Manager of the LSWR, Sir Charles Owens, wrote a paper for the Board of Trade on the subject of 'The Disadvantages of Competition'.

On 13 May 1911 the GWR and LSWR signed a non-competition agreement which handed the Ocean traffic to the GWR and closed the LSWR Ocean Terminal at Stonehouse Pool. In return, the revenue on all GWR/LSWR local competitive traffic between Plymouth and Exeter and the Ocean revenues were pooled and shared according to the proportions of the traffic each Company had carried in 1908.

Ocean trains had simultaneously a glamorous and a heroic air about them, because they carried gold and some of the richest people in the world, and because of their connection with the largest transatlantic liners of the day which were themselves in constant rivalry for the fastest crossing of the ocean. Although the GWR had the traffic without competition, the prestigious combination of great ocean liner and powerful locomotive ensured that all 'Ocean Liner' trains ran fast, and that the finest engines and the best coaches were used.

Whilst the GWR was consolidating its grip on Ocean traffic at Plymouth, it was also spending a very great deal of money to build an Ocean terminal on a virgin site on Fishguard Bay. This was opened on 30 August 1906, and served the greatest ocean-going liners until that most fateful of months - August 1914.

Fishguard's function as a port was slow to re-start after the Great War. Transatlantic ships never called again and traffic for Ireland did not recommence until 1920 and was then severely restricted by the Irish War of Independence against the British, followed tragically by a Civil War, but in 1923 the

traffic began to develop even to the extent of the re-introduction of the famous 'Day Excursions' from Paddington to Killarney.

The GWR's docks on the South Wales coast declined after the Great War since they were primarily coal-exporting points, but Milford Haven in West Wales grew ever busier with its fish traffic, while the docks at Avonmouth and Birkenhead handled an increasing import traffic throughout the 'twenties. Weymouth, as port for the Channel Islands and Brittany, took an increasing traffic in passengers and vegetables, but most of all Plymouth Millbay's prestigious trans-world Ocean Liner traffic grew annually until 1930 (see Appendix 4), and although it then decreased it remained considerable up to the outbreak of the next great war.

The Sound, half a mile on the landward side of the Breakwater, was always relatively calm, even if there was a sou'westerly gale roaring up Channel. The GWR tender (see Appendix 5), the *Sir Francis Drake*, would be tied to the liner and would lie snugly in the lee of the huge hull, rising and falling on the sheltered swell. A staircase was extended down the side of the hull to the level of the tender's embarkation point and a pair of sailors were stationed at the bottom to hand the disembarking passengers, men, women and children, safely on to the smaller ship. While this was going on the liner's derricks were slinging nets full of mails or luggage into the hold of the tender. At night this hazardous operation was carried out in a lamp-lit twilight. The tender then ferried its load to Millbay Quay where a through train to Paddington was waiting, formed with the best carriages available.

These trains were hauled at the start of the period under consideration by 'Star' Class locomotives, and by the 'Castles' from 1924. 'King' Class locomotives were not permitted over the docks line, and if one had been booked to work an 'Ocean Special' it would have been necessary to change engines at Plymouth North Road; as far as is known, a 'King' was never used.

On 5 December 1924 the great transatlantic liner SS *America* came into Plymouth Sound and dropped anchor at the Breakwater at 9.42 am. The GWR tender *Sir Francis Drake* was waiting and was tied alongside at 9.50 am. Some 4,134 bags of mail and 66 passengers were loaded, and at 10.50 am the ropes were cast off for the passage back to shore. On the way to the quay, GWR staff sorted out tickets and any other problems and the tender tied up at Millbay quay at 11.04.

Plymouth Millbay with the four GWR tenders moored, circa *1937. On either side of the pontoon are* Sir John Hawkins, *nearest the camera, and* Sir Francis Drake. (P. A. Hopkins)

Unloading, direct to the waiting Paddington express, began at once, and at 11.55 am the train pulled away with 45 passengers and 1,345 bags of mail, arriving in Paddington at 3.48 pm, 233 minutes for 227 miles, a very typical run.

The record for an 'Ocean Mail' from passing Millbay station to Paddington was 217 minutes with a 170-ton train – a 'Plym A' (see Appendix 6). This was a very remarkable time indeed, not least because there could have been no delays at all in the 227-mile journey. Moreover, there could be no scheduled path for an Ocean special – it had to be fitted into the regular train service as well as the signalmen were able, and there were likely to be delays along the way.

The running of a special was advised on a notice, received in signal boxes a day or two before it ran, but this could do no more than warn that one or more 'Ocean Specials' would run – no-one could say precisely when the ship would drop anchor in the Sound nor what load it would be delivering, until with the advent of radiotelephony the Company could be forewarned as to the number of passengers and mail bags to be disembarked.

When the tenders got back to the quay the Boat Train Inspector at the passenger landing stage could judge when the train would be ready to leave and would confer with the Passenger Train Controller on a likely 'path' for the train. Having decided on this, the Inspector would telephone Millbay Station

Inspector with the probable departure time and the designation of the train, and the latter officer would then start a 'box to box' message to run through every signal box to Paddington, such as 'Plym A 10.10 Millbay to Paddington'.

Thirty minutes before an up or down 'Ocean Special' was due to use the line between the Quay and Millbay Crossing signal box, a Pilotman, appointed by the Dock Inspector, walked from the quay to the Crossing box with a special form, signed by the signalman, to acknowledge that a passenger train was shortly going to use the line and to promise that no engine or wagon would be permitted to foul the line without the permission of the Pilotman. All points connecting sidings with the running line were clamped and padlocked by the Pilotman who kept the keys in his pocket. He also had to warn everyone working in the area – traders and stevedores – that a passenger train would pass by shortly. Five minutes before the actual departure time the Boat Train Inspector told the Millbay Crossing signalman to 'get the road' – saying something along the lines of 'Right away the Boat Train – Plym A – 10.10 Millbay to Paddington'.

The Millbay Crossing signalman then rang '4 bells' to Millbay station who did not reply until he 'had the road' from Cornwall Junction. Cornwall Junction then set the points for the Plymouth North Road direction and gave 'Line Clear' to Millbay Station, who returned 'Line Clear' to Millbay

Above and below 'Mill Bay Level Crossing Box' in about 1904, looking up the hill towards Millbay station. The wooden platform in the foreground was later demolished to make way for a double track across the road, as can be seen in the later (1953) and more distant view, which also shows Millbay Crossing's home and inner home (the latter with Millbay station's fixed distant beneath it). (British Rail, Larry Crosier)

Crossing - the latter signalman was not permitted to lower his signals for an up train (giving access to the Millbay Station section) until he had seen that the Millbay Station home signal was lowered.

With this done he closed his gates across the public road and pegged his block instrument in communication with the one at the Quay (situated in the Baggage Warehouse) to 'Line Clear'. Seeing the white 'Line Clear' flag appear in his instrument, the Boat Train Inspector stepped outside and gave the 'Right Away' to the train's guard whose duty it was actually to start the train.

Having 'given the road' to the Quay and closed his gates across the road, the Millbay Crossing signalman would watch anxiously for the column of smoke rising above the warehouses while road traffic built up at the gates. Sometimes the train might not start for 10 minutes after 'Line Clear' had been given, and even in horse-drawn days road traffic was heavy. The lengthy closure of Millbay Crossing gates often caused a queue of carts and motor cars which trailed along Millbay Road to Berry's Clock at the city centre, blocking the main streets in central Plymouth. The City police would arrive and ask

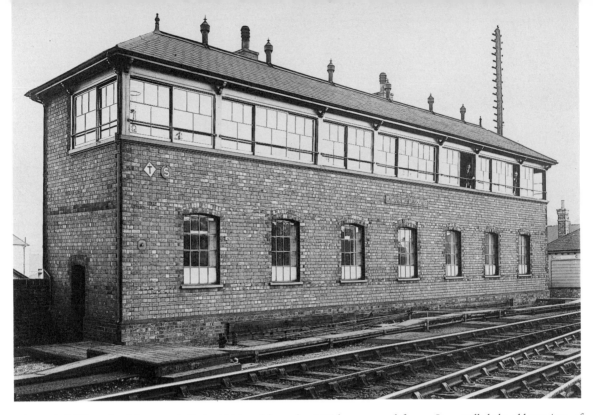

Plymouth Millbay signal box was built in 1914 and housed a 115-lever manual frame. It controlled the old terminus of the South Devon Railway, Millbay, the tracks to Millbay Crossing and the docks, and the carriage sidings for Plymouth North Road station.

Empty train-sets were brought here for storage and/or re-marshalling as the coaches were frequently booked to form other passenger trains. Carriage marshalling went on almost continuously and the newly formed trains were run by gravity, under the guard's hand-brake control, from the sidings on to the main line where their locomotive was coupled on. The box was the fourth busiest on the GWR in 1923 - a 'Special Class' job (see chapter 23) with a 24-hour average rating of 465 lever/bell operations per hour - and was worked by a single signalman with a booking lad.

Millbay Dock. 'Star' and 'Castle' Class locomotives hauling the Company's finest carriages came away from the quays between the stone warehouses. This view, somewhat out of period (31 October 1944), shows bomb damage and barrage balloons. (British Rail)

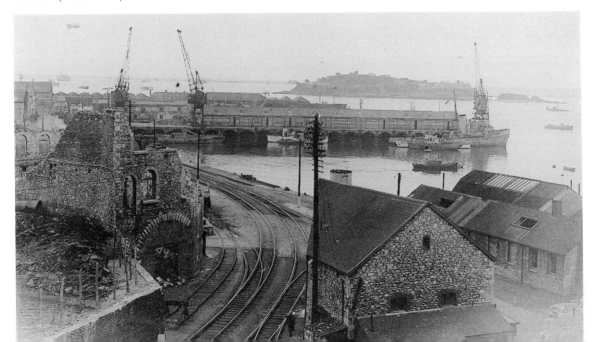

for the gates to be opened – but once 'Line Clear' had been given for the train to approach, nothing could be done unless the Docks Inspector and the Pilotman agreed positively to stop the departure of the train.

The railway lines were set in the cobbled quays, cheek-by-jowl with road traffic on the streets crossing the dockyard. To maintain safety a 'Flag Boy' was employed whose very responsible job was to walk ahead of the train to warn road users and make sure there were no road vehicles 'foul' of the tracks.

Millbay Docks were a world of their own and doubtless a very interesting book of memoirs could be written by a properly experienced person. One day in 1924 the SS *Arracon* from Rangoon called in Plymouth Sound to unload two elephants bound for London Zoo. The idea was to put slings around each elephant's belly, crane it over the side and down on to the GWR tender. The loaders tried the oldest and presumably the wisest elephant first but she – her name was Violet – stood on her head at the mere sight of the big canvas straps. After some time her Burmese attendant managed to get her to accept the slings, but then the loaders could not get Violet's portly body balanced in the sling, so every time the crane hoisted the animal fell forwards on to her head. All the while the other elephant, a younger and altogether more flighty creature, was trumpeting louder than the ship's siren.

However, after Violet had been lifted and dumped on her head several times, the gentle creature got the hang of matters, 'held still' and allowed herself to be swung over the side and lowered gently onto the *Sir Francis Drake*. The young elephant, having seen its companion lowered out of sight over the side of the ship, was then so lonely that it willingly consented to being strapped and hoisted just so it could rejoin its friend.

The two elephants stood quietly with their attendants on the deck of the tender as it butted through the salt spray, back to Millbay docks. The crew very kindly waited until the flowing tide had lifted the boat's deck level with Millbay quay so the elephants could walk across a level gangplank, but when the moment came Violet and her friend absolutely refused to budge and had to be slung ashore in their canvas straps.

From here they were to walk to the station. They set off plodding purposefully, trunks swinging, until they met an iron horse, Millbay's dock shunter, No 1369, hissing steam with a rake of rumbling vans in tow. The elephants were rooted to the spot by the

sight and refused to move until the engine had been reversed around a corner.

Off they went again only to come up against some honest GWR drayhorses, earning their oats. These drayhorses had to be wheeled around and hidden before the elephants would move. Finally they made it through the streets to Millbay station where they were boxed into a specially strengthened 'Python A' four-wheel van.

In 1924 504 liners called at Plymouth, almost equalling the number for 1913; 22,600 passengers were landed, 100 less than 1913, but receipts in 1924 were £36,000, £4,000 up on 1913. In addition, these 1924 passengers were carried in half the number of special 'Ocean Liner' trains used in 1913.

In those pre-air-travel days the transatlantic and indeed trans-world liner travel for business people was the only way to go, and in 1927, in addition to the usual French Line and Cunard liners, there came Blue Star liners inward-bound from South America and Bibby Line vessels from India (see Appendix 4). The inward-bound Baltic-American Line ships SS *Estonia* and SS *Lithuania* stopped to disembark passengers, not at Plymouth, but off Portland in July and August 1927.

On 9 July 1927 450 Americans were landed off the SS *Andania*; 350 went to Paddington but 100 went by special train to Fishguard for Killarney. The latter train, including a dining car, left Millbay at 7 pm and arrived at Fishguard Harbour at 5.12 am the next day.

Also in 1927, for the first time, *outward*-bound liners called at Plymouth, and this traffic also grew:

	1927	1929
Liners calling at Plymouth	74	80
Passengers embarking	3,704	3,491
Mailbags shipped	600	2,219

A lady passenger, going down on an evening 'Ocean Special' to Plymouth in 1927, dropped her false teeth out of the window passing Westbourne Park. A workman found them and handed them into the Station Inspector's office at Paddington. Meanwhile, the lady had reported the loss to the Guard who threw out a note as the train passed Slough. Slough informed the Station Inspector at Paddington who now knew to whom to address the teeth. He parcelled them and addressed them to the lady owner 'c/o S.M. Millbay' and sent them down on the 1.40 am 'Papers', a Penzance-bound train booked almost as fast as the 'Cornish Riviera'. A thoughtful tele-graph message to Plymouth North Road and Millbay Station Inspectors made certain that teeth and owner were reunited - the parcel was handed to her just as she was boarding the tender.

The Great Western Railway was short of money but its Commercial Department were rich in ideas and energy which they threw at the problem of how to make the railway pay at a time of deepening recession. Moreover, the Commercial people were backed to the hilt by those in charge of Operating. Nothing was too much trouble.

Early in 1928 someone in the GWR Marine Department at Plymouth realised that ship-loads of merely pleasure-cruising Americans and other nationalities were going past some of the most beautiful country in Britain without stopping to sample the delights of Babbacombe, Buckfastleigh and cream teams at Widecombe-in-the-Moor. The record does not name the originator of the idea, but he suggested that the ships be stopped and their passengers offered a 'land cruise' as part of their holiday.

Consequently the eastbound Holland-America Line SS *Ryndam* was persuaded to drop anchor off Torquay on the morning of 27 May 1928. One of the Plymouth tenders was waiting and brought ashore 400 tourists who were then given a two-day tour by GWR buses, trains and hotels, from Torquay around Dartmoor and back to the ship the following evening.

The trip was a roaring success, for the *Ryndam*, having upped its anchor and steamed eastwards, got only as far as Weymouth before the captain dropped anchor again and disembarked another 357 passengers into the welcoming arms of the GWR who feted them around Portland and Chesil Beach. For these efforts the Great Western earned £230 and was so pleased that it planned more trips.

The numbers of ships calling increased again and again. The Port of Plymouth was almost always open - although fog was a nuisance - and the GWR would always run a special train to London with passengers off the ship, just as soon as they could be loaded into the train - the carriages and locomotive were always waiting. The Great Western was in the business of running trains whenever its passengers required them.

On 10 July 1929 the GWR put into service a new tender, the *Sir John Hawkins*. The record year of all was 1931 when 788 ships called, eastbound and westbound, sometimes four a day. As the decade closed the demand for sleeping berths went beyond

that which the GWR could handle - 100 per train was not unusual - and the Company was frequently forced to borrow sleeping cars from the LMS.

In 1931 the GWR set out to develop a cross-Channel passenger traffic between Millbay, Le Havre and Bordeaux, using French Lines liners. The eastbound ships called at Le Havre after Plymouth, and westbound liners called at Plymouth before going on to Bordeaux from whence they set out for New York. During 1931 1,172 people made use of this very luxurious ferry service. To encourage the traffic the Great Western had built in Hull the *Sir Richard Grenville*, which was 35 feet longer and 5 feet wider than the existing tenders and had a very much improved saloon which, the GWR hoped, 'will be attractive especially for night landings and when the weather is bad'.

Sometimes foggy weather made the passage into Plymouth Sound impossible, causing the big liners to abort their call and go on to the Southern Railway terminal at Southampton. This was tedious for passengers in a hurry, who had to spend an extra full day on board the ship. In November 1928 a radio direction beacon was established on Start Point, Torquay, which was of some small use to vessels calling at Plymouth, and in 1929 a similar beacon was established on Penlee Point, overlooking Plymouth Sound.

It is remarkable how long a bad system will be tolerated before an improvement is made. Important radio messages from eastbound liners concerning their passengers' requirements at Plymouth were picked up at the Postmaster General's Land's End radio station and were relayed from there to the GPO station at Devizes for delivery to the Great Western. These messages were *apparently* treated like ordinary letters, as it is recorded that by the time the message arrived at Plymouth it was often too late to be acted upon - yet it was not until 1931 that the Great Western made 'representations' to the Postmaster General and arranged for these messages to be telegraphed promptly from Devizes to Plymouth.

The GWR believed in selling itself. Paddington's best canvassers were regularly sent to Millbay and put aboard a liner during the hour that she was at anchor in the Sound for the purpose of getting to know the Purser of each ship, to tell him what the GWR could offer and to leave GWR tourist and publicity literature in the ship's lounges and library.

From 1931 a GWR Inspector rode on the tender, whose job it was to interview all the passengers and make sure that the tourists amongst them were made aware of the delights of Devon – the GWR's 'Shire of the Sea-Kings' – that they received GWR tourist publicity, and that they were sold GWR tickets. Sir James Milne reported to his Directors that the efforts of these men were so successful 'that many people who had bought 3rd Class tickets were induced to travel 1st Class'!

Although 1931 was the peak year for the Plymouth 'Ocean Liner' traffic, perhaps the high-point of the service occurred in March and April 1937 when Cunard White Star informed the GWR that the RMS *Queen Mary* would call twice in each month, inward-bound, to set down passengers and mail to save a day on the journey. Each one of these calls by the ship disembarked so many passengers and so much mail that all four tenders and three special trains were needed to carry away the traffic.

17
Milk by rail

In 1921 the GWR's milk traffic was carried almost entirely in churns, as it always had been. It was a very labour-intensive and space-wasteful method, sending millions of gallons of milk in 'penny packets.' Glass-lined road milk-tankers had just come into use, while the GWR was running just three glass-lined milk tanks, although by April 1923 the Company had 57 such vehicles.

Milk was lost to the roads at a faster rate than any other rail-borne traffic. This was due to the inconvenience that all farmers experienced in having to take their churns to and from the railhead, and also to the loss of milk from pilfering and rough shunting which occurred *en route*.

From 1921 the Divisional Traffic Superintendents urged the Directors to get into the road-rail tanker collection service - to go around the farms to collect the milk and take it to the railhead - but the Directors remained for years remarkably reluctant to take this sound advice.

In January 1923 the Great Western approached Sir William Price, Chairman of United Dairies (UD), and suggested a co-operative scheme whereby UD would build the glass-lined rail-tanks, the GWR would build the railway chassis to carry the tanks, would make a rail connection into the existing UD depot at Wootton Bassett, and both parties would co-operate in building a new milk terminal at South Lambeth Goods depot where the GWR already owned land. UD, however, would not support the scheme because it already had a rail terminal at Mitre Bridge, Willesden, although it was willing to put milk on rail, but only at its price.

Early in 1926 UD approached the GWR to carry milk to its Mitre Bridge depot, but only at the same cost as if it was taken to Paddington. The GWR Directors were willing to agree to this if, in return, UD replaced on rail all the milk that it was by then sending to London by road from Moreton-in-Marsh and Wootton Bassett. No agreement was reached.

In February 1926 Sir Felix Pole warned the Directors of

'. . .the growth in recent years of road tankers of 2,000 or 2,500 gallons capacity, hauling milk from farms within 130 miles of London - Chippenham, Frome, Grafton and Burbage. These tankers can go into the farm yards which is immensely time-saving, since the farmer no longer has to go to the station. There is no pilfering, there are no returned empties and on top of this the farmers are being offered very attractive rates, considerably less than rail.'

The Chester Division Traffic Superintendent stated at the end of 1926 that

'In 1926 the rail-borne milk traffic from Rossett to Liverpool has declined from 41,000 gallons a week and now it is 6,000 per week.'

He went on to estimate that it would cost £600 to provide ramps and other terminal facilities at Rossett and Liverpool for road-rail tankers and the additional annual income from a road tanker collection and delivery service would be £1,500. The

Minutes do not record if anything was done about this.

On 27 January 1927 the Directors belatedly took heed of their Superintendents' warnings and agreed to install a daily rail-tanker service from the Wootton Bassett depot of UD and also reduced rates for the carriage of road tankers on rail. The really big operators like UD, Cow & Gate and Nestlé were offered a 30 per cent reduction for milk in bulk, either in a road-rail tank or in rail-only tank, the only stipulation being that the container had to be of at least 3,000 gallons capacity. Rail facilities were laid into the UD depot at Wootton Bassett and on 19 October 1927 the GWR's first milk-tanker train ran from there to UD's Mitre Bridge plant at Willesden - and this for the same rate as if the milk was going straight into Paddington.

In November 1927 205,000 gallons of milk were carried by this service, earning £828 for the GWR. Farmers were offered reduced rates for milk in churns if the traffic was reasonably large - milk in churns, over 1,000 gallons per annum, would attract a 15 per cent reduction, while over 2,000 gallons per annum in churns would enjoy a 20 per cent reduction. This reduction did not, however, remove the ordinary farmers' inconvenience and loss of time in having to make the daily trek to the railway sta-

tion, and there remained the problem of stealing or simple spillage from churns. As late as May 1931 farmers and the large dairies were complaining of loss of milk in churns due to pilfering and rough shunting and threatened to put the traffic on the road if the railway was not more careful.

From 25 December 1927 until 4 January 1928 there were heavy falls of snow which prevented the road hauliers from getting round the farms to collect, and as a result the farmers had to fall back on the neglected yet still faithful and reliable Great Western Railway. The road firms that failed their customers were Viner & Long of Frome, who sent 29,956 gallons by rail, Rose & Son of Bromham and Devizes (7,174 gallons), and Hosier Bros of Grafton (4,938 gallons). At this time Viner & Long used 1,500-gallon and 2,500-gallon road tankers to supply milk processing factories in Slough and London. The GWR quoted very competitive rates for bulk milk carriage in response to the threat from this firm, and in 1930 Sir James Milne reported to his Directors - with some satisfaction, I imagine - that Viner & Long 'had failed for £21,402'. When shall we again see the railway bankrupting road hauliers?

None the less, in 1930 the railway was still losing milk traffic to road hauliers and at last the Directors

The traditional way of handling milk was in churns, or 'cans'. This is the 10.15 am Paddington-Swindon on 9 February 1928, starting from Royal Oak and calling at all stations from Didcot to put off the churns of individual farmers. Some churns have come from the processing plant by GWR lorry, others have been loaded into 'Siphons' and ferried into Royal Oak by a local 'trip'. The handling - manual and by shunting-trip trains - of thousands of churns can hardly have been profitable, but the GWR Superintendents and General Manager were unable to persuade their Directors to abandon the traffic and had the greatest difficulty in getting them to adopt bulk-handling methods. (British Rail)

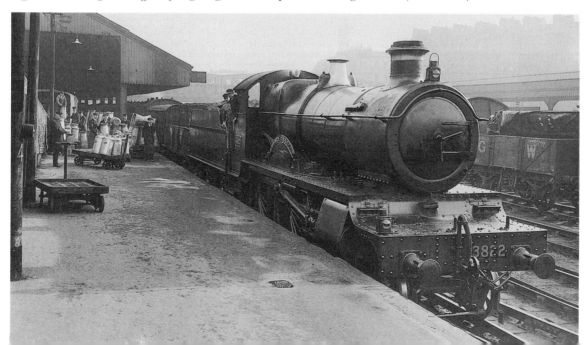

GWR automation - using this ingenious crane on a motor lorry, one man can cover a wide area and lift heavy milk churns without assistance. The scene is Bewdley on 13 June 1929. (British Rail)

agreed to investigate the feasibility of GWR-owned road-rail milk tankers for use between farms and the railhead, or between a UD depot and the railhead. A sub-committee of Divisional Superintendents was appointed, including F. C. A. Coventry of the GWR's Road Motor Division and the formidable R. G. Pole (Felix Pole's brother), the Bristol Divisional Superintendent.

Feasibility was established and in October 1931 the GWR Directors authorised expenditure on road-rail tankers for a 'Collection and Delivery' service around the farms in designated areas. The GWR tankers were on the road from February 1932, 10 years after the Divisional Superintendents had urged this service and after a large portion of the milk traffic had been irretrievably lost.

Milk collecting points were established in small towns like Bridport and Yeovil, and also 'out in the wilds' at places such as Thorney on the Yeovil-Langport line. The first GWR road-rail tanker left UD's Bridport milk processing plant for the GWR at Maiden Newton on 26 January 1933, depriving, I suppose, the branch train of a regular source of income.

Before 1927 there were very few dedicated 'milk trains' on the GWR, although a huge quantity of milk in churns was carried by parcels and passenger trains. Coming up the 'Berks & Hants' line in 1910, and for many years after, the only 'milk train' was the 7.5 pm from Trowbridge via Westbury to

Reading, carrying milk churns collected off passenger trains from Dorset, Somerset and Wiltshire. On the Swindon-Didcot section there was only the 9.10 pm Swindon-Paddington with milk from the Chippenham, Kemble and Cirencester areas.

After 1927 and more particularly from 1930, the number of milk trains increased and they ran over longer distances. By 1929, for instance, the Trowbridge-Reading service had become the 4.21 pm Weymouth-Clapham Junction, calling at Maiden Newton, Yetminster and Yeovil to pick up extra loaded 'Siphons'. During the Yeovil stop 'Siphons' were attached from Thorney as well as Yeovil.

On Sundays an extra milk train left Yetminster at 1.30 pm, arriving at Yeovil Pen Mill at 1.40 to be combined with 'Siphons' from Yeovil to form the 2.55 pm (Sundays only) Yeovil-Kensington. The Thorney depot dispatched two trains, the 3.30 pm and the 5 pm; the former terminated at Yeovil (Town). The timetable gives no indication of how the tanks and/or 'Siphons' were worked forward - either by a passenger train or perhaps going on to London via the Southern Railway route. The 5 p.m ran to Pen Mill and its vehicles were attached to the 4.30 pm (Sundays only) Weymouth-Paddington milk train.

A milk processing depot was built by UD at Whitland during 1929 and early 1930 - the new sidings and additional signalling in connection with this

Tiverton Junction looking towards Taunton on 28 January 1932, a bottleneck about to be opened out into quadruple track. A large amount of perishable traffic and freight came from Tiverton branch - a big 'Siphon' and a passenger brake-van in the Tiverton bay bear witness to this. In addition, the milk-laden Hemyock branch started from behind the right-hand platform, going, briefly, in the Taunton direction. (British Rail)

were installed during April 1930, and on 10 November 1930 the 2.55 pm (Saturdays excepted) Whitland (as famous a train - to railwaymen - as any express passenger) made its first run from the new plant to Mitre Bridge.

The train consisted of UD glass-lined 3,000-gallon tanks on newly Swindon-built four-wheel trucks. These were, however, badly designed, having to carry a heavy load at up to 60 mph or even more on a short wheelbase of only 10 ft 6 in. They

Shrivenham station after the quadrupling in 1933. No 5914 Ripon Hall is at the down platform on the new down relief line with a milk train.

The new down main is next left, the old down main has become the up main and the old up main, alongside the old station, is now the up relief line. Challow tracks were similarly reorganised (see chapter 21). (British Rail)

did not perform satisfactorily and were soon prohibited from running in trains which would travel in excess of 60 mph; neither were they to run at 60 mph for more than 75 non-stop miles. They were replaced in 1932 by the very practical six-wheeled trucks with a 13 ft 6 in wheel-base.

Also on this train were the first of the new 'Siphon J' 50-foot vehicles. These fine, eight-wheeled, ice-cooled and insulated milk vans with specially tight-fitting doors were designed for the carriage of milk in churns. Churns were a nuisance, but thousands were still in use and the Company built the 'Siphon Js' the better to care for churn-loaded milk over long distances. Eight of them were built at Swindon in 1930 with a further 27 during 1931-2. They could carry a load of 15 tons, the equivalent of 116 milk churns.

During the seven weeks to the end of 1930, the Whitland depot put 163,000 gallons of milk on rail. During the whole of 1930 almost three million gallons were carried from Wootton Bassett. Having got into bulk milk cartage, the GWR was able to supply milk to Nestl[82] and Cow & Gate factories as well as UD, and the vehicles they used were branded for the specific job they were on. Bulk milk haulage was a world within the world of the railway and seemed set fair to be a good revenue earner with low costs relative to churn-borne traffic.

Milk for London also came on to the GWR at Highbridge, originating from the UD Bason Bridge depot on the Somerset & Dorset Railway. The east-west S&D crossed the north-south GWR on the level at Highbridge and there was an north-to-east connecting curve between the systems. Milk traffic was transferred by four scheduled 'trips' - two were GWR-worked and two by the S&D - over the connecting chord.

Whilst on the subject of S&D/GWR transfers, it is interesting to note that in 1929, and as late as the summer of 1937, there was a 'Saturdays only' lunchtime express train from Burnham-on-Sea, S&D, to Paddington. This was a remarkable working, not least because the train crossed the GWR on the level to the south side and then reversed from the S&D line, over the chord, into the GWR station.

The GWR Directors were now used to co-operating with outside firms - and other railways - such were the changes brought about by harsh necessity, and in July 1933 the Company leased to UD, for £750 per annum, 7½ acres of land at Wood Lane, at the side of the Ealing & Shepherd's Bush (E&SB)

electrified line. Here UD built a modern milk processing plant, while the GWR spent £9,750 on sidings, access roads and signalling. An extra pair of tracks was laid, with a loan under the 1929 Act, alongside the E&SB giving the effect of quadrupling the section from Wood Lane to North Acton, although there was no connection *en route* between the two pairs of tracks. Access into and out of the depot was controlled by a 12-lever ground frame released electrically from the nearby Viaduct Junction signal box. The terminal was opened in 1934.

By 1936 the weekday service of GWR milk trains to London was as follows:

> 6.45 am Westbury-West Ealing
> 8.30 am Little Somerford-West Ealing
> 12.40 pm Reading-Paddington
> 2.25 pm Dorrington (RR - see below)-Marylebone
> 2.55 pm Whitland-Mitre Bridge
> 4.27 pm Weymouth-Kensington
> 7.20 pm Chippenham-Wood Lane
> 8.30 pm Swindon-Paddington
> 8.40 pm Chippenham-Wood Lane
> 10.15 pm Oxford-West Ealing
> 11.48 pm Newbury-Forest Hill (Southern Railway)

The 6.45 am from Newbury also carried passengers and called at all stations to Reading. The evening Kemble milk train also carried passengers and terminated at Swindon, the milk going forward on the 7.20 pm Chippenham-Wood Lane. Besides these there were local 'trips' with loaded and empty tanks and churns between West Ealing, Wood Lane, Mitre Bridge and Kensington. There was also a 5.40 pm Westbury milk which terminated at Wootton Bassett. The tankers on this may have been taken forward by the 2.55 pm Whitland, the 7.20 pm or 8.40 pm Chippenham. The 2.25 pm Dorrington ran daily to Birmingham and was 'RR' ('Runs if Required') to Marylebone. It came up the GWR to Banbury where the Great Western engine came off and an LNER engine went on the other end to take the train to London via Woodford Halse. The empties returned from Marylebone to Dorrington over the same route.

The 1936 timetable shows no milk trains running on the Birmingham 'New Line' to London, while the 10.15 pm Oxford was the only milk train to originate from north of Didcot, bringing milk

No 2973 with 16 empty four- and six-wheeled milk tanks and two six-wheeled brake-vans at Addison Road (Kensington Olympia) on 4 January 1933. The leading vehicle is a six-wheel flat truck carrying a United Dairies road tanker. The formation of the train suggests that it will be divided later in the journey - perhaps at Swindon - the front nine vehicles going to Chippenham and the West, the rear nine to South Wales. The rail tankers weighed about 12 tons empty and could carry 3,000 gallons of milk weighing 3½ tons. This empty train weighs about 230 tons. (British Rail)

from the Fairford, Worcester and Banbury routes which had been brought into Oxford by passenger trains.

Main-line milk trains in the 'twenties and 'thirties were usually hauled by express passenger engines of the second rank - 'County', 'City', 'Saint' or 'Star' Class (but almost anything could have been used) - and were given apparently easy schedules, but the loads could be heavy and a margin had to be allowed for recovery if time was lost at the picking-up points. Speeds became higher as time went by.

This example is the 7.55 pm from Chippenham in 1929:

Miles			
0	Swindon	9.20	
10¾	Uffington arr	9.38	33 mph start-to-stop
	Pick up tanks from Faringdon		
	dep	9.48	
13½	Didcot	10.10	36½ mph start-to-pass

In 1936 the 7.20 pm from Chippenham, as it had then become, was timed to average 44 mph between Swindon and Uffington, start to stop, a relatively difficult timing, but was then allowed an easy 30 mph average from the re-start at Uffington to passing Didcot. Running non-stop to West Ealing, the train was required to average 45 mph. At West Ealing traffic was detached, the engine changed and the direction of the train reversed as it had to go around the 'Greenford loop' to get on to the Wood Lane line at North Acton Junction.

By 1936 the pattern of milk trains was established and was to remain recognisably the same into 1961, with 'King' Class engines for motive power on the 2.55 pm from Whitland. The 'Milkys' were, with the 'hard-hitting' fish trains and the 'C' headcode 'vackum goods', heavy work for their skilled firemen, and great earners of revenue for the Company. The true costs are unknown, but they kept a lot of heavy traffic off the roads.

18

Fish traffic

The Great Western handled a steadily increasing traffic in fish throughout the period 1921-38, but 1939 showed a decrease owing to the outbreak of war in September. Some of the traffic originated from locations on the east coast and entered GWR territory at Banbury via the former Great Central route (LNER) at Woodford Halse. There were two trains from this direction in 1936, the 3.32 pm and 8.17 pm from Doncaster - the timings were different at weekends. Both of them called at Banbury and went through to Swindon, probably hauled by their LNER engine all the way. The 3.32 pm Doncaster was non-stop through Oxford, while the 8.17 called at Oxford, Middle Road, at 2.12 am to detach Oxford and Reading vans. At Swindon both trains were broken up and re-marshalled for Gloucester, Wales and the West of England. Vanloads of fish from the east coast were sent to Swansea South Dock fish market to be unloaded, sold and re-loaded for transit back to the East coast curing factories. The ways of commerce are strange!

Fish caught off the south and south-west coast of Ireland and some east coast fish was brought to Rosslare and thence to Fishguard on the ferry. Each day the Irish Traffic Superintendent's office in Dublin advised the Fishguard Station Master of the quantity of fish and its various British destinations. The Fishguard Yard Foreman and Shed Master then arranged for the necessary wagons to be marshalled and one or two engines per train to be supplied - the incline out of the harbour was 1 in 60 for a mile, with another mile at 1 in 90.

The fish was packed in crushed ice in rough wooden boxes about 3 ft 6 in long and 6 inches deep. These boxes were auctioned on the quay to the fish wholesalers, the lids were then nailed down and the boxes were brought, heavy with fish and ice and dripping slimy water, to the GWR to be weighed, invoiced, waybilled and labelled home before being loaded into the correct van according to destination. The vans were then marshalled in the proper order for being detached with the least shunting at the designated stations along the way.

There were two kinds of ventilated wooden vans for the traffic, some having a 12-foot and others an 18-foot wheelbase, but all of them fitted with the vacuum brake and oil-lubricated axle-boxes for long-distance non-stop running. These were known to everyone by their telegraphic code word - 'Bloater'. The combined fleet of 'Bloaters' numbered 147 and they were built at Swindon between 1919 and 1923 to replace an ancient and motley assortment of fish-carrying wagons.

There were four regular fish trains out of Fishguard, at 3.15 am, 5 am, 8 am and 8.30 am. The first two took fish caught on the east coast of Ireland, the later pair of departures catered for traffic from the south and south-west of Ireland - Bantry and Baltimore, Cahirciveen and Kinsale.

Each pair of departures had the same destinations: one train to Crewe and the North via the LMS line out of Carmarthen, the other to GWR destinations via Swansea.

Milford Haven had its own fishing fleet and was one of the top five fishing ports in the UK during the years 1921-39. In 1926 43,780 tons of white fish

It would be a fast and smelly trip for the guard riding in the caboose of this 'Tadpole A', surrounded by boxes of fish. The vehicle is branded 'To be returned to Penzance'. (Lens of Sutton)

and herring were landed at Milford and almost all of it went out by rail. In 1930 the GWR hauled 47,584 tons of fish from the port, 2,059 tons more than in 1929, for a revenue of £162,897, £5,996 more than the year before.

In 1931 a disaster threatened when the largest single operator of trawlers at Milford moved its operation to Hull and Fleetwood, but other trawlers moved in. Their catch never equalled previous hauls but still a good tonnage continued to be landed. In 1936 41,155 tons was hauled by the GWR for £131,713.

There were two regular fish trains out of Milford, the 3.15 and 3.50 pm, together with 'paths' for three specials on an 'RR' - 'Runs if Required' - basis: 5.10, 5.25 and 7 pm. Milford Haven Station Master's office advised, by single-needle telegraph, the stations at which the train would call, informing what wagons were on the train for that station and also the wagons to be detached there and sent on by another train to another destination.

The 3.15 pm was destined for the North via Carmarthen (Town) and the LMS line via Llandilo, Craven Arms and Shrewsbury to Crewe. This train was marshalled with an LMS brake-van next to the engine, then the Crewe traffic and the Crewe Transfers - the Liverpool, Manchester and Yorkshire traffic - with a GWR brake-van at the rear.

The 3.50 pm was the main distributor for the GWR and was often double-headed. Since before the Great War it had been known as the 'Trawl Fish' and was a Very Important Train. It was hauled in the 1920s by a '43xx' Class 2-6-0 or 'Bulldog' Class 4-4-0, which would have been heavy work for the fireman of a medium-sized engine. Later it was possible to supply a '29xx', made redundant off the 'fasts' by the 'Castles', or a brand new '49xx'.

In the 1920s the 3.50 pm ran non-stop to Landore where it stopped to detach wagons for Swansea, Neath, the Valleys and stations on the South Wales main line as far east as, but not including, Cardiff. Having detached this traffic it attached wagons off the 6.30 pm Swansea South Dock-Landore 'trip', which could be a fair-sized train, depending on the catch of fish. The fullest marshalling order from Milford was as follows: Engine - Cardiff - Newport - LMS via Gloucester - Paddington - Reading - Bristol - Birmingham - Aberdare - Landore Transfers - brake-van.

At Severn Tunnel Junction wagons for Bath, Bristol and westwards were detached at 8.40 pm and put on the 9.10 pm Cardiff-Bristol parcels. If this was not running, the fish vans formed a 'Special' to Bristol. Vans for Reading and/or London were also detached at Severn Tunnel Junction to be taken for-

2-6-0 No 5347 carrying 'C' headlamps (5 beats on the bell between signal boxes) with a fully vacuum-braked fish train consisting of seven four-wheeled long-wheelbase 'Bloater' wagons, a bogie 'Tadpole' (no caboose) and a six-wheel passenger-train brake-van in which the guard would ride. 19 October 1921. (British Rail)

ward at 9.55 pm, either by the following 5.10 pm (RR) from Milford Haven or, as an extension of the 3.50 pm Milford, running via Badminton.

The 3.50 pm Milford proper ran to Gloucester, terminated and was 'broken up' there at 9.50 pm. There were wagons for LMS destinations, which required to be 'tripped' across to the 'Midland', vans for Birmingham (GW) and Worcester, and for Stroud and Kemble, and these were shunted on to passenger or parcels trains by the station pilot engine. The Kemble line vans went forward on the 6.50 pm Neyland-Paddington mail train leaving Gloucester at 12.33 am.

The Great Western ran fish trains as 'C' head-code, fully vacuum-braked trains, and their importance in the hierarchy of trains was denoted by the locomotive's headcode – one lamp in front of its chimney and one over the right-hand buffer. They were belled through the signal boxes by the 'Is Line Clear?' code of 5 bells (GWR 1920 and 1936 Regulations).

A typical fish train was a heavy load for the engine and fireman – a 'full digger' – especially on the long haul from below the River Severn to the summit of the Cotswolds at Badminton. After the 1 in 90 drop for 2½ miles under the river, the train –

and fireman – faced 3 miles of 1 in 100, 2 miles of 1 in 80/90 and 10 miles of 1 in 300 to Badminton summit. This was followed by 10 miles falling at 1 in 300, 5 miles rising at 1 in 300 to Wootton Bassett and the slightest rising gradient for 7 miles to Swindon. The line fell slightly all the way from Swindon to Paddington, 77¼ miles. The 3.50 pm Milford's schedule from 'The Tunnel' was:

	Time	Average speed (mph)
Severn Tunnel Junc	9.55	
Patchway	10.22	22
Wootton Bassett	11.12	36
Swindon	11.20/30	37
Didcot	12.00	48
Reading	12.23/38	40
Westbourne Park	1.25	44
Paddington	1.30	18

As always with railway traffic there was the problem of the 'returned empties'. The nightly flow of loaded fish meant an equal return of vans and empty fish boxes, every box to be properly recorded, charged to the owner and the bill sent to him. All this was done by practical, competent men with a bit of pencil and paper.

The boxes were loaded into empty fish vans or

vacuum-braked open wagons and were sent down by the 11.35 am Ladbroke Grove-Neyland Fish Empties which went via Gloucester, picking up northern and LMS vans there, and Bath and Bristol vans at Severn Tunnel Junction. Just to complicate matters further, the empty fish boxes had to be segregated into those which had contained 'trawl fish' (white fish, such as cod) and those which had contained mackerel.

The 'Trawl Fish' was but one of a fleet of 'hard-hitting vacuum (usually pronounced 'vackum') goods' which stormed Great Western metals, for the most part by night. It was followed from the Severn Tunnel by the 'C' headcode 3.50 pm from Fishguard – the 'Irish Goods' – and arrived at Swindon at 11.20 pm. to 'knock off' some vans. The train got away smartly at 11.30 and was followed 5 minutes later by the 9.55 pm Bristol-Paddington 'C' headcode, which came (theoretically) non-stop through Swindon, but more likely had the distant signals against him. This was tight working, but the 'Trawl Fish' would pull away because the Bristol was booked to stop at Uffington to take water.

However, the driver of the Bristol would have to look sharp in taking water at Uffington because the 3.50 pm Fishguard was only 10 minutes behind him. The Great Western at work!

The same trains ran in almost exactly the same timings for up to 30 years, part of the way of life of hundreds of railwaymen and women, their titles as well known to the workforce as the 'Cornish Riviera' or the 'Bristolian' were to the enthusiast fraternity – and the 'Trawl Fish' earned more shillings per mile for the Company than either of these prestigious passenger trains.

The fish traffic cycle – loaded and returned empties, marshalling and re-marshalling – represented some of the best and also some of the hardest of railway work. But it worked well because it was handled by horny-handed veterans who knew what they were about.

19
Special freight traffic

Potatoes, fruit, flowers and broccoli comprised most of the seasonal 'block load' 'Specials' run for the benefit of a multitude of growers, French as well as English and Cornish. The first 'block trains' dedicated to a single company were the 20-van specials of baled blankets which ran through the 1920s from Smiths & Co of Witney consigned to Maples Ltd in London. They used to go up 'fast vackum goods'. At Paddington it would take 24 two-horse GWR carts to shift the consignment to Maples' store in the City - a wonderful procession of GWR horse-flesh along Oxford Street and Tottenham Court Road.

The railway was not a 'common carrier' of animals but it ran many specials for racehorses, fox-hunters, agricultural show animals, sheep, pigs and cattle to and from markets, or to Calne for Harris's bacon factory. Examples of the seasonal specials included those for Cheddar Valley strawberries, Pershore plums, Cornish, French or Channel Islands new potatoes ('Perpot specials') or broccoli ('Broc specials') up from Weymouth or Marazion, bananas from Jamaica, coming in through the Port of London, Avonmouth or Barry, and cattle from across the Irish Sea through Fishguard.

The Vale of Evesham plum traffic was worth

A 'block load' of Messrs Early's Witney blankets ready to leave Witney goods yard for Maples's London store on 27 September 1923. This was good business for the Fairford branch but how often did a department store, however large, require this number of blankets? A railway can carry produce but it cannot create the demand.

Lurking in the corner is a rather Broad-Gauge-looking Thornycroft lorry. Two or three of these carried the usual output of Early's factory once the roads improved. (British Rail)

Loading strawberries at Axbridge. The nearest wagon is a 'fruit' wagon bound for Sheffield, the others are milk 'Siphons', the nearest of them also chalked for Sheffield. Eight GWR staff are visible, one young porter with a flower in his buttonhole and a silver watch chain on his waistcoat.

Assorted growers, some in summery straw boaters, and one grower's daughter complete the happy scene some time in the 1920s. (Lens of Sutton)

£3,500 a year to the GWR so a late frost that killed the plum blossom would cost the Company that much. So important was this traffic considered to be that in May 1927 'Bulldog' Class 4-4-0 No 3353 *Plymouth* was renamed *Pershore Plum* as an acknowledgement of the GWR's connection with the trade, and was transferred to Worcester to haul, on occasion, trains of plums. Did No 4021 ever haul a train of new potatoes before it was renamed *British Monarch* in 1927?

Strawberry traffic had a season lasting through the month of August, right in the middle of the heaviest passenger traffic. The strawberries came from France through Millbay or Weymouth and from the stations on the Cheddar Valley line. Train-loads were taken to such important centres as London, Manchester, Edinburgh and Dublin. The working of this traffic was a short, intense peak of considerable operational complexity, all of which the GWR was pleased to accept.

During the 'twenties, and to a lesser extent in the 'thirties, Cheddar Valley line stations were fragrant with the perfume of strawberries, the road to each station crammed with horse-drawn or donkey-drawn carts as the 300 or so growers in the area hurried to the train and queued to get into the yard with their produce. Extra porters were drafted to Cheddar and Axbridge to help with the rush. Each consignment had to be weighed, paid and waybilled before being placed in the correct van according to

its destination. Whoever directed the loading at Cheddar had to have a great deal of skill and foresight - born of years of experience of the traffic - to keep the number of wagons required to a minimum and to keep the complicated job as 'simple' as possible, not only for Cheddar but also for the receiving stations along the line.

An absolute maximum of 1½ tons of strawberries was all that could be put in a truck weighing 7 tons! These trucks were then labelled and attached to the rear of a passing passenger train 'uphill' or 'downhill' according to the destination of the contents. Small consignments to diverse destinations were loaded into a van for Yatton and Bristol where they were off-loaded and put into the brake-vans of relevant passenger trains.

Perhaps a van-load had been loaded for Salisbury and Portsmouth and sent away via Witham (Somerset) and Westbury. Westbury would be informed (perhaps over the single-needle telegraph) that there was a van or vans for the Southern so that the shunters and signalmen there would be aware of the need to detach the van(s) from the incoming branch train and attach it to a Bristol-Portsmouth train. Yatton and Bristol would also need to know what small consignments were coming their way for re-loading into passenger trains.

Besides these difficult small consignments of a few punnets or a van or two, there was also the train-load traffic for wholesalers in the big cities. The 'Strawberry Train' was marshalled with about 14 trucks - perhaps two or three each for Manchester, Birmingham, Carlisle and Glasgow, and three or four for London - and left at 6 pm after loading all day. The GWR carried this traffic, with all the complication it involved, for slightly less than three farthings (³⁄₄ of one old penny) per pound weight (a penny then being 240 to the pound sterling).

Hundreds of consignments had to be placed in the right trucks, paperwork completed and all the right people advised. Whilst the ultimate responsibility for clearing this traffic devolved upon the Cheddar Station Master, he in fact had to depend on some very experienced and intelligent porters - never imagine that porters in those days merely carried suitcases. And when the job was over for another year, everyone felt they had done a good job, earned a few 'bob' extra and were quietly pleased with themselves.

The other soft traffic which seems completely unsuited to railway carriage - but which was carried in vast quantities - was tomatoes. The Guernsey tomato season helped to keep Weymouth docks and railwaymen busy from April to November. In 1938, for instance, a total of 2,670,000 baskets of tomatoes, each containing 14 lbs, was landed on the quay. To assist the dockers in sorting the boxes into their destinations, main ones - Manchester, Birmingham, London, Glasgow - had a colour-coded label.

The boxes were loaded into waiting GWR covered vans designated 'Fruit C', 200 of which were specially made for the traffic between 1928 and 1939. They had a 12 ft 6 in or an 18- foot wheelbase, vacuum brakes (some were dual-fitted with air brakes) and screw couplings so that they could be run in passenger trains, the GWR's intention being to deliver the tomatoes the day after landing at Weymouth. The vans were all gas-lit and were also used for parcels or PLA traffic.

Any kind of rough shunting of these vans would have had a disastrous effect on the squashy contents, and in 1938 the LMS introduced the 'Shoc-Van' where the van body could slide on its chassis under the control of springs, thus greatly reducing the effects of a heavy shunt. The GWR was quick to take up the idea.

Potatoes and broccoli were imported from France and the Channel Islands through Weymouth and Plymouth, whilst Cornish vegetables were sent by the train-load from Marazion yard at Penzance and from other centres, such as St Erth. Farmers brought their crated produce to their local railhead in trailers towed behind the family car, horses and donkeys. Railway wagons loaded at small stations had to be collected by a local shunting train and taken to a larger centre to be marshalled into long and heavy train-loads bound for London and the major cities of Britain. In the peak of the season St Erth was dispatching nine 'Broc' or 'Perpot' specials a day, and

The St Helier *tied up at Weymouth, having brought in passengers and tomatoes from the Channel Islands in about 1935.* (Clinker Collection/courtesy Brunel University)

the total output of West Cornwall in a season was over 30,000 tons.

The extra tonnages handled in the space of three or four weeks, or over the year, were dramatic. In 1928, up to 4 October, 21,231 tons of French potatoes were landed at Weymouth, an increase of 2,494 tons on the same period in 1927. Local GWR management arranged for a deputation of Cornish broccoli-growers to go to France and Germany to sell Cornish broccoli there, and as a result the first ever truck-loads of the vegetable were exported on 26 February 1929.

At the same time increasingly vast tonnages of broccoli were being imported from France through Weymouth. Between 5 January and 8 May 1930 16,815 tons came in, compared with 14,395 tons the previous year and only 8,860 tons in 1928; the 1930 revenue from this traffic was £25,219. French broccoli normally did not begin to arrive at Weymouth until 5 January but the 1932 season began on 13 December 1931, and 2,000 tons had passed through by 5 January. Extra locomotives, men, engines and wagons were posted to Weymouth for the rush, there were extra dock staff to load the produce, extra shunting power, extra trains to be run - the GWR, management and staff was never afraid of railway work. At the other end of the journey the GWR unloaded the produce and provided cartage to the market.

All this work the GWR undertook as fast as possible and for a very modest sum, yet the Company was unpopular with a certain unidentified section of the public. In 1924 a Government Committee, under the Chairmanship of the Marquess of Linlithgow (who?), produced a report on the cost and efficiency of the distribution of agricultural produce. This curious Committee which purported to investigate 'fair dealing' was so far removed from impartiality that it did not contain a single representative from any railway company; the loyalties of those sitting on the Committee is not known but may be guessed from the 'facts' they discovered.

The report accused the railways of slow transits and exorbitant charges, stating as fact that *one half* of the gross price received by the farmer at Covent Garden market went to the railway company in carriage charges. Great Western management was shocked and, I suppose, not a little hurt to be the butt of such lies, and the Goods Department were instructed to make a careful analysis of the costs of a broccoli purchased at Covent Garden. It was found

that the GWR charged 2s 2d to carry 1 cwt (112 lbs) of Cornish broccoli 305 miles to Covent Garden, while that same crate was sold in Covent Garden market for 10s 6d, from which the GWR researcher purchased 1½ lbs of the vegetable for 6d. The costs involved were as follows:

To the grower	1s 1d
Market commission	28d
Cartage to retailer's shop	28d
Railway carriage (305 miles)	35d
Retailer	4s 8d

Whatever the report alleged, the growers continued to use the GWR and placed more and more broccoli on rail up to a record 36,036 tons for the year 1937, a 14 per cent increase on 1936, and producing revenue for the GWR of £73,118.

Banana traffic was carried only in steam-heated, insulated covered vans, each fitted with the vacuum brake. The Great Western took great care of the fruit so as to develop the traffic - nothing, it would seem, was too much trouble for the railway in those days. In 1924 250 such vans were turned out of Swindon Works to handle the growing traffic in bananas, imported in steam-heated ships from the Caribbean by Elders Fyffes, landing in London, Plymouth, Avonmouth and Barry. The fruit was picked green and ripened on the journey from the docks to the wholesaler's siding, including its last few hours by rail. Even into the early 1960s the banana trains were a common sight on the Western Region, running at 60 mph up to the depot at Taplow behind 'Castle', 'Hall' and 'Grange' Class locomotives.

A large number of country towns held monthly fairs 'on the first Wednesday of each month' or some other regular day for the sale of sheep, cows or horses - or all three - and even cheeses, and of course the GWR was always keen to carry the animals or produce. The largest fair anywhere on the GWR was the annual 'Dalis' Fair held at Lampeter on 6-7 May where horses and ponies were the main traffic, but where there were also large numbers of cattle, sheep and pigs. At Kerry the number of cattle wagons in and out was the only increasing item of traffic throughout the 1920s.

Quite apart from the freight traffic generated by fairs like this, there was also an increase in passenger traffic as dealers came from the big cities and thousands of local people poured into the town. At Kington the dealers flocked in by rail (and, it must be said, by road as well) to buy the famous sheep of the area – the Clun, Radnor Forest and Kerry breeds. In August 1938, for instance, 22,000 sheep were on sale and 200 cattle wagons had to be worked on to the Kington branch and stored in anticipation of the traffic. On that August day the 2 pm Kington Cattle Special took away 30 loaded wagons, the 4 pm took 60 wagons and the 6 pm, if the records can be believed, was 'one quarter of a mile long'. I suppose that these trains were worked out to Leominster yard 'rough' – unmarshalled – and at Leominster they would be made up into trains for specific destinations. This was a job requiring the Leominster Foreman-Shunter and his men to exercise intelligence, an intimate knowledge of national geography and the routes by which the traffic should be directed. It was not simply a matter of slinging couplings over hooks with a shunting pole.

Cattle trucks designed to run in goods trains were known by their telegraphic codeword 'Mex', while a 'Mex B' was vacuum braked for passenger or express freight workings. Although designated as 'cattle' trucks, they were also used for sheep, pigs and goats.

The annual August Marlborough Fair was also very large and dealt largely in sheep. Extra staff were drafted in from other stations, a shunting engine was provided and Swindon and Westbury sheds were on notice to provide as many engines as would be required to work the 'Specials' away. The necessary cattle wagons were stored in sidings at Ogbourne and Savernake as well as at Marlborough.

Down the steep hill from the station lay Marlborough town where the GWR traffic canvassers were busy in the streets, looking for traffic, keeping an eye and an ear on the road hauliers and doing their best to undercut them, often quoting prices on their own responsibility to get the traffic. One ancient Great Western man who had gone out as a canvasser at fair times described his methods to me: 'I used to twist their arms up their backs and say "Come on, put it on rail, what d'you think you've got a railway for?"' An exaggeration, I suppose, but nevertheless showing the determination of GWR men to obey the Company's exhortation and 'GET TRAFFIC'.

My friend the late Albert Stanley was sent to assist at Marlborough for all the Marlborough Fairs from the early 1920s and recalled particularly that of 22 August 1926. Talking to me 40 years later on a once busy but then closed and vandalised station, he remembered the organised chaos of penning the sheep, helping to drive sheep into trucks, flocks having to be split and placed in several trucks, trying to count them after they had been driven into the wagon, the shouting as GWR staff argued with shepherds as to how many sheep there were in a truck, the frantic writing on scraps of paper, filling in forms, hurrying along lines of trucks, clipping on the labels – all this performed against a background of concentrated bleating from the thousands of sheep!

Albert looked back over the years, wondered 'how the hell we ever managed' and added disgustedly 'and now BR turn away traffic'. Albert's memories of Marlborough Fair were vivid and his recounting of them made such a great impression on me that when I was researching this book I tried to find out more about his experience. He was right to remember the 1926 Fair, for in that year the GWR recorded that 9,500 sheep were loaded into 217 wagons.

But the very bedlam and confusion of such large flocks and herds militated against putting the traffic on rail, and as motor lorries and country roads improved in the 'thirties the traffic was virtually lost to rail. To a modern manager it would seem like 'good riddance', but anything which made the railways less busy was deplored by the old-time managers and they fought hard to retain the traffic.

20
Signal & Telegraph Department, 1921–28

In 1921 the GWR maintained 1,407 signal boxes. In 1922 there were 1,645, when the Company had absorbed such straggling lines as the Cambrian and most particularly the Welsh valley lines, which were signalled not merely heavily but 'in duplicate' as competing lines drove up the same valley with rival signal boxes side by side. In October 1923 the Midland & South Western Junction came into the GWR, with about 21 boxes. By 1926 the GWR had signalling to maintain on about 3,700 route miles.

The Chief Signal & Telegraph Engineer in 1921 was A. T. Blackall, then aged 62, who had pioneered the establishment of this Department as a separate and independent entity. Blackall joined the GWR in June 1879 aged 19, the son of Thomas Blackall who was Signal Engineer of the GWR from 1885 until his retirement in 1893. Until that year the Signal Department had been part of the Civil Engineer's empire, but on 1 June 1893 it was placed under the control of the Chief Locomotive Engineer, William Dean, with A. T. Blackall, then aged 34, as his Signal Assistant. He gained the title 'Signal Engineer' in August 1897.

William Dean objected to the signalling side becoming an independent department. On the LNWR, GER and L&YR signalling was ultimately the responsibility of the Chief Locomotive Engineer, while on the LSWR, NER and Midland Railway signalling was under the Civil Engineer's Department. In May 1902 G. J. Churchward was deputising for the ailing (and shortly to retire) William Dean, and he could see the good sense in making an independent department out of this specialist subject. Consequently A. T. Blackall became Chief Signal Engineer of an independent Signal Department on the 15th.

The Telegraph Department was a separate entity run from 1855 until 1892 by C. E. Spagnoletti as 'Telegraph Superintendent'. His place was taken by H. T. Goodenough, who had begun his career as a boy in the telegraph office at Reading. In July 1903 Goodenough retired and his department was placed under A. T. Blackall with C. M. Jacobs as his Electrical Assistant. Thus the 'Signal & Telegraph Department' was created. For many years the merger was not much more than on paper, although great savings could have been made by amalgamating and reducing duplicated facilities at 'District' level.

In 1921 most of the separate 'Signal' and 'Telegraph' Districts were still operational. There were separate 'Signal' and 'Telegraph' Inspectors, technicians, maintenance gangs, offices, stores and small workshops. Whether this was an indication of lethargy on Blackall's part is uncertain - since 1903 he had, for instance, supervised the signalling of hundreds of miles of new railways as well as the design of standard locking frames and signal boxes.

Blackall retired in June 1923 and his place was taken by R. J. S. Insell with Charles Jacobs as his Assistant. Robert Insell had entered GWR service as a lad in the Drawing Office at Reading in 1881 and was appointed 'Draughtsman' on 24 March 1886. C. M. Jacobs had started his career as a clerk in the Telegraph Department at Hereford in 1882.

Gas-lit Swansea Train Control Office in the 1920s. (John Morris Collection)

Insell at once made a start on cost-cutting by merging the two sides of his Department, and in 1926 190 S&T employees were made redundant. However, early in 1928 Insell became ill and died on 25 March, with the mergers still far from complete. Jacobs then became Chief, although he would reach his 60th birthday in October that year and therefore had only five years' service left to give.

The GWR Directors were perfectly aware of this when they appointed him but they took the old-fashioned (and very proper) view that

'Mr Jacobs has proved to be an exceptionally able electrical, signalling and telegraph expert. There are young men coming on but they will require more experience before they can be considered

The Caversham Road frontage of the GWR Signal & Telegraph Works at Reading station in July 1922, the camera looking towards Caversham. Within these solid walls the Company pre-fabricated its timber signal boxes, lever frames and interlocking machines, signalling instruments, signals, level crossing gates and ATC gear, and mended station clocks and guards' watches. On the up side of the railway, $^3/_4$ mile west of the station was the S&T Department's timber yard and sawmill. (British Rail)

Birmingham Snow Hill after the 1910-12 rebuilding, seen from the North signal box in 1936. The tracks were packed skilfully on to a narrow (yet enormous) brick viaduct. Birmingham suburban coaches can be seen on the far left, with No 5167 placing coaches in the down bay on the right. From the brick arches to the glass roof and the trains which ran continuously beneath it, Snow Hill was a marvel of GWR engineering skill. (British Rail)

for the Chief position. It is therefore recommended that Mr Jacobs should be appointed Signal Engineer at £2,000 p.a..'

Jacobs continued the amalgamations of Districts. GWR Company Minutes state that new depots 'will be constructed at Slough, Hereford, Cogan and Treforest'; the Slough depot seems to have been built at West Ealing. However, at the end of 1928 there were still separate 'Signal' and 'Telegraph' Inspectors, staff and buildings at Frome, Chippenham, Swindon and Reading. Reading Signal Works was by then on short time and the number of staff had been reduced by 7.7 per cent, and wages paid over the year to S&T Department staff had been reduced by £3,509.

Jacobs retired in 1936 having reduced the size of his Department annually without in any way reducing its efficiency - on the contrary, it had introduced the largest and most difficult re-signalling schemes ever seen on the GWR.

Numbers employed by the S&T Department

1932	1933	1935	1936
2,505	2,305	2,036	1,959

Jacobs place as 'Chief' was taken by F. H. D. Page.

Insell and Jacobs had worked closely together since at least 1904 and even when Insell was 'the Guvnor' they were very much a partnership. They were not merely administrators - first and foremost both were extremely able, forward-looking engineers, well aware of the savings which could be made by the use of electricity. They were keen to reduce their Company's expenses by modern telecommunications and better signalling. Even before the Great War they had brought about the installation of power-operated signalling at several locations.

These early installations used batteries to operate signals and points. The first was at Didcot North Junction in 1905 when a new signal box was erected to house a frame of miniature levers controlling a layout which had previously required two conventional signal boxes. Current came from batteries charged by a petrol-engined generator. Signals and points were operated by electric motors activated by the movement of miniature levers; the levers were interlocked by mechanical means within the locking frame in the conventional way.

Track circuits to detect the presence of a train on a particular stretch of line had no role in this installation, and the conventional 60-foot 'fouling bar' attached to the inside of the rail up to the point blade was used to prevent facing points from being moved should the signalman prematurely replace the guarding signal to 'Danger' and then thoughtlessly move the facing point lever. However, the fouling bar provided only limited protection, although it was better than nothing.

Snow Hill station was controlled by two power-operated signal boxes using a battery-powered system designed by Siemens of London. The North box came into use in 1912 and the South box in 1913. The miniature levers, 2 inches apart, switched current to point and signal motors, but otherwise the routine of signalling was conventional, with bells and block instruments, although the latter were specially designed for Snow Hill. The installations remained in use until 1967. (Peter Barlow/Adrian Vaughan Collection)

Birmingham Snow Hill North signal box, seen here in 1960, was a Saxby & Farmer construction and was second-hand when erected here in 1910-12. It accommodated a relatively light power-frame enabling the box to be raised on the narrowest of girders. Electric operation of signalling gave space for tracks which would otherwise have been taken up by wide point-rodding and signal-wire runs. In 1923 it was the third busiest box on the GWR, after Ladbroke Grove and Old Oak Common West. (British Rail)

A similar battery-powered installation replaced two signal boxes at Yarnton, north of Oxford, in 1909.

When Birmingham Snow Hill station was rebuilt in 1910-12, space was extremely limited and electrical signalling allowed every inch to be used for track, since there was no need for the usual wide runs of point rodding and festoons of signal wires. Birmingham North box (second-hand, probably from Paddington) and Hockley housed battery-power-operated miniature lever frames in 1912; Birmingham South was brought into use in 1913.

An electro-pneumatic system was installed at Slough, Bath Road Junction, in 1913, almost certainly as a 'trial run' for the resignalling of Paddington; this latter scheme was abandoned owing to the onset of war.

Single battery-power-operated semaphore distant signals were installed over the 11 miles of the 'Swansea District Line' opened in 1913 and others followed, including those at Hungerford (1921).

Track circuits were in use from 1907, after Insell and Jacobs had satisfied themselves that the device was trustworthy and 'fail-safe'. Under this system the line of rails is divided into independent circuits of any length by an insulation at the rail joint, and a low-voltage current is fed from a battery through one rail to the coils of the relay and returns to the battery through the other rail.

When the track is not occupied by a vehicle, the current passes continuously through the coils of the relay so that certain contacts are held closed. In this mode the relay feeds current to electric lock circuits and to indicators in the signal box which show the unoccupied state of that track-circuited section. If, while the circuits are in this mode, the signalman depresses the lock release plunger applying to a signal, point or facing point bolt lever, current will energise a solenoid to lift the electric lock, thus allowing that lever to be pulled. However, when a vehicle's wheels come on to the track-circuited rails the current takes a 'short cut' back to the battery through the axles rather than through the relay. The relay is then de-energised, the contacts fall away and current is cut off from the relevant electric lock circuits, making certain levers inoperable. There were 870 track circuits in use on the GWR in 1921, 1,594 in 1930, and 4,672 by October 1945.

Using track circuits and battery-operated signals, Intermediate Block Signal (IBS) sections were installed in 1907, in preference to building signal boxes, on the quadruple track at Purley and, in

August 1910, at Basildon, west of Reading. The Purley signals halved the approximately 3-mile block section between Pangbourne and Tilehurst, while those at Basildon halved the similar length block sections between Pangbourne and Goring. Controlled from existing boxes at Tilehurst, Pangbourne and Goring, these signals did the same job as two 12-lever signal boxes and six signalmen - at less cost. Soon after this IBS sections were installed between Coton Hill North (Shrewsbury) and Leaton, and in October 1915 one was used to replace Flax Bourton Cutting box.

Having installed these IBS sections, little more was done with the idea until January 1927 when one was installed on the down line only between Wellington (Somerset) and Whiteball to break that $3\frac{3}{4}$-mile block section, most of which was on rising gradients of 1 in 90/80. IBS sections were also installed at Dudgeley, between Leebotwood and Church Stretton, on the down line only, to break a relatively long section on a steep incline. Brentham IBS section, between Park Royal and Perivale, was installed in 1932, and was used to replace Olton signal box, between Lapworth and Knowle & Dorridge, which closed on 25 June 1933 when the line north from Lapworth was quadrupled.

An IBS section was installed at Battersea on the West London Extension Railway between Chelsea & Fulham and Latchmere Junction signal boxes in 1938. The section was not actually halved - the IB home signal on the down (northbound) line was only 552 yards north of Latchmere Junction signal box, and was controlled from that box, while the up (southbound) IB home was controlled from Chelsea & Fulham box and was 1,336 yards in advance of that box, towards Latchmere.

In spite of the existence of the IBS system, a large number of conventional 'break-section' signal boxes were built during the 1920s and 1930s.

A revolutionary scheme was brought into use at Winchester (Chesil) in March 1922 when the life-expired lever frame was replaced with an electrically operated Siemens 'route setting' frame, a system which that company had patented in 1918. The equipment was powered by batteries which were charged weekly from the public mains of Winchester city, the existence of such a supply being a most important consideration in the decision to equip the station with this system.

The frame was 2 ft 8 in long and contained 16 miniature levers set at $2\frac{1}{2}$-inch centres interlocked by means of horizontal tappet locking in trays behind the console. The 16 levers were equivalent to 35 or 36 levers in a conventional frame, the length of which, at 4-inch centres, would have been about 12 feet.

The movement of a signal lever altered the necessary points ahead of the signal (route-setting), so there was no need for separate levers to operate the points. However, if an electrical failure locked the route-setting levers, it was possible to reverse a 'King' lever which unlocked six emergency 'point slides'. Each one of these controlled one set of points so that routes could be set up whilst a handsignalman with flags/handlamp took the place of the inoperable semaphore signal.

Behind each signal lever was a bank of four indicator lights, arranged vertically. When a lever was in the 'Normal' position only a red light was illuminated, and the signal controlled by that lever was at 'Danger'. To set a route and clear a signal, the signalman pulled the required lever towards him to a second notch where it was held by an electric lock while the system checked that all relevant track circuits were clear. When the track circuits were 'proved', the lights displayed changed to red and white and the lock lifted to permit the lever to move to a third notch.

Here it was again locked while the relevant points were motored to their proper positions and were checked through the electrical detection as being set correctly. The display now showed red-white-yellow. When this third operation was complete the lever could be pulled to the fourth and final notch

to motor the signal arm to the 'off' position. When the signal was properly lowered the light display showed white-yellow-green.

The Winchester layout used track circuiting to provide protection against the premature movement of points, thus superseding the 'fouling bar' system. This was the first time on the GWR that track circuits were trusted to supplant mechanical fouling bars as the means of 'holding' points in position during the passage of a train.

The Siemens system of route-setting was used to re-signal Newport (Mon) in 1927, during the major improvements and additions to the station, buildings and layout carried out between 1924 and 1930. A new bridge to carry quadruple tracks over the River Usk was built during 1924/5. Quadruple tracks could then be laid eastwards from the station the 50 chains to Maindee Junction, where the Paddington and Shrewsbury routes diverged. Westwards from the station, quadruple tracks had existed since 1912, after the construction of the second Gaer Tunnel.

Rebuilding work on the station included a fine, brick-faced, five-storey office block almost 80 feet high on the down side facing the street, new waiting and refreshment rooms, a passenger subway and lengthened platforms, together with an improved layout and electrically operated semaphore signalling installed during 1926-8. The widened layout was controlled by the East and West boxes using the Siemens route-setting system already installed at Winchester.

Newport (Mon) station and Middle signal box, which was abolished in the power-operated signalling scheme of 1926-8; photographed in about 1921. (Clinker Collection/courtesy Brunel University)

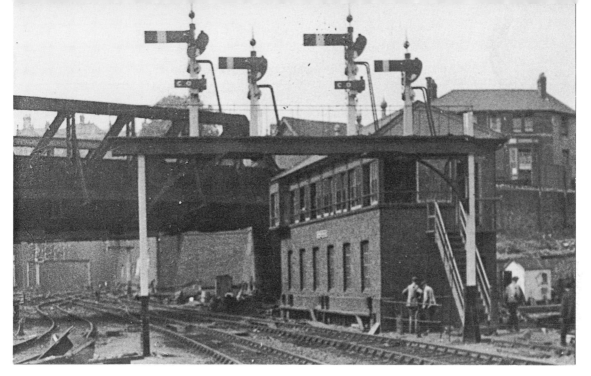

The West signal box was opened in 1912 with a 110-lever frame. Between 1926 and 1928 a Siemens route-setting frame of 144 miniature levers was installed to command the enlarged west end layout and that which was controlled from the former Middle box. Additional line capacity was obtained by signalling the relief lines, serving platforms 6 and 8, for 'each way' working between West and East boxes. These arrangements were brought into use on 24 June 1928, the year of this photograph. (Ray Caston/Adrian Vaughan Collection

The new East box was a plain-gabled timber building, set on a narrow pedestal at the side of the Shaftesbury Road bridge which cut across the end of a row of houses – the back wall of the signal box almost touched the wall of the adjacent house. The box housed a 96-lever Siemens route-setting frame of the same type as at Winchester, and by this means one signalman – with a booking lad – controlled the eastern end of the station and the eastern approaches thereto, permitting the abolition of Maindee West

The gantry controlling the down main and down platform lines and the 'scissors' crossing between the two at Newport. At first glance it would not appear that the signalling had been modernised but these signals, like all the others, were electrically operated through the Siemens 'route setting' system whereby the operation of one lever moved all necessary points and signals for that route. (Lens of Sutton)

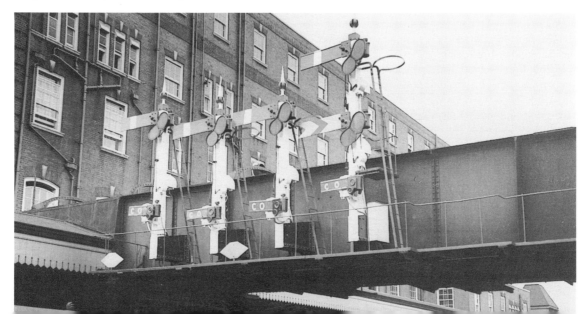

Junction box 50 chains eastwards across the Usk Bridge. The new Newport East box was brought into use on 29 May 1927.

West box was a brick, hip-roofed building dating from 1912, when it housed a conventional locking frame of 110 levers. This frame was replaced by a Siemens frame of 144 route-setting levers, thereby abolishing the Middle box situated on the northernmost platform. The West box then controlled from newport station to Gaer Tunnel. Additional line capacity was obtained by signalling the relief lines, serving platforms 6 and 8, for 'each way' working between West and East boxes. These arrangement were brought into use on 24 June 1928. No further use was made of the excellently compact Siemens route-setting system on the GWR.

In 1923 came the invention of the low-voltage electric motor and, with the acceptance by 1923 that track circuits could be trusted to protect layouts and to 'approach lock' facing points, it became possible for point blades and a facing point bolt to be operated by a 20-volt motor driven by batteries.

This system was first put to work at Gerrards Cross and Beaconsfield stations, whose platforms were served by long loops off the main lines. The points at one end were controlled by one box, which also controlled several other points, but those at the other end had to be controlled from a second signal box which had no other function than to operate the inlet and outlet points and associated signals. The battery-operated 20-volt system was installed in the West or Station box at Beaconsfield and at Gerrards Cross in October and on 11 November 1923 respectively, enabling the smaller signal boxes at both places to be closed, thus simplifying the signalling, saving six mens' wages and some maintenance costs.

The Signal Engineer was given a even more powerful tool in 1923 with the introduction of the Nicholson & Roberts hand generator, marketed by Westinghouse. This machine - known to the signalmen by the wryly sarcastic title of 'hurdy-gurdy' - was located in the signal box, and by means of churning the handle the signalman could send current to operate remote point motors and thus work points beyond the permitted range for rodding operation. The hand generator was a very neat solution to the problem of cumbersome and difficult to maintain battery 'cells' and, like the larger 'route-setting' system, was a device which had tremendous potential for saving money; large numbers of signal boxes could have been abolished, but the system was not immediately taken up, nor was it widely used during the period of this book.

The first points to be operated by hand-generated current were installed at Pencader Station box to replace Pencader Junction signal box, 34 chains north of Pencader, on 21 July 1929. Pencader Junction signal box controlled a single set of points and associated signals required to run trains to and from the Newcastle Emlyn branch, off the Carmarthen-Aberystwyth line. Exactly one month later Aberayron Junction box, 1 mile 24 chains north of Lampeter, was abolished when its single facing point and associated signals were worked by a hand generator in Lampeter Station box. These modernisations made the branch lines cheaper to run and thus helped to keep them open.

The hand generator could have been used to abolish many signal boxes, but it was not widely used. Some of the newly quadrupled stations of the 1930s, including Challow, Wantage Road and Lapworth, had hand generators to enable long platform loops to be operated from one box. The system was also brought into use on 23 May 1938 at Grovesend Colliery Loop signal box, to control the double track junction to and from the Swansea District Line to the Hendy Loop towards Llandilo. This junction had previously been controlled by Morlais Junction East box, which was abolished.

A cheap alternative to the hand generator for remote point operation was the continental system with a double wire. This system is described thus by John Morris in his paper for the Signalling Record Society:

'A continuous wire led from the signal box to the points, one side of the "circuit" always being in tension, the other side slack. Compensators with heavy weights kept the wire adjusted when it expanded or contracted due to changes in air temperature. At the points the wire went around a horizontal wheel. When the signal box lever was operated the resulting movement in the wire turned the wheel which drove a cam which drove the points and their bolt through a short length of rodding.'

Points up to half a mile away from the signal box could be worked by this method, which was none the less extremely heavy work for the signalman. The system was installed at a handful of locations; the first was at Park Junction, Newport, to abolish Gaer Loop box, the last at Johnston (Pembs), in 1935, to abolish Johnston West box.

The need for two small boxes, one at each end of a station (or other layout), was the result of the

A typical conventional mechanical signal box and its associated equipment in April 1928 - Llanstephan Crossing signal box, looking towards Sarnau.

This box was in operation by 1885 with 10 levers, but had a 23-lever frame, controlling goods loops and a crossover, when this picture was taken. The nearest signal post carries Carmarthen Bridge's up distant signal and a miniature arm routing to the up goods loop. The latter arm was repeated by 3-foot arm bracketed out from the concrete post of the up home signal next in rear, on the bend. (British Rail)

Another unmodernised - indeed primitive - installation at Exeter, photograhed in 1925. Level crossings were the bane of railway operations everywhere and especially where a road crossed through a station complex. At Red Cow Crossing, Exeter, the Exwick road crossed the whole 'fan' of tracks right at the platform ends of this station busy with shunting, bank engines, arrivals and departures. At this time there were no 'wicket' gates - they came later. Pedestrians had to wait to cross until the main gates were opened for carts and lorries. The gates were bolted and unbolted by a lever in the Middle signal box - the cast-iron 'gate stop' can be seen protruding from the ground at the left-hand end of the gate - but the gates were opened by a crossing-keeper, possibly the man on the right. The wait at Red Cow crossing must have been legendary in Exeter. (British Rail)

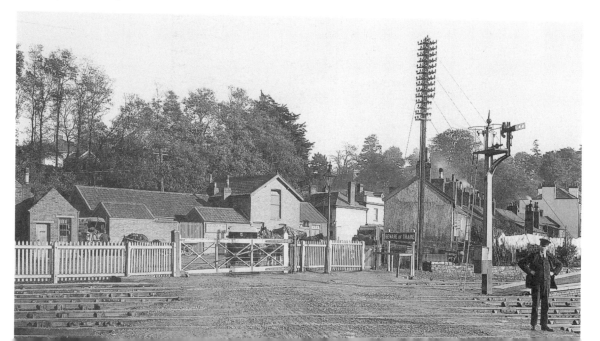

Board of Trade's 19th-century rule which restricted the length of rodding from a signal box to a set of points to 150 yards. Years of experience - and lobbying from the companies - got the rule relaxed to 250 yards, and in 1925 it was further relaxed to 350 yards. This enabled the GWR to abolish some boxes as their functions could now be taken over by a nearby box by purely mechanical means.

Money for investment in labour-saving devices became increasingly difficult to obtain just as the need to reduce operating costs grew ever more urgent. However, using all the means at their disposal the GWR S&T Department was able to economise on signal boxes as follows:

Signal boxes:	Abolished		Installed
Renewed			
1925	12	11	16
1926	12	3	10
1927	18	7	10
1928	26	6	3
1930	19	3	-
1931	26	13	-
	113	43	43
	43		

Net reduction, 1925-31: 70

On 19 January 1925 the 45-lever Waltham Siding box of 1893 was taken out of use to be replaced by a new 43-lever box, the prototype for a new type of signal box construction (classified 'Type 9' by the Signalling Record Society). The new Waltham Siding box was curious and most un-Great Western in its crudity. The walls were made with hollow concrete blocks, 18 in x 10½ in x 2¾ in, filling a steel framework. The stairs were internal, and the roof was plain gabled and had slates or thin tiles hung 'diamond' fashion. There was a badly proportioned deep blank space horizontally above the windows below the eaves, and the sliding windows were ugly with small square panes. Waltham cost £650, when a brick box of the same dimensions would have cost £870. Insell wanted the design to be adopted as the standard. Timber boxes were cheaper to build, he said, but were more costly to maintain and were only erected in exceptional circumstances.

Happily, the 'production models' of the 'Type 9' design were more refined and handsome than their prototype. Whilst retaining the cheap concrete and steel construction they had pre-1914 hipped gables, standard GWR windows and a properly proportioned space between the tops of the windows and the eaves. In fact, they returned, as far as possible, to the outline of the 1896-1906 Standard.

Nineteen were built. The first and also the largest were erected at the rebuilt and enlarged Cardiff Queen Street in 1928 - North box with a 200-lever frame and South box with a frame of levers numbered to 153. There was another at Neath General West. The greatest concentration of these boxes was between Swindon and Didcot, at Shrivenham, Ashbury Crossing, Challow, Wantage Road,

Insell's prototype signal box at Waltham Siding using a steel frame and concrete block walls. Fortunately the design was later civilised with a hip-gabled roof and improved fenestration before going into general use.

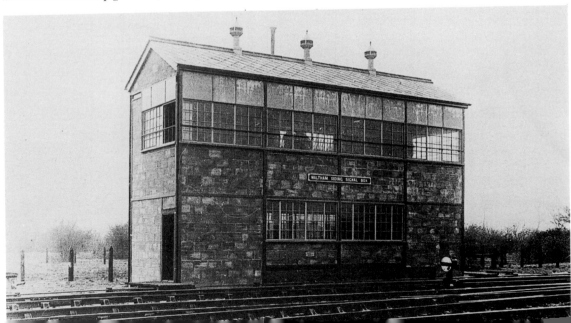

Foxhall Junction, Didcot West End and East Junction. Some, if not all, of these were built by the contractor Hinkins & Frewen. Others were built at Kemble in 1929, Bridgwater (1932), and Ruabon Middle, Canton Sidings, Cherry Orchard and Frome South (1933), after which no more appeared.

The levers housed in the signal box were interlocked with each other to prevent conflicting movements being set up. There were dozens of patents for the mechanical contrivances to do this, but the most successful was the compact and versatile 'tappet' system invented by James Deakin, an employee of the signalling contractors Stevens & Sons, and patented by that firm in 1870.

One of the GWR's Chief Engineers, Michael Lane, had patented an interlocking system in 1863 and from that the Company developed its own highly idiosyncratic system known as 'twist' locking, a curious title derived from the shape of an important component of the mechanism. Although the Stevens patent on tappet interlocking lapsed in 1883, allowing the free use of the tappet principle, the GWR was content with its own method.

The 'twist' system of interlocking did not lend itself to 'conditional locking' (ie 'lever X interlocked with lever Y only when lever Z is reversed'). In addition, the mechanism required signal levers to be $5\frac{1}{4}$ inches apart, which meant that signal boxes were longer, taller and wider than would otherwise have been the case with 'tappet' locking. This was particularly the case with the larger boxes with 100 or more levers.

Another GWR interlocking system, working on a principle similar to the Stevens 'tappet' system, was the 'stud' type. The first stud frame on the GWR was one composed of five levers installed at Exeter City Basin Junction on 30 November 1891. The levers were still relatively widely spaced, at $5\frac{1}{4}$-inch centres, but this type of interlocking was more amenable to the fitting of conditional locking. However, it could not be used for frames of more than 37 levers, and in 1906 the GWR locking experts finally swallowed their pride and adopted the principle of the Stevens tappet system in designs of their own making. The interlocking mechanism was arranged to lie flat or horizontally, and the levers were once again at $5\frac{1}{4}$-inch centres. The first such frame entered service in 1906, its location uncertain.

In 1908 the GWR adopted the 'vertical tappet' system which took up less room than the horizontal tappet, the levers being set at 4-inch centres. Again the location of the first installation of this type is uncertain.

In 1923 the 1908 system was improved to increase the amount of locking which could be effected by the machinery, and this system then remained the standard until the last interlocking frame was produced for the Western Region of British Railways in 1966; some of these frames are still in use in 1993.

In 1914 an American three-aspect, upper quadrant, semi-automatic semaphore signal was installed as Paddington Departure signal box's starting signal and distant for Westbourne Bridge. The arm was red with an amber aspect for the 'Caution' position, and it was the first signal on the GWR to carry such a light; it was also the first upper quadrant signal on the line. One other three-aspect semi-automatic semaphore was erected at the southern end of Wolverhampton Low Level tunnel in 1923. This acted as the down starting signal for Wolverhampton South and the distant signal for the North box. In the same year the GWR-owned Ealing & Shepherd's Bush electric railway was equipped with three-aspect semaphores, using an amber light at night for 'Caution'. Many of these signals were fully automatic, worked by the occupation of track circuits ahead.

In 1921 a few standard GWR distant signals between Paddington and Southall were given yellow arms with black chevrons and amber lights. Then, in February 1925, the Ministry of Transport made it one of their 'Requirements' that distant signals be given yellow arms and lights. The GWR took no action until 1927, but by the end of that year yellow arms and lights had been installed on all distant signals between London, Bristol and Plympton, and London and Birmingham, and a start had been made on the Oxford to Worcester and Cheltenham, Cheltenham to Tyseley, Birmingham to Wolverhampton, Worcester to Hereford, Swindon to Ledbury, Rotherwas to Cardiff, Westbury to Cogload and Westbury to Weymouth routes.

Some of the new distant signal arms may have been of a new type - vitreous enamelled steel with a half-round bead stiffening the top and bottom edge. There is uncertainty as to when these new arms came into use; some authorities think as early as 1919, but the S&T Department's Annual Report to the Directors for 1927 states that 'A number of non-corrugated, vitreous enamel signal arms have been obtained and are experimentally in use. Trials are

Period piece at Wrexham North. The top arm is wooden of a style in use since 1887 (the twin-glass spectacles date from 1892), while the distant arm and the middle stop arm are made of beaded and enamelled steel, a type dating from about 1927. The left-hand arm is wooden, to a design in use before 1920, and directs to a goods line. The 'Calling On' ('CO') arms are in beaded and enamelled steel but to a pre-1920 design which was superceded by 1936 by a red arm carrying a horizontal white stripe. A 'CO' arm lowered authorised a driver to pass the main signal at 'Danger' and proceed cautiously as far as the line was clear but not to pass any other signal at 'Danger'.(Lens of Sutton)

being made with tubular steel posts from the use of which, if found to be satisfactory, economy in cost both of provision and erection is anticipated.'

These new steel arms carried the old-style spectacle plate and were fitted to wooden and concrete posts. Concrete posts had been in use since 1917, when fine trunks of pine were scarce. Tubular steel posts came into use around 1926. In 1928 the Departmental Report stated that 'four tubular steel signal posts and 14 concrete signal posts have been installed together with 243 wooden posts'. Concrete posts were dropped in favour of steel around 1930 and the steel posts superseded wood from 1934.

Tubular steel posts carried the beaded-edge steel arms, but these had a 'solid' casting for the spectacle

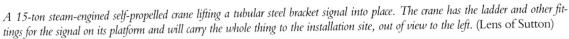

A 15-ton steam-engined self-propelled crane lifting a tubular steel bracket signal into place. The crane has the ladder and other fittings for the signal on its platform and will carry the whole thing to the installation site, out of view to the left. (Lens of Sutton)

plate; the old-style 'built-up' spectacle was never fitted to a steel post.

Communication between signal boxes and between stations was generally conducted over the ancient single-needle telegraph. Telephone circuits between offices at many moderate and larger-sized stations had existed since the turn of the century or soon after, but I am concerned here with what might be described as 'train operating' communications.

The vastly inflated wartime traffic highlighted the need for swifter and easier means of communication. There were some, rare, telephone circuits prior to 1924, but it was really after that year that telephones between boxes began to be installed. Frequently the telephone was used in addition to the single-needle, as is demonstrated by a 1920s GWR complaint to its staff. A decision made in the course of a telephone conversation would be confirmed by the single-needle - because in that way a written record of the agreement was made. It was many years before the single-needle was completely abolished between signal boxes, stations and telegraph offices. I believe I am correct in saying that there was a single-needle circuit in use between Reading and Newport (Mon) until 1964.

In 1924 an electric 'tele-type' instrument circuit was installed between Paddington and Birmingham Snow Hill; these were the GWR's first 'tele-printers' and remained in use for many years. In the same year the first GWR automatic telephone exchange was installed to serve the dozens of offices at Paddington station. From the same year trunk telephone circuits were installed in stages from Paddington down to Bristol, Swansea, Chester and Penzance.

The GWR pioneered the 'Motor Trolley' system of track maintenance in July 1928 on the newly singled line from Andoversford Junction to Cirencester, and from Cirencester to Rushey Platt Junction, 1½ miles north of Swindon Town. With the aid of the motorised trolley, two gangs of nine men, instead of four gangs totalling 36 men, were all that was required to maintain the 27 miles of single track, and the wages of two gangers and two sub-gangers were saved. The motor trolley system used the 'Ganger's Occupation Key' arangement (Annett's Key) to interrupt the electrical circuit between the two signal boxes that controlled the staff intruments for the block section and thus prevent a staff being withdrawn while the trolley was on the track.

In 1929 the system was extended to cover the North Pembrokeshire branch, Whitchurch to Whittington, Banbury to Cheltenham, the Helston branch and the Severn & Wye Joint line, a total of 163½ miles saving £4,600 per annum. In 1930 the system was further extended to cover Swindon Town to Marlborough, Witney to Fairford, and Over Junction to Ledbury. By March 1932 450 miles of single track were under the new system of maintenance, saving the Company £10,370 per annum since 1928.

21

Signal & telegraph and civil engineering, 1921–39

The last major addition to GWR route mileage was a 9-mile northwards extension of the Kingswinford branch which left the Stourbridge Junction-Wolverhampton line at Kingswinford Junction to Baggeridge to connect with the Earl of Dudley's steelworks railway.

The extension was built for double track but was laid as a single line from Baggeridge to a forked junction with the Paddington-Chester main line at Oxley, just north of Wolverhampton. The Act for this extension had been obtained in 1905, when it was also intended to build a branch from Wombourn to Bridgnorth; the new line, without the branch to Bridgnorth, was opened on 11 May 1925. The only work of any note on the line was the steel girder bridge carrying the line over the canal at Tettenhall. The line was originally a 'Blue route' - allowing nothing heavier than a '28xx' 2-8-0 or '31xx' 2-6-2T to pass over it - but during 1931 its underbridges were strengthened to 'Red route' standards, permitting all but the '47xx' 2-8-0 and 'King' classes to work over it.

Probably the most difficult civil engineering job undertaken during the years 1921 to 1939 was the driving of a new 1,589-yeard-long single-track tunnel between Colwall and Malvern Wells to duplicate the existing tunnel and permit double track to be extended through the ridge from Malvern Wells Tunnel box to Colwall.

The old Colwall tunnel, 1,567 yards long, was opened in 1861 through the ridge of the Malverns. The rock is volcanic and because of its intense hardness the tunnel was constructed as small as

possible, without any ventilation and on a 1 in 80 gradient falling towards Malvern. As locomotives became larger it became especially horrible, the roof of the tunnel being only 12 inches - even less in places - above the chimney of a Churchward '29xx', labouring hard up the steep grade deep inside the hill.

Work on the new tunnel began in February 1924 using pneumatic drills and dynamite, and it was opened for traffic on 1 August 1926 after an expenditure of £18,673. The new tunnel rose on a 1 in 90 gradient, was vented by a shaft at the upper end and was very much larger in cross section than the old one - 18 feet from rail to roof and 17 feet across. The largest engine then likely to use the tunnel, the 'Star' or '29xx' Class, now had a 4-foot clearance between the chimney and the tunnel roof.

In addition, the easier gradient enabled Class 'A' locomotives (the average 0-6-0 saddle tank) to haul an extra five loaded Class 1 (coal or mineral) wagons, while Class 'E' engines ('28xx' 2-8-0s, for instance) could take an extra ten Class 1 wagons. The Malvern banker was needed less as a result.

The old tunnel was to have been used for up trains, where they would be free-wheeling down the 1 in 80, but in fact it was found to be so unsafe, due to geological faults, and so narrow that no self-respecting railway could use it. It was therefore abandoned and was evidently leased or sold to the Admiralty. The old line leading to the tunnel became a 'refuge siding', used to allow a faster train to get by. Normally trains reversed into such sidings, but at Colwall they went into the refuge 'head first' and reversed out to continue their journey through the new tunnal.

The old Colwall signal box of 32 levers was demolished and a new one built. This contained a 40-lever frame to work a double-track layout, and was brought into use in August 1926. It was built to the 1906 standard design with hipped gables and decorative blue bricks at the quoins and window casings; this was a relatively expensive design superceded in 1920-2 by a cheaper design using plain gables.

During the 1920s the GWR carried out several large improvement schemes for stations and layouts. Newport has already been mentioned, and an even larger scheme involved the remodelling and widening of the track layout over the 3 miles from Old Oak Common to Paddington. At the Paddington end this required the setting back of the goods shed wall to make room for tracks, as well as other large and difficult construction work.

Newton Abbot station, which had remained more or less unchanged since Broad Gauge days, was completely rebuilt and the layout mightily enlarged. The locomotive depot and Divisional locomotive repair shop (built in 1893) were also considerably enlarged. A new locomotive erecting shop was started at Caerphilly, a new goods depot was begun at Bristol Temple Meads, and the replacement of the Brunellian girders of the 17 spans forming the eastern and western approach viaducts to the Royal Albert Bridge was started. The rebuilding of Cardiff

(Queen Street) was also begun, and improvements at Cardiff and Swansea (High Street) stations was mooted. During 1926 the GWR spent £446,117 of its own money on improvement works.

The Newton Abbot improvements of 1926-7 cost in excess of £48,000. The new refreshment rooms and waiting rooms were brought into use in December 1926, and the new booking hall, cloak room, parcels office and the footbridge between the platforms were completed the following year. In 1924 a boiler washing-out plant was installed at the locomotive shed, and in 1926 a 65-foot turntable was installed together with improvements to the coaling stage and a new office block.

The greatly enlarged station layout was controlled from the 206-lever East box - opened on 3 April 1926 - and the 153-lever West box - opened on 25 April 1927 - both of them constructed in timber with plain gables. The lever frames therein were the new standard type with some short levers to work battery-powered points, semaphore signals and ground discs in 'banner' form.

In 1929, as the Depression deepened and unemployment became embarrassing even to the Government, that august body of men saw what they thought was a way to relieve unemployment by encouraging large public works, and that summer passed the Development (Loans & Guarantees) Act which enabled the privately owned railway companies to receive grants or cheap loans of public money to carry out improvements to their railways.

By the mid-1920s Newton Abbot was bursting at the seams and ripe for enlargement. In 1926 the station was rebuilt, and this view of the east end shows the enlarged platforms under construction. (British Rail)

A closer view of the east end at Newton Abbot. The Moretonhampstead branch turns away to the left beyond the junction signal, with the old East box behind. Note the '31xx' tank shunting in right distance. Note also the GWR photographer's leather box, carrying his photographic plates, part-covered by his jacket. The plate box is a familiar feature of GWR official photographs. (British Rail)

One of the Government-assisted works approved in 1930 was the continuation of improvements already taking place at Paddington. Here crane engine No 18 helps in the rebuilding, hoisting for our inspection precast concrete sections which will support the new platforms are hoisted. The old and new 'Arrival' boxes are to the right of the engine on either side of the bridge. (8 October 1933 British Rail)

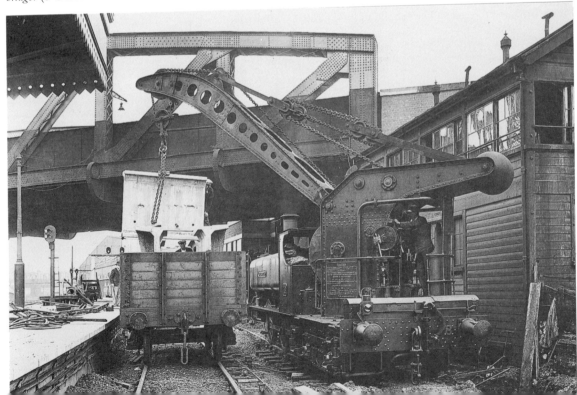

Funding was subject to Ministry of Transport approval which would only be given to projects which would employ large numbers of men.

The list of important works which became possible to undertake once the money became available is too vast to describe in full, but the sheer vastness of the programme of essential improvements is an indication of how desperately underfunded the GWR and all railways had been since long before 1921. During 1930 literally dozens of 'Government Assisted' new works schemes were approved. Unfortunately 'electrification' was not put forward, but below - taken from GWR records - are some of the major schemes approved and carried out:

Continuing the enlargements and improvements already taking place at Paddington and the extension of two-aspect colour-light signalling westwards as far as Southall West Junction

A new station alongside the existing one at Bristol Temple Meads, the enlargement and re-signalling of the layout in the station area and the quadrupling of the lines, stations and bridges from Filton Junction through Temple Meads to Portishead Junction (Parson Street)

A comprehensive rebuild and quadrupling for Taunton and Cardiff (General) stations

The rebuilding and enlargement of Swansea (High Street) station

Quadrupling of the tracks from Olton to Rowington Junction (later cut back to end at Lapworth)

Rebuilding the layout at Didcot station to abolish the East End box

Quadrupling between Wantage Road and Challow, and Ashbury Crossing to Shrivenham

Quadrupling the tracks through Cullompton, Exminster, Sampford Peverell, Stoke Canon, Tiverton Junction and Wellington stations

Provision of avoiding lines around Westbury (Wilts) and Frome

New engine sheds for Cardiff East Dock, Didcot, Kidderminster, Laira, Landore, Pantyffynon, Radyr and Treherbert

A new hand-operated lifting bridge at Haverfordwest

Construction of new or greatly enlarged goods warehouses at Small Heath, Soho (Birmingham), St Austell, Swansea, and Wolverhampton Herbert Street.

Another improvement was the extension of the Paddington colour-light signals. This example, photographed in 1940, is on the up relief line exactly 1 mile west of Paddington station near Subway Junction. The colour-light heads are mounted on the old semaphore bracket. (British Rail)

All of this work was completed by the end of 1934 although the Haverfordwest bridge, which was renewed without serious delay to trains, was not restored to double-line working until February 1936.

In addition there were dozens of relatively small jobs done solely with GWR money. Starting in 1929 the GWR began to install pressed steel sleepers with integral chairs, and at the end of 1930 59 miles of track had been relaid using the new sleeper; six years later 260 miles of track was on steel sleepers. Other jobs included the provision of an extra siding or prefabricated concrete warehouse, widening of a road bridge, a new telephone exchange, or the building of a halt (in 1930 'upwards of 14' of these lineside platforms were constructed, with a further 15 in 1932).

The main line from Plymouth, Cornwall Junction, to Penzance had been built as single track, and most of it was doubled between 1893 and 1900 as the timber viaducts were replaced by wider masonry arches. During the period of this book the only sections of single track main line in Cornwall were across the Royal Albert Bridge ($\frac{1}{2}$ mile), from Scorrier to Drump Lane ($1\frac{3}{4}$ miles), from St Erth to Marazion ($3\frac{1}{2}$ miles), and from Ponsandane to Penzance, $\frac{3}{4}$ mile.

Challow station during quadrupling, looking towards Swindon; this was another of the Development Act projects. The wooden station, dating from 1840, was demolished and a new station built 50 yards further east; the 1840 goods shed was spared. There is considerable activity in the goods department – a horse and cart and a lorry have arrived with grain, another truck is loaded with beet, more trucks are loading down in the yard, and a horse-box and water tank are nearest the camera. The 1874 signal box stands beside the down main line, dwarfed by the gleaming new box, the 'civilised' version of Insell's prototype. The down and up main lines will become up main and up relief lines respectively when the job is done. (British Rail)

The 347-yard long, 12-foot high Penzance viaduct, between Ponsandane and Penzance, was replaced by a stone embankment on which a double line was laid, and this was opened on 24 July 1921. St Erth to Marazion was opened as double track on 16 June 1929, and the only 'doubling' work to be assisted by a grant under the 1929 Act was the 1½ miles from Scorrier to Redruth, completed on 13 April 1930. The ½ mile between Royal Albert Bridge signal box and Saltash station is single track to this day.

The last of the Brunel timber viaducts in Cornwall were on the Falmouth branch - Pascoe, Penrhyn and Penwithers were replaced by embankments in 1923 and 1926; Perran by arches in 1927; the superb Ponsanooth viaduct, 217 yards long and 139 feet high, by an equally magnificent masonry structure in 1930; Ringwell and Carnon in 1933; and College Wood, 318 yards long and 100 feet high, in 1934. This left only two Brunel timber viaducts - Gamlyn and Dare - on the Dare branch in South Wales which were replaced in 1947.

At Rogerstone and Banbury gravitation 'hump' sorting yards with grid-irons of sidings were constructed with the aid of Government money, and the existing yards at Severn Tunnel Junction were enlarged to accommodate an extra 1,529 wagons, all this starting in 1930. At the Banbury and Rogerstone hump yards the points leading to the sidings were worked pneumatically through electrically controlled valves operated from a Descubes push-button console in the 'Hump Ground Frame'. Rogerstone hump came into use on 3 June 1931, Banbury exactly one month later.

The wagons were pushed steadily over the summit of the hump by the shunting engine; the under-shunter used his pole to uncouple the wagons according to the 'cut' plan and the trucks were then allowed to free-wheel into the correct siding, as the points were switched in front of each 'cut' by electro-pneumatic operation from the control cabin. Given a very skilful set of men, wagons could be marshalled - or sorted - quickly into trains.

'Up' and 'Down' hump sorting yards at Severn Tunnel Junction with electro-pneumatically operated points were constructed from 1937. The Down hump was brought into use on 11 October 1939, the Up hump on 5 November of that year. The consoles used were an improved pattern of the Banbury ones, looking more like the 'panel' control consoles of the 1960s.

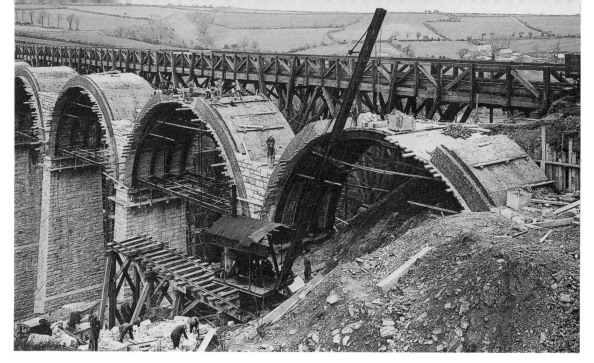

Long after the demise of Brunel and Queen Victoria, craftsmen were still able to build magnificent structures. This is the brick and masonry viaduct at Ponsanooth, on the Falmouth branch, on 26 March 1930. The new bridge will replace the masonry and timber viaduct designed by Brunel in the 1850s as a temporary measure. Brunel gave his timber viaducts a life expectancy of 10 years, but by regular replacement of the timber struts that at Ponsanooth lasted until 1930. The maximum height above the valley floor was 139 feet, length 215 yards.

College Wood timber viaduct lasted until 1934 and the last, the Dare viaduct in South Wales, survived until 1947. (British Rail)

Banbury Hump Ground Frame, dating from 1931, in use in 1955. (Peter Barlow/Adrian Vaughan Collection)

The Descubes 'push-button' control console for the electro-pneumatic point switching system at Banbury Hump Yard. (Peter Barlow/Adrian Vaughan Collection)

The Automatic Train Control (ATC) system was extended over a large part (but not all) of the GWR's double track routes system with the help of Government loans. This meant equipping 2,000 locomotives and laying well over 1,000 ramps with all their attendant batteries and circuitry (see Appendix 2).

At the start of 1929 the system was in use between Reading and Paddington, this installation dating from 1908-10. At the end of 1929 it had been extended to Oxford and Swindon, and from Old Oak Common to High Wycombe. By the end of 1930 the system had reached Taunton via Westbury and via Bristol, East Usk Junction via Badminton and via Gloucester, to Hatton via Bicester, to Aynho Junction via Oxford, and to Hereford and Stourbridge Junction via Oxford. By 7 October 1931 the ATC had reached Swansea, Plymouth and Wolverhampton. One of the sections never equipped with ATC was Clarbeston Road Junction to Milford/Neyland.

In April 1933 the GWR Directors formally approved the wholesale introduction of an electrically operated lock on the lever operating the signal which controlled the entrance to the section ahead (the 'section signal'). Such devices had been in use since 1907, installed in particular circumstances, but now the Company's policy was the universal installation of this important safety device.

This system maintained an electric lock on the section signal's lever which was released only when the signalman in advance pegged the instrument for that line to 'Line Clear'. Without this device the 'section signal' lever was free to be pulled even if there was a train in the section ahead and 'Train on Line' was showing on the instrument. This piece of important safety work did not qualify for a Ministry of Transport grant/loan because it would not have employed many men, and in the same Minute by which the GWR Directors approved the universal adoption of 'locking with Line Clear', they also had to state that the cost of universal installation was too great to permit the programme to go ahead 'except at certain places like junctions'. 'Locking with Line Clear' was by no means universal even in 1970.

The story of the modernisation of Bristol Temple Meads station by the quadrupling of its approaches and the bridges and stations along the way over the 7 miles from Filton Junction in the north to Parson Street in the south, and rebuilding of its Bath Road locomotive depot, is an epic of engineering history, too long to be told properly here - and while this was going on the Company was also rebuilding Taunton, Cardiff and Swansea stations!

Bristol Temple Meads station lay on a curve, on arches, and crammed between two waterways. The city cattle market lay at street level 'inside' the curve on the south side, while the goods shed and yard lay at ground level on the north side. Prior to re-building, three double lines - from Gloucester (LMS), South Wales and Paddington - converged at South Wales Junction, about 500 yards east of the station. Instead of continuing as six tracks, they merged into four, fanning out to reach the various platforms as they crossed the Floating Harbour bridge which was 150 feet from the platform ends.

At this point the tracks were running roughly east-west into the Old Station, but the through tracks swung due south on a long curve through the 1876-built station. At the south end all through traffic came across the New Cut bridge on a simple double track - one up and one down line to and from Taunton.

This was a very niggardly arrangement and delays were routine; trains too long for a platform had to 'draw up' to get the rear vans to the platform, and in

A pre-First World War photograph of locomotives queuing to get on to Bristol Bath Road engine shed because of the bad siting of the inadequate servicing facilities on the shed. A Dean 'Single' is standing across the Weston-super-Mare bay track, and the Locomotive Yard signal box can be seen behind the chimney of the engine. This was the view from the extreme southern tip of the down main platform, the only one to bridge the New Cut. (pre-1914. Clinker Collection/Courtesy Brunel University)

so doing the front of the train then blocked the exit from an adjoining platform.

The GWR passenger-engine shed for Temple Meads, Bath Road, was sited south of the New Cut bridge, on the down side, with a single connection from the down main to the shed. Queues of engines are known to have formed, blocking the main line, as locomotives inched their way into the crowded depot. The remarkable thing is that the Company's punctuality record was as good as it was once their difficulties are understood.

To improve matters the New Cut bridge was widened. It had been about 65 feet wide to carry the

Like the previous photograph, this one also illustrates the extreme inadequacy of Bristol station from at least 1900 until the rebuilding of 1930-4.

This is the west end, up side, of Temple Meads. The track on which the men are working is the up main with the up main loop going to platforms 3 and 4 respectively. The building on the left is not the original B&ER terminus but a B&ER carriage shed. Two carriage shunting horses are in a 'lean-to' shelter at the front of the building. The tall chimneys on the right rise from the back wall of the old B&ER headquarters building, in use here as the GWR Bristol Divisional Superintendent's offices. The platform behind the workmen is the 'Fish Dock' which occupies the site of the original B&ER terminal station. (Clinker Collection/courtesy Brunel University)

Bristol Temple Meads west end, complete, in 1935. Five new platforms and a widened track space all bridge the New Cut, and colour-light signals are controlled from three new signal boxes. (Clinker Collection/courtesy Brunel University)

down main platform, the double track main line and the 'Weston bay'. It now became about 312 feet wide to carry 15 tracks, including proper access to the locomotive depot and four platforms. Concurrent with this work came the rebuilding of the Bath Road bridge to 190 feet span in order to bridge the widened tracks – this was achieved without interrupting the city tramcar service which passed over it.

Temple Meads east end in 1934. The layout has been improved by removing the central platforms under the 1876 roof and by building a new station alongside, out of sight, on the left. The 1876 extension roof to the old terminal station is on the right, Bristol East signal box in the centre. This was in brick with 16th-century-style doorways to the locking room - one can be seen to the right of the locomotive's smokebox - and the same effect was produced around the locking room windows. The box was known as the 'Coffin Box' because of the tapered plan at this end, due to the narrowing of the platform.

LMS Class '5' 4-6-0 No 5044 is revesing an LMS coach on to GWR carriages past some colour-light signals, not yet in use. Another gantry for colour-lights is on the extreme right. (Clinker Collection/courtesy Brunel University)

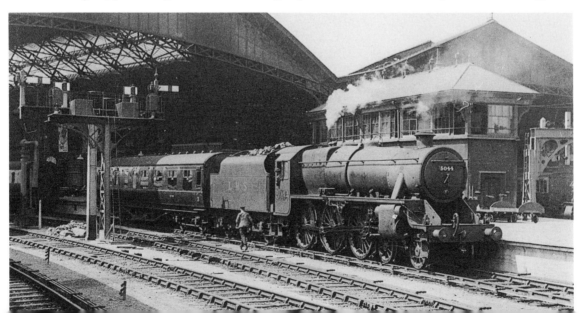

The east end approach tracks of Temple Meads in 1935 seen from the new power-operated East signal box. (Clinker Collection/courtesy Brunel University)

South of the New Cut the land was raised to provide space for a large new locomotive depot. The new shed was 210 feet by 167 feet covering 10 tracks, and there was a 150 feet by 50 feet four-track repair shop. The coal stage was built in brick, double-sided, 90 feet by 32 feet, and supported water tanks with a capacity of 135,000 gallons. There were two turntables, neither of them under cover. The allocation of locomotives to the shed was about 90 engines.

An area of the cattle market was filled in to rail level and the down side approach road was buried to provide room for three platforms (five platform faces), and a greatly enlarged GPO sorting office with its own platforms or loading docks. The new passenger platforms were covered by GWR standard awnings supported by cast iron columns and were provided with very handsome buildings, railway offices, refreshment and waiting rooms faced with Carrara glazed blocks on a granite plinth.

At the east end the Floating Harbour bridge was widened from about 130 feet at mid-stream to about 360 feet to accommodate 20 tracks and three extended platforms.

The south wall of the station, alongside which the third new platform was built, was pierced with arches to give access to the old No 1 which was then re-numbered No 8. Of the four platforms which lay under the great arching 1876 roof, the middle two were demolished, but their tracks were retained as through lines, with 'scissors' points at the centre of

both of the long platform lines to enable two trains to stand at one platform and the rearmost train to leave via the scissors and the through line. Scissors crossings were also provided between the platform and through lines at No 3 platform.

Five mechanical signal boxes had been necessary to control the Temple Meads station area: from the west they were Pylle Hill Junction, 42 levers (where the Bristol Avoiding Line rejoined the main line); Bath Road Engine Shed, 14 levers; Bristol West, 61 levers; Bristol East (built on the platform and constructed in brick in an 'Elizabethan' style to match the station), 105 levers; and South Wales Junction, also having 105 levers.

These were replaced with three signal boxes - East, West and Locomotive Yard - each containing a General Railway Signal Co 'draw-slide' frame having 336, 328 and 32 draw-slides respectively. The new West box numbered its draw-slides from 33 to 368, and it is possible that the empty space for 33 slides was intended to take over the functions of the 32 slides installed in the new Locomotive Yard box.

Some work began in 1930, while other contracts, such as that for the new locomotive depot at Bath Road, were not let until 1931. Stapleton Road, Horfield, Ashley Hill, Bedminster and Parson Street stations had to be more or less rebuilt for quadruple track, new carriage sidings were laid at Malago Vale, new signalling installed and a large engine shed built. Some jobs were completed sooner than others, and the work was finally complete in August 1935.

Bristol was a railway crossroads, a vital centre of railway communications, and the work was carried out without closing the station to the very heavy train service. Whilst Cardiff, Taunton, Bristol and Swansea stations were being rebuilt, the average minutes late at their destination for express trains in January, one of the worst months of the year for operating because of weather conditions, quite apart from delays due to rebuilding, were as follows:

	Minutes late at destination		
	1932	1933	1934
West of England expresses	13.6	10.0	4.8
South Wales expresses	11.3	11.0	5.6

Cardiff station platforms were rebuilt in the same style as Bristol and the tracks quadrupled for a distance of 1¾ miles from Newtown West to Leckwith Junction, the latter opened in 1931 as part of the new scheme. Eighteen bridges were reconstructed, including the massive stone 'Taff viaduct' which carried the old Taff Vale Railway from Queen Street station over the GWR tracks, round and

down into the GWR station. To do this the Company actually suspended the passenger train service for a week and ran buses between the two stations.

At the west end of the station the bridge over the River Taff was widened from 78 to 175 feet, and west of Canton engine shed, where the Leckwith Road crossed the main line on the level, an embankment was raised to take the railway across on a bridge.

The new station was signalled electrically with power-operated points and colour-light signals worked from two signal boxes - East and West. These were built of brick in a modernistic style similar to that used at Bristol Temple Meads, and each housed Westinghouse Type 'L' power frames with miniature levers set at 2-inch centres - 151 levers in East box, 339 levers in West. West box also took over the work of the old Penarth Junction box, working power-operated points and colour-light signals.

Each point and signal had its own lever, as in a conventional lever frame, the colour-light signals showed the same aspects as ordinary semaphores, and ordinary block telegraph signalling was used to

The Westinghouse 'L'-type power frame at Cardiff West, brought into use on 7 July 1934 to replace Cardiff West (75 levers) and Penarth Junction (120 levers). With the similarly equipped East box, this controlled the greatly enlarged station layout. These were the only 'L' frames on the GWR. The one shown here was the largest in Britain, with 339 levers grouped to work the up side and down side, one man on each section, sharing a booking-lad. The megaphone on the floor is for communicating with drivers; note beside it the conventional four-lever detonator placer. (British Rail)

keep the trains apart; of course, the layout was fully protected by track circuiting. Safety interlocking between levers was achieved electrically.

Swansea High Street station was thoroughly inadequate even before 1914 with only two platforms, respectively 360 and 580 feet long and a one-coach bay. It was closely surrounded by slums and was generally an insalubrious place. Main-line express trains could not be accommodated and the usual practise was for express trains to and from Paddington and West Wales to carry a 'Swansea portion' of two or three carriages. The train would stop at Landore to detach the Swansea portion, which was then worked into the terminus by a Pilot engine.

After modernisation, Swansea High Street had four platforms each 900 feet long, a bay of 600 feet, an extra track out to Landore and, on newly built-up ground, a large acreage of carriage sidings. Express trains to and from West Wales and Paddington now worked direct into the terminal and continued on their journey after another express engine had been attached to what had been the rear of the train. The platforms were extended on brick arches over the complicated road intersection of Bargeman Row, Jockey Street and Upper Strand, the latter passing under the platforms at a 45-degree skew.

The resulting brick arches were acknowledged by the Ministry of Transport Inspector to be the most fiendishly complicated examples of skew-arch, spiral brick-laying ever done in England - and that was said in the full knowledge of what had been achieved in the 1890s in the brick arches built for subways in the Central London Railway underground stations.

Swansea had waited since before 1914 for a better station - in 1915 North Dock Junction signal box had been erected just off the end of Swansea High Street platforms, and was large enough for a 120-lever frame but in 1915 contained only 40, obviously in anticipation of a larger station. In 1925 it had received the larger frame and in about 1927 the old Swansea High Street box was closed, its functions transferred to the lever frame in North Dock Junction which was then renamed Swansea High Street. There were still enough levers left over to enable the enlarged layout of 1934 to be controlled from there.

At Cogload Junction, 4 miles east of Taunton, trains originating from London, Wales, the West Midlands and the North of England merged with the London traffic via Westbury, and local trains from Yeovil, all to run along a double track (only one down and one up line) to Taunton station. From Creech Junction, 2 miles west of Cogload, this bottleneck had also to accommodate trains to and from Taunton and Chard. Taunton station was then under its overall roof dating from Bristol & Exeter Railway days and was thoroughly inadequate for the traffic of 1930.

During 1930-32 the cramped layout in Taunton station was rebuilt and the line quadrupled from Cogload to Norton Fitzwarren. New signal boxes were provided for Creech Junction (78 levers), Taunton East Junction (147 levers), Taunton West Station (135 levers), Taunton West Junction (67 levers), and Norton Fitzwarren (89 levers).

The station layouts at Wellington, Sampford Peverell, Tiverton Junction, Cullompton and Stoke Canon were also quadrupled, with new signal boxes at all these places except Wellington. Here the East and West boxes had been abolished in 1922 in favour of a new central box with 67 levers on the up platform. The new Sampford Peverell box, with 50 levers, came into use in February 1932, the new Tiverton Junction box with 125 levers opened in September 1932, Cullompton, with 49 levers, in October 1931, and Stoke Canon Junction, 57 levers, on 25 October 1931.

Most of the new boxes from Cogload Junction to Stoke Canon Junction were built expensively in red brick with hipped gables, similar in outline to the 1906 standard but without the decorative blue bricks, lacking the ornamental timberwork under the eaves and with an internal staircase. The exceptions were the 1906 timber signal box at Cogload which was re-used after being moved from the down to the up side of the line.

Silk Mill Crossing retained its 1899-vintage 17-lever timber box, but it was set back 14 feet on 16 December 1931 to make room for two extra lines. The level crossing gates here spanned four tracks, and would have been heavy to move on a fine day, so it seems likely that in a high wind they were close to impossible to swing shut. The old Silk Mill Crossing box survived until July 1940 when it was replaced by a large red brick box, similar in design to the rest of the Taunton boxes, and housing 53 levers.

Norton Fitzwarren signal box prior to the rebuilding of the station and layout housed 35 levers. Here the Minehead and Barnstaple branches, single tracks but regarded as secondary main lines by the GWR, diverged from the main line to Penzance. The quadrupled tracks from Taunton were extended to Norton Fitzwarren and new, long platforms serving the four lines were built. This enlarged layout required a new signal box and an 89-lever hip-roofed timber box was brought into use on 14 February 1932.

The signalman would have had a very difficult job with the token pick-up/set-down for the branch lines, so auxiliary token instruments were provided on the platforms and a Leading Porter was delegated to the duty of token exchange, the tokens being released by the signalman in the signal box.

'Avoiding Lines' to bypass Frome and Westbury were opened in December 1932 and January 1933 respectively. Four new signal boxes were also built; from east to west they were Heywood Road Junction (39 levers), Fairwood Junction (28 levers), Clink Road Junction (29 levers), and Blatchbridge Junction (28 levers). They were simple plain-gabled all-timber buildings.

In 1936 work began, again with the help of Government loans or grants, on doubling the single-track section from Norton Fitzwarren to Bishop's Lydeard on the Minehead line and to Milverton on the Barnstaple line. Norton Fitzwarren box was extended to house 131 levers, and the junctions were relaid to permit 40 mph running over them; 'splitting' distants were provided for each route. The line to Bishop's Lydeard was opened as double track in October 1936 and the Milverton section was completed in 1937. This speeded the working considerably and removed the complications of the token exchange at the busy junction.

In 1936 Government loans or grants also helped to rebuild the huge goods shed and sidings at Hockley in Birmingham, to quadruple the line between Wood Lane and North Acton, and also to double the Hatton-Bearley section and the Cornelly-Porthcawl section, together with the enlargement of Porthcawl station. This work was completed in late 1938 or during 1939.

Exeter and Plymouth, Gloucester, Oxford, Banbury and Leamington stations were all in need of renewal, but of these only Leamington enjoyed any large improvement; Plymouth was toyed with and a little decorative work seems to have been done at Exeter.

The 1877 GWR/LSWR Joint station at Plymouth North Road had been scheduled for renewal in 1898. A full set of drawings was made for a magnificent station with arched steel and glass roofs but nothing came of the plan. The station was even more in need of rebuilding and enlargement by 1930, and in 1932 it was given some additional coverings to the platforms by means of standard GWR awnings. In 1937 the Houndiscombe Road bridge under the tracks at the east end of the station and the Saltash Road bridge at the west end were both widened to take four rather than two tracks. Then in 1939 a new platform 7/8 was brought into use. A subway was constructed from No 8 to No 2 by the middle of the war, leaving the old footbridge from No 2 to No 1. At this stage the work was suspended until after the war.

Between 1937 and 1939 Leamington station's passenger facilities were completely rebuilt in the modern style, with a shining white concrete facade which cleverly managed to combine 'thirties functionalism with a dash of the neo-Georgian.

Work on improving the Par-Newquay branch began in about 1914. Doubling the line between St Dennis Junction and Tregoss Moor was commenced, but after some of the distance had been doubled and that much extra line had been laid, the extra was lifted and sent to France for the war effort. The work recommenced after the war and the double track from St Dennis to Tregoss was opened for traffic in 1921. The line from Goonbarrow Junction to Bugle was doubled in 1930. St Columb Road loops were extended by 220 yards to accommodate 15-coach trains between 1931 and 1933, and in 1936 Luxulyan and Roche crossing loops were extended to allow 15-coach trains to pass. In 1938 the platforms at Newquay were extended, but the war halted further work until 1946.

Some large works sanctioned under the 1929 Development Act but not carried out are worthy of mention. The 7-mile railway to Looe from St Germans would have required very heavy engineering work: the masonry arched viaduct at Millendreath, 287 yards long and 123 feet high, the Keveral viaduct, 343 yards long and 144 feet high, Looe tunnel, 700 yards long, and Seaton, 2,288 yards. A hotel and a golf course were to have been built by the GWR at Looe. The centre-line of the railway was laid out and some contracts were let during 1937, but then the scheme was dropped.

Another important 'non job' was the proposed reconstruction of the Southern Railway's access to Exeter St David's. From the tunnel near the top of the 1 in 37 incline between the Southern's Queen Street and St David's stations, a new embankment was to have been built on a gradient of 1 in 100 to

Par station looking towards Penzance in about 1925; the St Blazey/Newquay line line diverges to the right. A down express has left a coach on the main line which the branch engine, a 'Metro' Class 2-4-0T, will attach to its train, giving this small engine a four-coach load for the steeply graded (1 in 37/41) line to Newquay, which was the subject of various improvements in the 1920s. (Clinker Collection/courtesy Brunel University)

carry the track over the GWR on a bridge to a double-track High Level station built on level track parallel with and above the GWR station. It was then to have continued at a 1 in 100 descent into what is now Riverside Yard and to run parallel with the GWR out to Cowley Bridge Junction.

This would have simplified of the layout at St David's including, of course, the abolition of the junction at the west end; both the West and East boxes were to have been abolished and a new, larger, Middle box erected. The plan, however, never got beyond the drawing-board.

Harking back to Brunel's original plan for the South Devon Railway, a plan was put forward and parcels of land were purchased for a new line, inland, between Exminster and Bishopsteignton, to avoid the sea-wall section.

A fresh burden was placed on the Company when, as early as May 1936, it was ordered to carry out work to protect vital railway staff and installations from air attack, to lay in stocks of emergency repair material and to begin to train staff in air-raid precautions. The total bill for this work was £5,226,000, of which the GWR's burden was £788,000. The GWR had asked the Government the vital question: 'Who is going to pay for the labour and materials?' Precisely two years later all the Company's Minutes were able to report on this question was that no reply had been received.

'It is not proposed to incur any substantial expenditure until this question is settled,' said the Minutes. Sir James Milne, the GWR General Manager, wrote with informed pessimism to his Directors in May 1938: 'It is probable that difficulty will be experienced in obtaining supplies of sandbags in an emergency. The companies have been negotiating for a bulk purchase of 10 million bags and for 300,000 yards of sacking. One million bags have so far been purchased of which the GWR has taken 100,000, which, with 50,000 yards of sacking, have cost £1,450.'

22
Railway Air Service

In late 1932 the Great Western management saw the possibility of air travel competing with long-distance train travel, so decided to be first into the business. In March 1933 the Company proposed to Imperial Airways that the latter should operate a passenger air service on behalf of the GWR. The route, Cardiff (Pengam field)-Teignmouth (Haldon field)-Plymouth (Roborough field), was chosen and a service of two flights in each direction began on 12 April 1933.

Pengam (dep)	9.15 am	1.45 pm
Haldon (arr)	10.5 am	2.35 pm
Haldon (dep)	10.10 am	2.40 pm
Roborough (arr)	10.35 am	3.05 pm
Roborough (dep)	11.25 am	3.55 pm
Haldon (arr)	11.55 am	4.20 pm
Haldon (dep)	12 noon	4.30 pm
Pengam (arr)	12.50 pm	5.20 pm

Three-engined six-seater Westland 'Wessex' monoplanes were used; they were painted chocolate and cream, had the GWR badge on the tail fin and 'Great Western Railway Air Service' on the fuselage.

On 22 May the service was extended to Birmingham (Castle Bromwich field) and the service was reduced to a single flight in each direction. Passengers were taken by road from the various air fields to Plymouth Millbay, which was close to the city centre, Teignmouth/Newton Abbot, Cardiff and Birmingham Snow Hill stations. Passengers using the plane to take them on holiday sent their suitcases by train PLA - 'Passengers Luggage in Advance'.

The service was suspended for the winter on 30 September 1933, having flown 62,400 miles to carry 714 passengers, 104 lbs of freight and 454 lbs of mail. Imperial Airways submitted all the income, £1,664, to the Great Western and then sent the bill for their costs in flying the operation - £8,190. With only six-seater planes it is hardly surprising that a huge loss was made. In spite of this, the Southern and the LMS asked to join the scheme in January 1934 and in March the 'Railway Air Service' (RAS) was registered as a Company with the intention of flying internally and to European destinations.

The RAS re-started on 7 May 1934 with a service from Liverpool (Speke) to Birmingham. Here passengers changed for Plymouth via Cardiff and Teignmouth, or Cowes via Bristol and Southampton. Four de Havilland 'Dragon' twin-engined biplanes were used, wearing a green, red and silver livery and the logo 'RAS'. The seating capacity was greater now, but demand outstripped supply, passengers were turned away regularly, and at the end of the season a loss of £7,000 was made. What was needed was an 'airbus', something with a large capacity, but of course that was to be years into the future.

For 1937 the flights were rearranged to use three instead of four planes. The service was: Cardiff-Bristol-Exeter-Plymouth and Liverpool-Birmingham-Cheltenham-Bristol-Southampton-Ryde-Brighton. On Sundays only from 14 July to 12 September they flew Cardiff-Bristol-Ryde-Brighton. The redundant fourth aircraft was sold back to de

The first flight of the RAS air service. (National Railway Museum, York)

Havilland for £1,650, and the estimated loss for the year was put again at £7,000.

In 1938 the service remained almost unaltered – the Liverpool-Ryde service made an extra call at Gloucester – but the estimated loss on the year's trading increased to £7,500.

The RAS was before its time – there were no suitable planes to make its far-sighted plans profitable. One wonders why the GWR even began it, knowing beforehand that it would make a loss, and then continued to run it after four loss-making years. The companies involved knew that a European war was approaching – they had been car-

rying extra rail freight traffic to build military airfields since 1935 - yet shortly before the outbreak of that war they instituted their first service into Europe.

The last peacetime service began on 22 May 1939 with an ambitious service making it possible to travel from Glasgow to Berlin or Prague in a day. However, on the outbreak of war, 3 September, the planes of the RAS were commandeered for Government service, providing internal communication between the Armed Forces.

Sir James Milne stated that running the air service had been 'experience cheaply bought'.

23
Labour history

Great Railway Shows and other glossy 'Heritage' displays of railwayana, whilst they reflect the visitor's face in flashing paint and brass, do not reflect the difficult living conditions of the railwaymen and women, nor of the hundreds of thousands of hard-working unpaid railway wives who kept the men's homes together, fed them and washed their clothes daily so that they could return, refreshed, to the fray. It was the daily struggle of these men and women which kept the railway going. One would not think of their lives as 'glossy'.

Railway work was strenuous and skilled for all railway workers - for footplate staff, shed staff, factory men, shunters and permanent way men it was in addition dirty, difficult and actually dangerous. What made them take up the daily challenge was the need to eat and keep a roof over their own and their children's heads.

Whilst actually at work the men were buoyed up by their morale, the teamwork in their difficult yet curiously satisfying employment, their comradeship, their pride in their ability to do a skilful yet difficult job and, for many men, their pride in the Great Western Railway. They were, in modern parlance, 'the "A" team', and they would keep the railway rolling. This morale, as will be seen, did not derive from high wages; high morale cannot be bought with money alone. Railwaymen were relatively happy because their work was useful, skilful, satisfying - and reasonably secure.

In the period of this book railwaymen were increasingly poorly repaid for their hard work and loyalty. 'Old hands', in recalling to me the 'twenties

A shunter portrayed in an official photograph from 1940. He has the heavy three-link coupling raised on the curly steel hook of his shunting pole, keenly observing the speed of the approaching wagon, and with perfect timing and deceptive ease he will fling the link over the opposite coupling hook at the split second that the buffers of both wagons strike and are compressed back on to their stocks. A scene as old as the railway. (British Rail)

The goods guard, another unsung hero of the railway. Riding in his 'Toad', he kept a sharp look-out for hot axle bearings and breakaway wagons - the three-link couplings could snap if they got a sharp tug. All through the long night haul he remained alert to the ups and downs of the road and the signals, and used his hand-brake (his fingers are resting on it) to retard his heavy van and thus keep the couplings drawn out. Just below his hand is the lid of a sand box and the lever he would operate to put sand on the rails to assist his brake. He maintained a log of the run and performed shunting along the way. His was a lonely, responsible and sometimes dangerous job performed under any conditions of weather day or night. November 1940. (British Rail)

The passenger guard's job was altogether more pleasant but no less responsible, with the added problem of dealing with the public. Giving 'Right away' at Paddington, July 1940. (British Rail)

and 'thirties, would say, when commenting on the poor pay, 'but at least the job was fairly secure and that was worth something'.

GWR footplate crew wages remained static from 1879 until 1911, while other GWR wages rose and fell during that period. Food prices, however, rose 20 per cent in the same period. Hours of work remained about the same, at 10 to 15 a day, and there were many bones of contention between the staff and the Directors, one being the refusal of the Company to recognise any trade union.

In the summer of 1911 there was the threat of a national railway strike and the GWR Directors tried to head it off by granting an extra 6d a day to their engine crews and small rises to the other staff. When the strike began on 17 August 1911, support for it amongst GWR men was far from complete.

David Lloyd George, for the Government, stated that 'the railways will be protected at whatever cost. The whole food supply of the community, its very way of life, depends on the railway service.' Soldiers, each carrying a loaded rifle, its bayonet fixed for instant use, patrolled the tracks and guarded signal boxes. Cavalry faced picket lines at stations. The strike ended on 19 August without the railwaymen - on whom the very way of life of the whole community depended - being given any improvement in *their* way of life.

In September 1915 wartime hyper-inflation forced the Government, which was then in charge of the railways, to grant the first of several increases. Prior to August 1919 promotion for footplatemen on the GWR, and the LNWR, was rigidly by seniority. A cleaner passed his examination on the engine and the Rule Book and was then placed at the bottom of a list of about 2,850 firemen, Class 3 to Class 1. The aspiring engine driver gradually rose to the top of the list of Class 3 firemen, as the Class 2 men moved into Class 1, and as the Class 1 men moved up to become Class 3 enginemen, and so on. Each man was obliged to take his promotion as it arose, no matter where the vacancy occurred. The system was called 'Classification' and it meant that a man did not get a pay rise until he stepped up into the next grade, a step which might take many years.

A better system was adopted by the Midland, Great Central, South Eastern & Chatham and Great Northern railways amongst others. Footplatemen on these railways got their pay rises up to the top limit automatically. On the Midland Railway there were no 'passenger' or 'goods' grades of enginemen - fire-

man received the full rate after three years, while drivers went on to full pay after four years.

The GWR/LNWR 'Classification' system obliged the promoted man to remove himself and his family to wherever the vacancy happened to arise - anywhere between Paddington, Penzance, Birkenhead and Fishguard! If a young fireman or young driver refused to accept a move, he had the choice of becoming a shed labourer - provided that a vacancy existed for one - or leave the service.

An older driver, one who was required to move up from Class 2 to Class 1, who refused to move for some weighty family reason was sometimes allowed to stay where he was provided that he undertook formally to forfeit all future wage rises. But this agreement was only binding on the man - not the Company. It sometimes happened that a man would be ordered to move to another shed and uproot his family after the Company had agreed to him staying put.

On the GWR prior to 1919, the Company, paternalistic though it was, still retained the right to have complete control over the lives of its 'servants', and naturally many men found this aspect irksome and wanted it changed. 'Classification' really was a silly, dictatorial system because all over the GWR system there were uprooted men trying to get home by a system of 'mutual swaps' - and this was permitted so long as, in the first instance, you moved at the Company's command.

In 1914 the locomotivemen's union, ASLEF, won the right to an eight-hour day for locomotivemen, but agreed to its suspension for the duration of the war on condition that it would be reinstated when the war was over. The Great War finished on 11 November 1918 and the next day ASLEF went to No 10 Downing Street to ask that the eight-hour day be introduced immediately. The men had worked terribly long hours, frequently hungry, sleeping rough, away from home for days at a time, and their efforts had been acknowledged as vital to the outcome of the war. Yet it was only after a great deal of huffing and puffing that the Government agreed to give back to the men rights which their union had loyally and patriotically abandoned in 1914.

From 22 March 1919 the working day for all railwaymen was reduced to 8 hours without any reduction in wages. The reservation of one engine to one or two drivers belonged to the era of the 10/12-hour day, and could less easily be operated on a three-shift, eight-hour day, although it was still 'the

The residue of clinker and stone from tons of coal burned over a long journey had to be shovelled out through the narrow fire-hole by a labourer using, relatively speaking, a tea-spoon on the end of a 12-foot-long iron handle. It was tedious, laborious and slow - but it was a steady job for all that. 29 June 1934. (British Rail)

done thing' to consider an engine as 'belonging' to a certain driver or pair of drivers.

The 'Classification' system was abolished in August 1919 when ASLEF negotiated standard rates of pay (see Appendix 7) for all British locomen; the rises were to be paid when a certain length of service was achieved. ASLEF also asked for - and was given - a nightwork rate of 'time and a quarter', Sunday work and nightshift overtime at 'time and a half', 12 hours rest between shifts if possible, and never less than nine hours. The problem of the drivers' and firemen's eyesight tests remained. These varied from company to company, many of them were decidedly eccentric and a common system was required.

The National Union of Railwaymen (NUR) followed ASLEF with a request for standard rates of pay for all its members with a minimum of 51 shillings (£2 11s) for a guaranteed 40-hour week. At this time the railway companies' working expenses were double what they had been in 1913 and wage

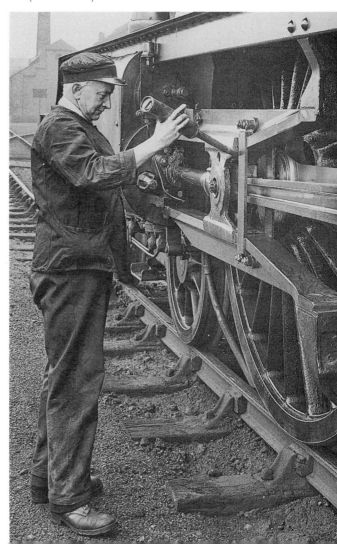

Oiling round No 5020 at Old Oak Common shed. The driver uses his 'long-feeder' oil can with the air of an artist. What cannot be photographed are his contortions to oil the inside valve-gear and big-ends. He must get between the driving wheels at the firebox end and lie on top of a big-end to reach some oil-pots. Movement of the engine at this stage could result in the big-end ripping open the driver's stomach. Hence the use of 'Not to be moved' signs at each end of the engine. 29 June 1934. (British Rail)

costs had trebled; the cost of locomotive coal in 1919 was 30 shillings a ton compared with 13 shillings a ton in 1913. Steel tyres for locomotive wheels, which had cost £10 in 1913, cost £40 in 1919. The Government refused to agree to the NUR's requests and a strike was called to start at midnight on 26/27 September 1919. ASLEF came out in support.

Ninety-three per cent of the GWR's Traffic Department struck work and 65 per cent of the locomotivemen. The Company appealed to their retired staff to volunteer to run the railway and volunteers arrived in sufficient numbers to run an emergency train service. On 4 October over 600 trains were run and on 5 October the strike was called off, but with certain gains to the men. These included: standard rates of pay, nationwide, for each grade; no adult railwayman to receive less than 51 shillings a week for a guaranteed week of 40 hours so long as the cost of living remained 110 per cent higher than in 1913; and a conference to set new wage rates.

The basic wages of railwaymen had been augmented by a 'Cost of Living' allowance, introduced during the Great War, to enable the men to buy food as prices rose; in 1920 the cost of living was deemed to be 120 per cent higher than that of 1913, the last full year of normality. This was an *allowance* (of dubious calculation), not a wage, and was reduced as the Government's 'Cost of Living' index fell.

Signalmen's wages during the period of this history were governed by a system of classification agreed on 20 March 1919. This listed every possible operation which a signalman could carry out and each operation was awarded a number of 'marks'. For instance:

	Mark
Push or pull a lever	1
Open or close gate	5
Bell signals for a through train	6
Telephone message received or sent	3

. . .and so on. A signal box was assessed by making a minute record, over 24 hours, of every action the signalmen made in connection with signalling trains. The total of 'marks' was added up and multiplied by the number of trains passing the box on the day of the census, then this figure was divided by the average number of trains passing the box over the preceding 24 days.

Master of all he surveys - the signalman at Wells East Somerset Box poses for the camera in 1935.(Dr Ian Scrimgeour)

The 'Class' of a box was then established from this table:

Marks	Class wages	Standard allowance	'Cost of Living' (sliding scale*)
375 and over	Special	£3 15s	4s 0d
300-374	1	£3 10s	4s 6d
225-299	2	£3 5s	6s 0d
150-224	3	£3 0s	8s 0d
75-149	4	£2 15s	10s 0d
30-74	5	£2 10s	12s 0d
1-29	6†	£2 6s	14s 0d

* Reduced as 'Cost of Living' index fell
† Class 6 was merged into Class 5 in 1939

The 'marks' system was an attempt to reach a fair assessment of the work performed in a signal box, but there many arguments - after the survey - as to whether a certain box should have been in a higher grade. 'Trust you to take the marks on a quiet day' was a favourite grumble, and signalmen at level crossing boxes sometimes took extraordinary measures, involving the co-operation of the public, to increase their marks.

These basic wages for signalmen (relief signalmen were paid slightly more) were established provisionally on 20 March 1920 and confirmed in May 1922. The wages were then not increased for almost 20 years. On the contrary, the reducing price of food, according to the Cost of Living index, reduced the Cost of Living allowance to zero; moreover, reductions were actually made to the standard rate of pay.

After the Grouping of 1923, with the railway companies back in private ownership, wages and working conditions were negotiated by the unions and companies through the National Wages Board (NWB), set up under the 1921 Railways Act. From the outset and until 1936 the companies pressed for a reduction in wages and for the NWB's decisions to be made binding. When this latter seemed likely to become the case, ASLEF went on strike. The strike lasted from 20 to 29 January 1924; the NUR did not join it, but ASLEF won the point in any case.

The Great Western's wages bill was more than trebled by the coming of the eight-hour day. In answer to this the Company did not close down miles of track, nor make thousands of men redundant. Instead the Directors looked for more traffic and tried to reduce expenditure by reducing wages directly and indirectly by losing a few hours out of a job here and there. It was a tinkering, 'good housekeeping' operation, making the servants run the very old-fashioned house as efficiently as possible.

What the Directors did *not* do was reform the management system. They preferred to lose their brilliant General Manager rather than save money - and earn more money - by taking his advice and modernise from the top downwards to make the railway more efficient.

Some signal boxes were closed, and more were equipped with the 'block switch' so that they could be taken out of circuit at slack periods to save wages. Branch-line engine sheds were closed and Station Masters at small stations were made redundant and their stations brought under the control of a larger one.

If any staff were made redundant during the 'twenties, they seem to have been taken on elsewhere because throughout that decade the number of people employed on the GWR rose to a record of 110,729 by 1930. The greatest redundancies came about in the 1930s - in March 1932 103,839 people were employed by the GWR, by March 1935 the total was 98,500, but thereafter the numbers increased, reaching 100,600 in 1937.

In 1927 the GWR's gross income was £31,460,000, but wages for that year were approaching £22 million and all other costs were rising - hence the call for a cut in wages and a reduction of staff as part of the drive for economy. On 29 July 1932 300 top-link engine drivers aged 60-65 were asked to retire as from 27 August and take their pension from the 'Enginemen's and Firemen's Mutual Assurance Society' (MAS). This Society had been founded in 1856 by Great Western footplatemen and was placed on a sound footing in 1865 by Driver Henry Kirtley, later Locomotive Superintendent at Paddington. The Company supported the Society and donated annual lump sums starting with £500 in 1865 to head off a wage demand. Membership of the Society bound the men more closely to the Company since if they resigned they lost their subscriptions.

The men retiring early received their lump sum payment of £40 from the MAS fund and their weekly pension of £1 2s 6d. The latter was augmented by an extra 10 shillings - 5 from the Society and 5 from the GWR - until the man reached 65. The Company reckoned that, over five years, they made a nett saving in wages of £107,000. The GWR was the only railway to lay off its top drivers; other companies laid off cleaners and down-graded the higher-graded men. Whilst to the men involved the money-saving measures doubtless seemed petty, taken overall the Company saved large sums of

The No 3 (wooden) platform of Paddington station at about 10.50 am on 21 August 1926. In spite of what must have been at the very least 'a warm day', the stalwart GWR employee - Platform Foreman or Train Guard - retains his dignity by not divesting himself of his heavy top coat. But then, several of the passengers are also wearing hats, coats and fur collars! (British Rail)

money which helped to keep it in business and therefore safeguarded the jobs of the majority of the staff.

In 1915 a very large engine shed to serve Newport (Mon) was built on green fields well to the west of the town. It was called Newport, Ebbw Junction and at that time it was well away from housing. The shed replaced the old GWR shed at Newport High Street shed and to some extent the Alexandra Docks Railway shed at Pill, or Dock Street as the locals called it.

Railwaymen had a long trek to get to Ebbw Junction shed, so a free bus and tram service was introduced to get the men to work and an agreement was made whereby enginemen transferred to Ebbw Junction from High Street or Dock Street sheds could book off duty at those places and be paid a walking time allowance to their homes. These arrangements were terminated in May 1930 as an economy measure,helping to save £99,945 that year.

Whilst this unburdened the Company it trans-

ferred the burden to the fragile economies of hundreds of enginemen and shed workers. Furious protests from the men resulted in the Company paying compensation totalling £1,070 to 396 workmen and providing a shed for their bicycles at a cost of £80. The Company also agreed to continue to run staff trains between Newport station and the shed, but insisted that the men would have to pay workmen's fare for their tickets.

The annual total income of the GWR in 1928 was £35,527,000, half a million less than 1927, while total expenses were £29,408,000, £588,000 more than 1927. The economies which had been made were not enough to keep pace with rising costs and falling revenue, and in August 1928 the Directors and top Officers volunteered to take a 5 per cent cut in their fees and salaries, while the rest agreed to a pay reduction of 2½ per cent. The savings in Directors' fees was £180,590 in 1929 and £171,000 in 1930 if the GWR balance sheet is to be believed. This two-sided voluntary agreement lasted until 12 November 1930, at which point the

GWR asked the National Wages Board to make the reduction 'official'. The reduction in Directors' fees was *not* included in this.

On 17 February 1931, after 17 days of deliberation, the NWB approved – and made obligatory from 1 March – the hitherto voluntary 2½ per cent cut in railwaymen's wages provided that this did not reduce the wage below 41 shillings per week and that not more than 6 shillings was deducted. Overtime rates were cut from 'time and a quarter' to 'time and one-eighth', Sunday pay was cut from 'time and a half' to 'time and one-third' and, where 'double time' was allowed, this was cut to 'time and two-thirds'. However, the NWB also raised the minimum pay for a driver from 84 to 90 shillings (£4 4s to £4 10s) a week, and engine cleaners aged 20 earning 42 shillings a week were to receive 48 shillings a week when they reached 22 years of age. These arrangements saved the GWR £667,000 in a full year.

The railway police were not subject to these cuts at first, but their wages too were reduced as from 18 March, saving the Company a further £2,300 per annum.

In November 1931 the companies asked for a 10 per cent reduction in wages. The NWB was evenly split on this – those members drawn from business agreed, those from the unions were against, while the Chairman, Sir Harold Morris, was in favour of a reduction of less than 10 per cent which would still have saved the companies £800,000. However, the companies wanted the full reduction, so no agreement could be reached and no further pay cuts were made. The resentment caused by the 2½ per cent cut was so strong that some old-hand railwaymen were still swearing about it 30 years later.

The railwaymen were not alone in having their wages cut at this time, but they were the last people to have the cuts restored and for the next six years the railway trade unions and the Company argued and haggled and threatened. In 1934 the trade unions threatened to strike, so the GWR agreed to restore wages as follows:

Basic weekly wage	Deductions
40s 6d (£2 0s 6d)	None
42s 6d	6d
44s	9d
44s 6d	1s

However, this only applied to the 'main' railway grades – footplate crews, shed staff, porters, signalmen, guards and shunters. Shopmen were suffering a 4 per cent wage cut and restaurant car staff had yet another sort of wage cut.

On 5 July 1937 the overtime rate of 'time and a quarter' was restored together with the pre-1930 rates of pay to all staff whose basic weekly wage did not exceed 44s 6d a week.

Thus from that date most railwaymen and women received pay rises to restore their wages to the levels of 1928! Of course the purchasing power of those shillings in 1937 was much less than it was in 1928, so the railway people were still not paid as well as they had been nine years earlier.

In July 1939 the minimum wage for adults was increased to 45 shillings per week, but no other concessions were given and the unions once more threatened strike action. Negotiations resumed, but then war broke out and the unions, reluctant to take advantage of the 'National Emergency', settled for what the railway companies felt they could afford to give. Engine drivers' pay was then 13 shillings a day and 'passed firemen' with 10 years service got 12 shillings. Firemen not passed for driving received 10s 6d per day.

It is worth noting here, however, that the GWR's nett income for its last full year of peacetime operation, 1938, was £1,842,820 less than 1937. The dividend for Ordinary shareholders in 1938 was 3 per cent. So while the railwaymen were not well rewarded for their loyal and skilful work, neither did the shareholders reap more than a very modest income.

24
The General Strike, 1926

For the old-hand railwaymen I once knew and who are now all passed away, the 'Great Strike' was a matter of enormous importance. Forty years later it was part of their legend; they often talked to me about it, and they would want me to explain it here as they, who took part in it as working people, saw it.

The atmosphere of the 1919-26 period for working men has to be understood. Several of my old friends had fought in the trenches in the Great War. One, Sid Tyler, the gentlest man I knew, said to me once, with great seriousness, 'I was bayoneting Germans before my 16th birthday'. He had joined up aged 14 in August 1914, out of pity for his father's heavy burden; his mother had died and left his father with a large family to look after and a daily job of work to attend to.

After the war thousands of ex-soldiers were angry

Some of the staff at Challow in about 1924, representative of the old-hand railwayman who recounted their memories of the 'Great Strike' to the author. From the left: two platelayers, 'Duchess', Tom Gillman, Harry Strong, Bert Reynolds, the Booking Clerk, and Station Master Achibald Drew. (Adrian Vaughan Collection)

and disillusioned – by what they had seen, by what they had been obliged to do, and by the sheer incompetence of those in charge. They had had enough of the old order, enough of the ruling classes, and they were not going to go back to the old days of 'forelock pulling' – these were the stated feelings of the men I worked with, men I knew to be mild and gentle people.

In Russia the Bolshevik V. I. Lenin had seen the war-weariness of the people and promised them peace and a new beginning. The Tsar and 'all existing social and economic conditions' were overthrown in order to build a new and fair society. The revolution began in October 1917 and after a civil war was complete in 1921. The question of the need for a change in Russia was drowned in an ocean of blood.

The British Unions seemed to speak a language similar to that of Lenin. There was an unprecedented political militancy amongst millions of British workers who also wanted a change after the horrors of the Great War. And there was, in some quarters, a great fear of revolution in Britain.

In January 1919 the coal-miners of Britain, still under Government control, voted overwhelmingly for a strike over pay and hours. The Prime Minister Lloyd George appointed Lord Sankey as Chairman of a Commission, composed 50/50 of mine-owners and members of the National Union of Mineworkers (NUM), to look into the grievances. Sankey recommended nationalisation, shorter hours and better pay for the miners. Of course the owners disagreed, but Lord Sankey's casting vote was for the miners. But this majority of one was not enough for Lloyd George, and the great 'Man of the People' ignored the inconvenient report.

The miners seethed and finally went on strike for the implementation of the Sankey Report in September 1920. After a three-week strike, which threatened to include the railwaymen, the miners secured a pay rise. It was the threat of this joint action of railwaymen and miners which spurred the Government to introduce the 'Emergency Powers Act' giving it powers in any future strike to declare a 'state of emergency' and rule by decree.

In 1921 the mines were handed back by the Government to their owners, whereupon the miners went on strike to force the full implementation of Sankey Report. The NUM tried to get the railway unions to back them, but when the strike began on 15 April the miners found themselves alone. Other union leaders, fearful of where concerted action

might lead, would also not give their support. So much for the Establishment's fears of 'Bolshevik' union leaders.

Coal was imported, the strike was broken and the miners were forced to return to work for lower wages. Forty years later, old-hand rural railwaymen recalled the breaking of this strike and spoke of 'betrayal' and of 'Black Friday'. They told me that it was their feeling of shame for the way the miners had been treated which led them to support the miners when next they got the chance, in 1926.

In 1924 British miners felt strong enough to threaten a strike for the Sankey Report to be implemented. Their famous slogan was 'Not a penny off the day – not a second on the day'. The newly elected Labour Government of Ramsay MacDonald replied by subsidising the poor wages paid by the employers and by appointing Lord Samuel to look into the problems. MacDonald must have known the outcome before Samuel completed his 'Inquiry' because while his Lordship was thus engaged, this Labour Government was preparing for a fight with the miners – their staunchest supporters! Coal stocks were built up and emergency plans for transport were organised. However, neither the miners nor the dreaded Bolshevik trade union movement as a whole made any preparations for a fight. In November 1924 Macdonald and his Labour Government were replaced by the Tories under Stanley Baldwin, who of course continued the preparations for a show-down.

Early in 1926 Samuel recommended the nationalisation of the mines – one day – but in the meantime recommended that the miners' wages be *reduced* by the removal of the Government subsidy. This report was, needless to say, at once accepted by the Government, whereupon the miners struck work. The TUC was very reluctant to call a General Strike, for fear of where it might lead. However, some workers were going on strike in any case – not for their own gain but in support of the much-maligned miners – so the TUC had no choice but to follow their members' example and declare a 'General Strike'.

The General Strike was the battle which had been so fearfully expected ever since 1917. 'Red Revolution' was supposedly waiting behind the Strike. The Conservative Government, the man who had endorsed the Samuel Report, the 'Socialist' Ramsay Macdonald and a large part of the British populace took fright.

No effort was made to improve the miserable

wages and the terrible working conditions of the miners, which would have resolved the problem and removed the supposed threat of Revolution; instead the injustices were left to fester while the Government invoked its Emergency Powers Act and made tremendous efforts to break the strike, including the operation of the railways with a skeleton staff of volunteers.

The NUR gave the Great Western Company 24 hours notice, on 2 May 1926, of their intention to call out their members on strike. At once Sir Felix Pole issued the following notice:

To the Great Western men
Whom Do You Serve?

Each Great Western man has to decide his course of action but I appeal to you all to hesitate before you break your contract of service with the old Company, before you inflict grave injury on the railway industry and before you arouse ill feeling in the railway service which will take years to remove.

The railway companies have demonstrated that they can settle their differences by direct negotiation. The mining industry should be advised to do the same. Remember that your means of livelihood are involved and that Great Western men are trusted to be loyal to their conditions of service in the same manner as they [the men] expect the Company to carry out their obligations.

When the strike began, at midnight on 3/4 May, it was joined by 98.8 per cent of GWR drivers, 99.5 per cent of firemen and 92.2 per cent of signalmen. Sir Felix Pole was thoroughly astonished by the response. The only comfort he could find was that the numbers of GWR locomen joining the strike was less than that on the LMS, where footplate support for the stoppage was all but total.

The Great Western activated the contingency plans worked out for earlier strikes. Railway clerical staff who had already taken and passed the signalling examination volunteered, as well as some Station Masters and District Inspectors. Temporary staff were recruited to be porters, operate signal boxes, drive and fire locomotives, look after horses and generally run the railway.

Earls, Lords, medical students and undergraduates, engineers, retired railwaymen, railwaymen previously dismissed for theft, all were recruited, 'trained' and put to work. There was absolutely no shortage of volunteers for the 'plum' jobs on locomotives or in signal boxes, but no-one - absolutely no-one - volunteered to go down the mines and hew coal.

By noon of the first day of the strike, the 4th, 60 young men, mainly university students, were sitting in the GWR's signalling school at Royal Oak listening to a lecture on the rules; on the 6th they were all at work in boxes in the London area. The Company was very proud of the way it trained people to be signalmen or drivers and made the ridiculous boast that 'fully qualified' signalmen had been produced in two days.

Felix Pole's alarm over the near totality of GWR staff going on strike in support of much-maligned fellow workers caused him to lose his sense of fair play. Volunteers recruited from outside the railway were asked to fill in a questionnaire which included one question which was deliberately and cunningly misleading: 'Are you interested in the possibility of full-time employment?'

This encouraged many people - including an ex-driver from Westbury (Wilts) who had been sacked for theft - to believe that if they volunteered for work they would be offered full-time employment. None of these people could have known that Pole had, simultaneously with the issue of the questionnaire, privately ordered that 'no volunteers are to be kept on after the emergency.'

Pole also published in the national press and broadcast on the radio a tolerably hysterical speech, the subject of which was the 'victimisation' of and the 'conspiracy' against Britain by the trade unions - as if working people were not British. He said:

'The Trade Union invariably asks that there should be "no victimisation" at the end of a strike. The present strike differs from previous strikes in that it is not associated with any dispute with the GWR - the victim is the Great Western - indeed the whole country is being victimised by a strike which is the blackest spot in the history of labour in this country.'

When one considers the disgraceful living and working conditions of all miners - and their wives and children - which had existed without improvement for 50 years, it might be thought that it was this appalling situation which was the blackest spot in the life of a so-called civilised country.

Pole's broadcast continued, full of outraged blimpishness:

'That thousands of men with no grievance against their employer should have been "instructed" to leave work and that so many of them should have done so passes all comprehension.'

Having wilfully blinded himself to the humanitarian reasons of his workforce, he could only take refuge in the 'conspiracy' theory, that fantasy so beloved of the comfortable, which covers all eventualities but fits no facts:

'It can only be explained as a deep conspiracy against the State. Thank God such a conspiracy cannot succeed and can only result in the discrediting of its promoters and the disillusionment of those who have been used as pawns in the game.'

On the 10th Pole issued another notice, as unpleasant as that which he had issued on 6th. This new notice *invited* all railwaymen whose 'ordinary work has ceased or *is not of direct value to the conduct of the Company's business* during the present emergency' to *volunteer* for work which was of *actual value* in running trains.

Though couched in terms of 'invitation' and 'volunteering', this was actually a test of loyalty, a trap along the lines of 'Whom do you serve?'. Those men and women who had remained at work during the strike doing their own job, clerks in goods stations for instance, were, by this notice, deemed to have *joined the strike* if they refused to assist in breaking the strike by going out as train guards or signalmen. Individual conscience had no place on the GWR at that time, Pole had become a dictator and those who wanted to keep their jobs did what they were told - and some were punished with dismissal. Those that were sacked were reinstated weeks or even months later, but they never received the wages they had lost due to Pole's cruel edict.

As each day of the strike passed, more Great Western signalmen returned to work until, on the last day, 12 May, 12 per cent of the total were working. A few GWR locomotive crews also returned to work before the strike was called off - 152 drivers and 94 firemen, 2.5 and 1.5 per cent respectively of the total - but on the LMS not only did all locomen stay out to the very end, but there were also fewer LMS signalmen at work on 12th than on the 4th.

The success of the GWR in running trains with volunteers and non-striking railwaymen is shown here:

Passenger, Milk and Perishable trains

24 hours ended 9 pm	No of trains	% of normal mileage
5 May	194	7.05
14 May	1,245	27.24

On the last day of the General Strike, 12 May (the miners remained on strike until Christmas and beyond), there were 288 volunteer drivers and 473 volunteer firemen working on the GWR.

Special attention was given to conveying milk to London. Each day between 3,000 and 10,000 full churns were delivered to Paddington, Ealing or Kensington, and the Government and the United Dairies Co thanked the GWR for the efforts that were made. On the other hand, the flow of freight through the system was suddenly stopped, leaving, for instance, 62,000 privately owned coal tubs, both loaded and empty, stabled in goods loops, refuge sidings, cattle dock sidings and blocking sidings in marshalling yards. These and all the other stranded wagons caused untold problems for the movement of freight for months after the strike was over.

There were a certain number of accidents due to the inexperience of the volunteers, including derailments at Swansea High Street, Plymouth, Ealing and Old Oak Common, amongst other places, and several buffer-stop collisions, including one at Oswestry. There were also incidents of burned fireboxes and otherwise damaged boilers. This being the case it is difficult to believe the GWR claim that 'no passengers were injured' on their trains during the strike.

Quite a number of volunteers complained of injuries received, so they said, as a result of their railway work. In July 1926 one S. G. Huband was awarded £6 by the GWR for lumbago which he claimed was the result of his working as a volunteer fireman. Another volunteer, Mr Salt, was given £5 for injuries received when his volunteer driver failed to stop at the buffers in the bay platform at Oswestry. Miss Auslia, who said she had hurt her back whilst working in the Mint stables at Paddington, was given 5 guineas. It is remarkable fact that many of the injuries claimed were of an invisible nature.

There was minor malicious damage done to GWR track during the strike - rail-keys removed, rocks placed on rails, fencing stolen for firewood. A permanent way department trolley was stolen at Taff Bargoed and used to carry coal hacked from an outcrop on the lineside. A GWR platelayer, one G. W. Farnham, was convicted at Plymouth of damaging a bus whilst swearing at the blackleg driver. He was sentenced to 6 weeks hard labour and dismissed from the GWR. Another platelayer, H. Keylock, waylaid Signalman Tyler on his way to Bridgend West box and prevented him from going on. Keylock was given the option of a £5 fine or 14 days hard labour, and then received double punishment as he was also sacked from the GWR.

In Swindon, Reading, Cardiff, Swansea and many other towns there was intense excitement, and feelings of hatred towards non-strikers boiled over. Criminal damage was inflicted on the property of men who worked during the strike; gateways were filled up with barbed wire, front doors were daubed with paint or tar and windows were broken. In Swansea the General Secretary of the Strike Committee, William Dupree, was, amongst others, convicted of intimidation and was dismissed. His dismissal was upheld by the National Wages Board and he himself said that his actions and those of the Strike Committee were 'foolish, unwarranted and without justification'.

The strike was called off 'unconditionally' by the TUC. The workmen took this to mean 'no conditions on either side', but the employers took it to mean 'unconditional surrender' by the unions, which indeed was the case. The Government, thankful to be over the worst, begged the railway companies to 'act cannily' and not punish their men in case this should lead to another strike. Emotions ran as high after the strike as during it and, indeed, I know that some men kept up their feud with 'blacklegs' for the rest of their lives.

The Great Western's policy on taking back their striking workforce was that men returning to work during the strike were at once taken on 'provided that their services can be utilised in any capacity', but 'no man who has played a leading part in the strike nor any striking Supervisor is to be allowed to return without the express instructions of this office'. Returning railwaymen signed this statement: 'You are hereby re-employed on the understanding that you are not relieved of the consequences of having broken your contract of service with the Company'.

Work was short because traffic was disrupted and the unions agreed to the suspension of the guaranteed week so that men could at least work two or three days. The GWR agreed to do this from the 31st, 'in such a way as will not harm the Company and not to be applicable to men who did not join the strike'. So those who had joined the strike would be employed on a 'casual' basis whilst those who had worked during the strike got a full week's pay even if they did not work a full six days. This increased the bitter feelings between striking and 'blackleg' railwaymen; the guarantee of a full week's pay was not restored to all staff until 11 April 1927.

The men saw all these various punitive actions of the Company as 'intimidation'. As far as they were concerned, the country had been crying out for its goods and passengers to be moved for the previous nine days, yet here was the GWR saying that there was insufficient work on offer to warrant immediate re-employment of all its staff. The popular view amongst the men was that favourites were taken back first and others were punished by being left out. The GWR case was that the 'Great Strike' had severely disrupted the country's trade - there was, for instance, a severe coal shortage owing to the continuing strike of the miners - and a 50 per cent train service until 12 July was all that was necessary (or possible given the coal shortage) to cater for the traffic.

At Oxford there were some railwaymen whom the Company refused to re-employ. Oxford's railwaymen, meeting in the Labour Party-funded Ruskin College - which had been the headquarters of the Oxford Strike Committee - resolved and informed the GWR that they would all 'work to rule' until the erstwhile strikers were reinstated. The Company replied that anyone 'going slow' would be sacked. The men gave in and the others remained dismissed. Because Ruskin College had been used as the headquarters of the Oxford Strike Committee, the Company announced that it would no longer permit any member of its staff to attend courses there or any other 'Labour' college.

When the 1926 garden-party-giving season began, the Lord Mayor of London and the Mayors and Lord Mayors of other cities invited groups of working people who had not joined the strike to go to the Town Hall or Mansion House for a municipal tea and tour around the Corporation's treasures. On 29 June the Lord Mayor of London invited 1,500 'loyal' workers, including 150 Great Western men.

At Oxford the invitation for '12 loyal workers' came to the Station Master's office. That gentleman handed it on to his clerk, who gave it to the leader of the Strike Committee, who invited himself and five of his colleagues on the Committee, one of them being my friend the late Driver Albert King, who told me the tale. Albert and his colleagues enjoyed their tour of the City plate and the meal which followed and they all managed to keep straight faces as His Worship thanked them for their 'loyalty'.

This 'loyal' and 'disloyal' label really hurt Albert and all railwaymen. As they saw it, in August 1914 they had peacefully given up their newly won eight-hour day in the interests of the nation's war effort. Later Albert, amongst 25,479 other Great Western employees, had *volunteered* for military service. Aged 18 he joined the Oxford & Buckinghamshire Light Infantry and had risked his life for his country in Flanders trenches, which is more than the Mayor – with all his talk of 'loyalty' – had done. Those were Albert's feelings, typical of thousands of railwaymen.

That year of 1926 was a disastrous year for the GWR, and, indeed, for the striking miners, who were starved into submission and went back to work for less wages than at the start of the strike. But before this happened the whole country was running short of coal which gave rise to a certain panic in the Baldwin Government. On 27 September 1926 the General Managers of the four railway companies were informed that they were to reduce their coal consumption by 25,000 tons a week – a 12½ per cent reduction – so that coal could be diverted to households and public utilities!

The railway managers pointed out that with insufficient supplies of coal, the railways would be unable to carry coal from the pits to the homes and factories, whilst the weekly saving of 25,000 tons of coal, spread around the country, would not keep many home fires and factory furnaces burning.

In reply to this common sense, the Ministry of Transport became pompous and threatened to commandeer the companies' stocks of coal as a national strategic reserve and dole it out to such causes as the civil servants thought deserving. One wonders what had happened to Lloyd George's idea of the railways being vital to the very existence of Britain, for with insufficient fuel the railways' capability to serve the nation would be reduced.

The companies offered to hire extra wagons – at Government expense – which would be filled with coal and would be stored on sidings – for which the Government would pay rent – to form a strategic reserve. This would cause overcrowding in marshalling yards but at least the railways would have all the fuel they needed in order to carry the country's traffic. The Government agreed and thousands of tons of coal were stored in this way.

The silly sequel to this silly story is that exactly one month after trying to confiscate the railways' stocks of coal and thus reduce railway services, the Government 'intimated' that they, the railway companies, should not make any cuts in their train services!

25

Great Western paternalism

In 1921 no fewer than 110,000 people were employed on the GWR (see Appendix 8), and in the eight weeks ending 17 July 19 people were dismissed: four for theft, three for being 'AWOL', two each for drunkenness, stealing fares, unsatisfactory conduct, indecent behaviour and continual lateness, one for Privilege Ticket irregularities, and one for travelling without a ticket.

In the next two months 25 people were dismissed: eight for theft, eight for unsatisfactory conduct, five for being 'AWOL', two for drunkenness, one for misconduct and one for misuse of GWR property. ('General Manager's Fortnightly Report to Board of Directors', PRO: RAIL 250)

The reasons for dismissal remained the same throughout the period, and those listed above include most of the usual categories. 'Theft' was perhaps the most common and men were sacked for stealing literally a paper-bag full of coal or half a dozen eggs. The GWR Staff Magazine stated in 1923 that incidents of theft by GWR staff from wagons and elsewhere in 1922 were 'much greater than before 1914' and that 'men of previously high standing such as guards and drivers were being sent to prison.'

During 1923 instances of dismissal began to decline. Thirteen were sacked in October, after which the monthly dismissals never again reached double figures. Up to 1930 eight dismissals a month was about the average and thereafter, until 1939, the monthly average dropped to about six, the population of the GWR declining from 110,000 to 95,000 during the same period.

On 24 November 1927 Station Master F. B. Pugh of Cleobury Mortimer, seeing the auditors arriving at his station, was seized by a fit of sheer panic and committed suicide by jumping in front of a goods train which was entering the station at that moment. It was then discovered that £2,068 was missing from the accounts, money which had been embezzled by Pugh 'in a most ingenious way'. The Coroner's jury returned a verdict of 'Suicide during temporary insanity'.

In 1929 there were some serious embezzlements by staff. The reports do not usually mention amounts, but the loss of £184 at Waterford and £426 at Birkenhead Goods Depot were singled out for mention as if these sums were unusually large. Theft or embezzlement and ticket irregularities, which amounted to theft, if discovered always resulted in dismissal.

Very occasionally there was the more exotic cause – 'Criminal conviction in Police Court', 'Immoral conduct', 'Behaviour offensive to a lady', 'Indecent assault', and 'Attempting to assault the Station Master and refusing to accept transfer to another station' (which suggests that the attempted assault would have been overlooked if the man had subsequently agreed to a transfer).

In 1934 a new reason for dismissal entered the scene – 'driving the Company's motor car without permission'. Perhaps some canvasser had used his Company car for a family trip to the seaside.

Every month around 100,000 GWR employees were either not caught or managed to keep their hands out of the till, in spite of the hardship they suffered from low wages. Tube cleaner Hodges at Bristol Bath Road engine shed found £7 lying on the ground and went to much trouble to discover the owner. He also found £3 in his coat pocket, placed there by mistake, and again went to a lot of trouble to discover the rightful owner. In appreciation of his honesty he was presented with a 400-day clock by his mates.

It would appear that the Great Western Railway was by no means as overbearing and bureaucratic an organisation as is present-day British Rail (the General Strike period excepted). For instance, GWR employees were not gagged - they were not forced to sign a statement binding them to secrecy with regard to all railway matters as present-day BR employees must do. They were not pestered with psychiatrists after passing a signal at 'Danger', neither were they harrassed by time-wasting and ridiculous regulations from a 'Health and Safety at Work' Executive. Provided that financial malpractice or indecency were not involved, it seems to be the case that the GWR had a gentlemanly interpretation of the Rules and Regulations.

The signalman at Ashley Hill Station box, Bristol, brought to work a dog called Jack, and he and his canine friend worked the box together from 1908 to 1921. The dog used to take the kettle in its mouth to the station for water, took telegrams from the signalman to the Station Master, and fetched the signalman's newspaper from the shop in the High Street. If it was necessary to hold a flag from the box window the dog did it, standing on his back legs, flag handle in his mouth. This might have been in contravention of Rule 65(a) of the Rule Book which forbade 'unauthorised persons' from interfering with the signalling, and of Rule 66 which obliged the signalman to keep his box private 'and not allow other than authorised persons to enter'. But not only was the dog tolerated by Station Master and District Inspectors, but also the rule-breaking was encouraged to the extent that photographs of the dog, flag in mouth and train passing, were sold to the public for the benefit of the Railway Orphans Fund. The signal dog, Jack, died in January 1921.

It was a matter of concern to the GWR that many of its employees lived in bad housing, and in 1922, after a Government shift of policy has prevented local authorities from building any more council houses, the Company felt themselves obliged to help. The subject was debated by a managerial Committee on 6 April 1922, who felt that the Company did not have the money to build or buy

Three reasons why the GWR worked as well as it did: superb engineering, highly skilled and experienced staff, and a commitment to 'the Job' in return for a secure future and a steady, if unexciting, wage. There was great comradeship and this 1921 pictures says it all. The gent in the trilby is said to be Fred Ward, Ranelagh Loco Yard foreman; the locomotive, Fawley Court, was an Old Oak Common engine at the time of this photograph, and so, almost certainly, are her crew. They are about to work a 'hard hitter' to South Wales. (Adrian Vaughan Collection)

houses for their staff except in special cases - remote locations for instance. But they made an agreement with building societies to assist GWR employees in borrowing money and building their own houses.

However, the Committee foresaw that this would not be beneficial to all members of staff because the rate of interest charged by the societies was relatively high, and in addition there were surveyors' and solicitors' costs. It was therefore further decided that the GWR would run very little risk if it was to advance to an employee 90 per cent of the survey-or's valuation of a house for periods not exceeding 20 years at 5 per cent, and charge only out-of-pocket expenses in connection with the legal work. The GWR Housing Committee noted that

'. . .other companies, particularly the North Eastern, have adopted schemes of this kind which have not only afforded tangible assistance to their men but also reduced the amount paid in removal allowance.'

It was especially recommended that such a scheme should be started at once, in Southall.

Signalmen Walt Thomas and Alf Joyce, stationed at Uffington, took advantage of this scheme, bought some land from the Craven Estate in Uffington and together built a fine semi-detached house. Walt Thomas's side was called 'Chepstow' and remained a signalman's (and ex-signalman's house) until the 1980s.

The workforce was insured against accidents at work by the National Insurance Act and by the Workman's Compensation Act, but the Company occasionally thought to go beyond the strict letter of the law where the law did not provide compensation for employees.

For example, Mrs Hamer, wife of sub-ganger Hamer, was the crossing-keeper at Cerist, Llandiloe. On 20 December 1923 she was at work and had her four-year-old nephew staying with her. She went out to see to the gates as a train was coming and the little boy wandered on to the line. At the very last moment Mrs Hamer saw the little lad between the rails with the train bearing down. She ran, dived to the boy with arms outstretched and had both arms amputated by the engine's wheels. The little boy was killed.

The GWR Directors awarded Mr Hamer an extra £1 a week for six months and this award was extended for a further six months 'as the man's difficulties have not decreased'. It was then decided that the award should stand for another six months and that after that the amount should be reduced annually to 15, 10 and 5 shillings, and at the end of that, the fourth year, terminated.

Mr Cox of Reading Signal & Telegraph Works, complained that his heart condition was brought on by his job. Medical evidence did not, however, support this, but having had his case put before them, the Directors took the view that 'in view of his straitened circumstances' they would pay him a pension of £1 per week.

On 15 August 1927 Driver A. Corbett of Banbury was crushed between buffers. £300 was paid to widow under the Workmen's Compensation Act, but then came an appeal to the GWR Directors from Corbett's son, 15 years 9 months old, who was apprenticed to a piano-tuner. His apprenticeship was due to end in December 1928 when he would earn 30 shillings per week. Meanwhile he needed subsistence money and asked for a lump sum. The GWR Directors, at their most paternalistic, saw the folly of giving a young lad a lump sum and instead agreed to pay him pocket money at £3 a month from September 1927 to December 1928. There are plenty of other such cases in the Company's records.

The Company was always ready with larger or smaller donations to assist the expenses of public events to which they might well be carrying passengers. For example, in July 1927 the Company donated 10 guineas to Plymouth Civic Week and 3 guineas to the Fishguard Bay Regatta. Besides this the Directors had for many years made it their practice each month to make donations to charitable causes and in particular schools and hospitals. In July 1927 they sent £50 to Montgomeryshire Hospital and £25 to St Stephen's School, Clewer. Often the list was much longer.

The GWR also made donations towards parochial Coronation festivities in 1937; villages as far apart as Appleford, North Bovey and Rogiet (for Severn Tunnel Junction) receiving £3-5 towards the cost of their celebrations.

There were many 'institutions' on the railway which added a little something to the friendly atmosphere - for instance, the official retirement presentation when the GWR gold watch was handed over by the Divisional Superintendent in his office, with other senior officers present (not a brief handshake by an official who could not be bothered to get out of the train on which he had arrived), followed by an unofficial restaurant dinner for the man and his wife paid for by the Superintendent.

Another institution was the Station Garden Competition, which had been going on since at least 1900. In 1921 and for many years afterwards the sum allocated for prizes for the latter was £400 for 12 Special prizes of £6 each for the best-kept garden in each Traffic Division, and 197 Ordinary prizes ranging from 15 shillings to £3 10s for gardens considered worthy by the Divisional Superintendent. The top gardens tended to be the same year after year, until the keen gardener retired or was moved elsewhere. In 1924 the winning gardens were Kidlington, Charlton Kings, Bloxham, Yatton, Ely, Hall Green, Torquay, Clynderwen, Gresford, Lostwithiel, Tram Inn and Pontdolgoch.

It would probably be asserted by modern railway managers that the station with the finest garden also had the most underemployed staff and, having inspected the superb gardens, they would make the gardener redundant. Obviously this was not the attitude of real railwaymen - and the GWR Directors were railwaymen. In about 1923 they intensified the gardens competition by the official issue of hanging flower-baskets specifically for those stations which had no other form of garden, and allocated £14 10s prize money for the best-kept baskets. The money had to be shared between 17 winning stations, so the Directors obviously believed in the Olympic principle - that taking part was the main reward.

An institution as venerable as the station garden competition was the annual outings of office salaried staff - the Divisional Superintendent's HQ staff or members of the Company Secretary's staff. The last-mentioned people had taken a day out together every year, except during the Great War, since 1912, and almost certainly before that. The outing followed a very regular, sober and generally conservative pattern as befitted the standing of those people working in such an important office. Each year a list circulated the office asking who wanted to go on the outing and where would they like to go. The same people went, year in, year out, and the same people refused to take part, year after year. The lists are preserved and the acid comments of certain people may still be read.

Those taking part paid their subscription to a fund to cover transport (beyond the railway), food and drink on the day. The Company Secretary always contributed £5 and his Assistant £2 10s, even though they never went on the trip (so as not to overawe the proceedings). Other very senior people did go, including the Company's Chief Cashier, for years a Mr D'Albertson.

A typical itinerary consisted of a train to some rural station, and thence (whisper it) by motor bus - even in 1912 - for a tour. Lunch was taken in a good hotel and after lunch a telegram was invariably sent back to the office informing the Guvnor - and all those miseries who had opted out - what a wonderful time the tourists were having. After dinner the tour continued, and at the end of the day, back at the station, the bus driver got 10 shillings before the party boarded the express for the ride home to Paddington with dinner taken in the restaurant car.

The Bristol Divisional Superintendent's staff on an office outing, circa 1932. The first man on the left, in the trilby, is Arthur Price, an office senior, who dealt with passenger train matters. The man at the back right of centre in the trilby with a pipe in his mouth is Steve Cray, whose knowledge of all matters relating to train working in the Bristol Division was legendary. To his right, in a black hat, is Miss Margery Riches who married another member of the office, G. H. Soole, and who became secretary to the Divisional Superintendent, R. G. Pole. (Clinker Collection/courtesy Brunel University)

In 1930 the office went to Kemble for a tour to the source of the Thames, the Roman villa at Chedworth and around such gems as Burford and Bibury. They got a better tour than they bargained for because the motor bus driver lost his way, but the tourists soothed his embarrassment and signified their delight at the mystery tour by giving him 12s 6d instead of the usual 10 bob. Had he realised the revolutionary nature of this gesture, he would have been very flattered. The driver's 10-shilling 'gratuity' was always included in the budget for the day's outing, because these were the top secretariat staff of the railway and very orderly people. These records are preserved at the Public Record Office.

In 1931, there was, in addition to the usual office grumps, a certain air of impoverishment about the whole affair. The usual expansiveness was lacking, due, no doubt, to a feeling of sadness at the mess the country was in and the consequent lack of prosperity of the GWR. The list circulating the office, canvassing for support for that year's tour, began with the sombre words: 'In view of all the circumstances we are not sure whether to have the outing this year at all.' Of the 18 people who usually went on the outing, six declined to go.

The national financial situation was becoming bleak and the suggested tour was relatively short. The list asked who wanted to go and whether 'the Buckinghamshire woods' or Blenheim Palace (home of Lord Churchill, the Chairman of the GWR Board) would be a suitable venue. Mr S. B. Taylor wrote grumpily 'No - a Saturday off duty instead.' Below this Mr D. Swain wrote 'You would', and nothing more. These two were bracketed together on the list by Mr Knock, the organiser, with the comment 'These never attend and their remarks do not apply'. A regular attender, Mr Hunt, wrote 'No - too many people getting married'.

In the event, qualms about indulging in luxury at a time (almost) of national mourning were suppressed and both venues were combined. Mr Knock chartered a 30-seater charabanc from the GWR depot at Slough for a 'privilege' rate of £5 15s to take the party from Slough to Oxford and Blenheim Palace through the leafy, hilly Chilterns. They looked around some of the university buildings at Oxford and went on to Woodstock where a dinner for twelve cost £9 1s 6d. After that they sent the usual telegram back to the office and went into Blenheim Palace grounds for a specially guided tour. The tip for the bus driver, garden guide and Woodstock waitress came to £1 12s 6d and the entire cost of the trip was £17 10s including train fares to Slough.

The 1938 outing on 28 May was on the grand scale of pre-1914. Twenty-two people rode in the Weston-super-Mare slip coach at the rear of the 8.55 am Paddington-Pembroke Dock. The coach was slipped at Stoke Gifford and attached to the regular shuttle service to Bristol and Weston, arriving at 12.15. Here they walked across to the Locking Road station where the Bristol Divisional Superintendent had, at their request, stabled a 1st Class dining car where lunch was waiting. The menu was: salmon and salad or cold roast lamb with mint sauce, hot peas, hot new potatoes, fruit salad, ice-cream, cheese and biscuits and coffee, and the price was 4s 5d. Perhaps this was at 'privilege' rates.

After lunch they sent S. G. Rowe, the Company Secretary, his greetings telegram. The piece of paper

The interior of an Edwardian restaurant car of Churchward design, such as might have been enjoyed by the Divisional Superindendents staff outing. Into the 1920s 1st Class diners were served in pre-war splendour: silver cutlery, fresh flowers, crisp and spotless linen, leather and mahogany chairs, a Brussels carpet and a moulded plaster ceiling 8 feet high. But risings costs led to economies - and the adoption of the 'Quick Snack' style of eating. (British Rail)

on which the party composed their message is preserved in the Public Record Office and it is amusing to see how the originally wordy greeting was carefully cut down until they had a decent balance between extravagance and miserliness - Rowe had, after all, contributed £5 to their outing. They allowed him two more words than was absolutely necessary: 'The Office send all good wishes whilst in the West Country'.

With clear consciences they then took off for a tour of Cheddar Gorge, visiting the caves, on to Wells for the cathedral, and getting over the hills to Bath in time to catch the 6.29 pm to Paddington. The Great Western dining car of that evening train up from Bath offered them the choice of: consomme or lobster; roast beef and Yorkshire pudding, or roast chicken and bread sauce, or cold meats; vegetables; salad; sardines on toast; ice-cream; jelly; cheese board. A meal chosen from this selection cost 5s 6d. Wine, spirits or coffee was extra. The express was booked at a modest speed so there was no chance of them spilling the consomme.

26

Swindon Trip

The great annual exodus from Swindon - the Works holiday popularly known as 'Trip' - first took place in 1849 when the Mechanics Institute organised a day trip to Oxford for 500 of its members. In 1905 24,500 people went away in 22 special trains on a six-day holiday from Monday to Saturday. No-one was forced to go away from Swindon, but the men were compulsorily locked out of their work and lost one week's wages as a result.

The factory had to be closed down once a year for essential maintenance work - stationary boilers de-scaled, air compressors overhauled, roads repaired, and work of that sort, carried out by 3-500 men who stayed behind - so the holiday was a good way of sweetening what some saw as a compulsory 'lock-out'. To strengthen this point of view is the fact that in some years the work took longer than seven days, the Works remained closed for that extra time and the workmen lost the wages for the extra day or days that it stayed shut. The loss of wages due to a week or more off work caused hardship to many families, but from 1913 the stoppage was arranged to take place for six days from the first Friday in July so that the men worked until the Thursday evening and had four days pay to look forward on the following pay day. From 1938 the seven days were fully paid for by the Company.

Six weeks before the great day of Trip, 12,000 workmen handed in their individual Privilege Ticket requisition forms, showing where each family wanted to go and how many would be travelling. From these forms the destinations required and the numbers going to them were calculated. The Company always tried to reduce the 'train miles' run, so the planning of the Trip trains was done very carefully. In 1926 the most popular destinations were Weymouth ('Swindon-by-the-Sea') with 6,307, Weston-super-Mare with 5,463, and London, with 4,020, followed by 5,400 to all the Devonshire and Cornish resorts. For their part the children and housewives saved their pennies in earnest and 'Roll on Trip' appeared in chalk on walls all around the town.

The epic nature of Trip was not in its high speed - on the famous 'galloping ground' from Swindon to Reading, 68 minutes was allowed for the 41 miles, start to stop. The epic was in the immaculately smooth organisation of an evacuation of upwards of 25,000 thousand men, women and children in a matter of a few hours - mostly in darkness. It was a perfect example of the brilliant 'staff work' of the HQ officials and the practised expertise of all ranks of the Great Western Railway in carrying it out.

Once all the men had handed in their Trip forms, a day was set aside for a conference of Divisional Officers. This was to plan where the necessary engines, coaches and crews were to be found when the railway's resources were already stretched in the height of the summer holiday period. They then had to scheme empty stock and loaded train movements to run the operation in the most economical way possible.

Overnight on 1/2 July 1926 a total of 25,146 people, including 8,100 children, left Swindon in 25 special trains, requiring 57 Brake-3rds and 295 corridor coaches. These trains were marshalled at Old Oak Common, Didcot, Taunton, Exeter, Cardiff, Bristol, Stoke Gifford and Swindon, and arrived at Swindon in complete readiness for their journey, clearly labelled and carrying with a 'Reporting Number' on the locomotive for the benefit of the signalmen along the way. A special Trip timetable was printed and distributed to all concerned, and by this means the Trippers were told beforehand the number of the train by which they were to travel.

Works families living in the Highworth, Purton and Wootton Bassett areas were brought into Swindon by special trains formed by the engines and coaches which normally formed the 'Workmen's' trains to the factory.

The departures took place in two phases: five trains from 8.30 pm on 1 July to midnight, and 20 trains between 4.25 am and 7.10 am on the 2nd.

Train No 1, for Penzance, arrived at Swindon from Old Oak Common at 4.30 pm on Thursday 1 July, formed from 10 3rd Class coaches with a Brake-3rd at each end, and hauled by an Old Oak Common engine. The train and engine was stabled on the down side siding at Swindon East box and left for Penzance at 8.30 pm from Swindon station's down main platform.

Train No 2 was for Plymouth, St Ives and Penzance and was marshalled at Didcot. It arrived at Swindon at 8.15 pm and was also stabled on the down side at East box. It was formed from 12 3rd Class coaches, divided into three sections by three Brake-3rds: one coach and a Brake-3rd for Plymouth, five and a Brake-3rd for Penzance, and six and a Brake-3rd for St Ives. The St Ives branch engine ran 'light' up to St Erth especially early to meet the Trip special, and a special 'light engine' was booked out from Penzance shed to St Erth to assist the branch engine haul the seven coaches down the branch. The engine to work the whole train from Swindon came up from Plymouth, double-heading some regular service, and set out for the West Country from the down main platform at Swindon at 9 pm.

The nine coaches and two Brakes forming Train No 3 for Plymouth and Newquay came from Didcot, and the engine from Plymouth. The coaches were again stabled on the down side, then the Plymouth engine joined them and drew them to Swindon station, down branch platform, so that trains 2 and 3 were standing together on each side of the island platform. No 3 left at 9.15 pm and arrived in Newquay at 4.5 am.

No 4, to Swansea, Pembroke and Aberystwyth, was formed at Didcot and consisted of 11 3rd Class coaches and three Brake-3rds. It was hauled by a Cardiff engine from Swindon and started from the down main platform at Swindon at 11.23 pm.

No 5, to Birkenhead and Manchester (with a contingent for Blackpool), was formed at Swindon and was hauled by a Swindon engine. The train comprised 10 coaches and four Brake-3rds, divided into two sections, one for Birkenhead and one Manchester; it ran via Oxford and Birmingham. Six coaches with a Brake-3rd at each end were detached at Wellington (Salop) to go to Manchester via Market Drayton and Crewe, where the Blackpool contingent changed into a service train, the LMS having been warned of the number of passengers to expect. The remaining 'four and two' went on to Birkenhead via Chester. This train left Swindon at midnight and brought the first phase of the operation to an end.

The second phase of the operation began in the small hours of Friday morning as empty trains began to arrive from Bristol, Taunton, Exeter, Cardiff, Old Oak Common and Swindon itself to form the Trip specials. Twenty trains were required – 256 3rd Class coaches and 66 Brake-3rds. Whilst these trains arrived and were shunted to sidings at Rodbourne Lane, parallel with the main lines, the usual traffic of the railway had also to be dealt with. Some of the carriages were later drawn into the station for loading, but most of them remained in the sidings and were loaded from the ground by ladder.

Getting on to trains in the dark from the ground was a delightful novelty of Trip which never failed to please the children, but the operation was carried out with great good sense, for in spite of the huge numbers involved, those 20 trains and 25,000 men, women and children were loaded and sent away like the proverbial clockwork.

The last train of the morning, the 7.10 am from Swindon to Portsmouth and Bournemouth, had 10 coaches – three 3rds and a Brake-3rd for Bournemouth, five 3rds and a Brake-3rd for Portsmouth – and ran via the M&SW section to Andover and thence by the Southern to Eastleigh where the Portsmouth section was dropped to be taken on by a Southern engine. The remainder of the train then continued through Southampton to Bournemouth. On arrival the engine left the coaches at the station and went to turn on the Branksome triangle, causing an annual stir amongst the Somerset & Dorset enginemen on Branksome shed. It returned to Bournemouth, picked up its coaches and went back to Eastleigh where it collected the empty coaches of its Portsmouth portion (which the Southern had worked back most promptly) and sped back to Swindon via Romsey, Andover and Marlborough – an interesting day out for Swindon men.

Trippers in small groups for holiday destinations not served by Trip trains travelled free on specified public services to such places as Andoversford, Calne, Cirencester (Town), Coalpit Heath, Faringdon, Foss Cross, Tetbury, and Wantage Road. In addition, in 1926 29 adults and one child went to Jersey by the 5.55 pm Swindon-Weymouth. People travelling beyond the destination of a Trip train paid a reduced fare for that part of the journey – Crewe to Blackpool at 4s 4d return per adult, for instance.

Having sent all these trains out, Swindon had then to receive them all back again the following week and dispose of the empty coaches.

27
Great Western accidents, 1921–29

The GWR had a good safety record and killed only three of its hundreds of millions of passengers between 1921 and 1939. However, there were a lot of crashes and derailments during that period, some more, some less serious, and at least 13 Great Western men were killed. Every year the railway suffered serious damage from bad weather (see Appendix 9), then the mens' loyalty to the Company and 'Pride in the Job' shone through in their efforts to keep the job going. A representative selection of these incidents are recalled here.

At 11.40 am on the morning of 22 September 1921, the 10.25 am passenger train from Plymouth to Crewe was offered to Dawlish from Teignmouth and accepted by Dawlish under the 'Warning Arrangement' - 3-5-5 on the bell to Teignmouth. This was done because the Dawlish signalman was about to foul the up line with the 9.10 am Exeter to Newton Abbot goods which had to shunt from down to up main through the crossover at the west end of Dawlish station, only a few yards ahead of the up home signal. The Teignmouth signalman warned the passenger train driver that the line ahead of the up home signal at Dawlish was occupied within the 'clearing point' usually kept clear beyond a signal for obvious safety reasons, but the driver approached the home signal too fast and ran past it at 'Danger', colliding with the goods train.

The engine of the goods was slightly damaged and four wagons were badly smashed while the leading bogie of the passenger train's engine was derailed and both lines were blocked. No-one was hurt although several people complained of 'shock'.

The Exeter breakdown crane was called but it was very difficult to get it to the site because of other trains standing on the down line between Exeter and Dawlish, which had to be shunted to clear the main line. When the crane and its vans arrived the derailed wagons were dumped on the beach before the job of rerailing the passenger loco could begin. Meanwhile through traffic was either cancelled or diverted over the Teign Valley line via Heathfield. Normal working was resumed at 7 pm.

The driver took the blame but GWR officials also decided that the Dawlish up distant signal had not been placed far enough to the rear of the home signal so it was re-sited. The cost of the accident, not including the re-siting of the signal but including claims from passengers, amounted to £630.

Four days later, on 26 September, Ganger Edmonds and seven men of the Clifton Down permanent way gang were working in a sharply curved cutting on the double track of the Clifton Down branch. The 7.10 am Avonmouth passenger train came round the bend as a goods train was passing in the opposite direction, so the men working in the track on which the passenger train was running did not hear it approach. The curvature gave a driver no more than 180 yards forward visibility; he braked as soon as he saw the gang at work on the line before him but could not stop, ploughing into the gang at 15 mph. Five men were killed, including Ganger Edmonds, and the other two, who jumped clear at the very last moment, were injured.

Steam-engined self-propelled cranes were used to clear wreckage after an accident such as that at Dawlish, as well as lifting track sections during relaying, hoisting bridge beams and so on. Here a 45-ton-lift crane, one of its two cylinders clearly visible, lifts the bogie of a 'Gane'-type wagon circa 1947. (Lens of Sutton)

Great Western gangers' 'Pride in the Job' could become an obsession - like a house-proud housewife. Men I worked with who had worked on the GWR 'gangs' in the 'twenties have told me that 'when an old Ganger set you to work you didn't straighten your back until he told you to.' Edmonds appears to have been such a man. The two survivors reported that two of the dead men had asked Edmonds to post a look-out but he had refused - one less shovel to do the work. Those who jumped clear had just stopped work for a surreptitious straightening of their backs and thus saved their lives.

But of course 'Pride in the Job' is very important. A serious accident was prevented by the ganger of the Dawlish-Teignmouth length on 11 March 1923. He was patrolling his length along the sea-wall in cold, torrential rain at 8 o'clock that morning and was keeping a sharp look-out, doubtless with landslides on his experienced mind. He was 300 yards west of Parson's Tunnel signal box when he saw fissures in the cliff face; if the rock fell it could easily block to

up line. Parsons Tunnel box was not switched in so he hurried on 1½ miles to Teignmouth and raised the alarm.

Single line working was put into force over the down line and a handsignalman was placed near the impending landslide. At 8.30 am next day the cliff face fell and blocked both lines, but the trains came to no harm. Traffic was diverted over the Heathfield line and via the Southern Railway, and after three days of digging the earth was cleared from the down line to enable single-line working to be resumed while the rest was cleared.

In the darkness of the small hours of 3 January 1925 the embankment between Tir Phil and Brithdir collapsed leaving the rails suspended over an 80-foot gap and the telegraph wires broken. At 5 am the signalman at Pontlottyn South box had to get 'Line Clear' from Brithdir signalman (Tir Phil being switched out) for a southbound LMS goods train and, being unable to make any contact, he filled in his 'Institution of Time Interval Working' form and gave it to the driver. He told him to pass his signal at

'Danger' and to go forward with great caution towards Brithdir.

The morning was pitch dark and only the fireman walking in front of the train would have prevented what was to occur. The men stayed on the footplate and eased their train forward, but half a mile south of Tir Phil station they ran on to the track festooned over the hole in the embankment and were falling into space before they realised their danger. The LMS driver and fireman were killed.

Every year from 1921 to 1939 some part of the GWR was affected by snow-storms, gales and/or floods and landslides which brought a section of the line to a halt or brought down the telegraph wires, forcing 'Time Interval' working to be adopted. The Welsh lines were usually the ones affected but there were also 'incidents' at exposed places such as the Cotswolds or Salisbury Plain.

The unsung heroes of all these incidents were, of course, the working men - the gangers, Signal & Telegraph Department linesmen, locomen, and porters and signalmen too, who struggled to work in spite of all, or, if they were already at work, suffered the wet and cold to keep the job going.

A terrific storm of wind and rain arose on 28 October 1927 which raged for 48 hours and caused enormous damage throughout Wales. On the GWR the worst damage was in the Harlech Bay area from Aberystwyth to Pwllheli where the gales combined with high tides to create a surge which flooded low-lying land around river estuaries. Between Ynysglas and Dovey Junction, Barmouth Junction and Penmaenpool, Talsarnau and Penrhynduedreath, long stretches of track were washed away, bridges displaced, telegraph wires, poles and signal posts blown down.

Traffic was suspended until 7 November. At Barmouth Junction four Company-owned houses were flooded, all but washed away and left feet deep in mud, so the families that lived in them lost almost everything they owned. While their houses and families were suffering this, the railwaymen from those houses were out on the track doing what they could to put matters right, and when the job was finally cleared up the damage to GWR property was estimated at £34,250, and the following 'gratuities' were paid by the Company to the staff.

A. Hange, Signalman, Barmouth Junction, £35
H. Jones, Station Master, Arthog, £30
A. Evans, Station Master, Barmouth Junction, £15

P. Evans, Shopman, Barmouth Junction, £12 10s
R. Jones, Porter, Ynysglas, £5
E. Venables, Signalman, Barmouth Junction, £2

The South Wales Valley lines often suffered damage from mining subsidence, and the line up the Rhymney Valley, from Newport on the GWR main line northwards through New Tredegar to Rhymney Lower, was seriously affected. On 27 September 1928 the down (southbound) line was taken out of use between McLaren's Colliery signal box and New Tredegar Colliery signal box, 57 chains further south, owing to severe subsidence, and single-line working, using the old up line, was instituted between those two places.

Double track recommenced at New Tredegar Colliery signal box and down trains swung over a crossover from the single line (the old up line) to regain their proper track. The distance between the up home signal and the crossover it protected was less than 440 yards, and consequently the New Tredegar Colliery signalman was not allowed to accept an up train from the New Tredegar Station box, 50 chains to the south, if he had already accepted a down train on the single track from McLaren's.

On 9 October 1928 the signalman in New Tredegar Colliery box accepted the up 9.12 Newport to Rhymney Lower passenger train from New Tredegar Station box, forgetting that he had already accepted the down 10.3 Rhymney Lower-Pengam miners' train from McLaren's.

Both trains approached New Tredegar at the same time, but the up train failed to stop at the home signal - although it was climbing a 1 in 98 gradient - and crashed head-on into the down train as it was about to go through the crossover to regain its proper line. Fourteen people were injured and one man, a miner from Bargoed colliery, was killed. He had the dubious distinction of being the first passenger fatality on the GWR since 1916. He was 44 and earned £3 15s a week on which he kept a wife and several children. His widow received £2,000 from the GWR.

On 24 April 1929 Signalman Saffin, a very capable and experienced man, was on duty in the 46-lever Aller Junction signal box, near Newton Abbot. At 8.23 am No 2857 arrived at his up main starting signal with a 47-wagon freight from Plymouth. At the rear of the train next to the guard's brake-van was a crane wagon and its match-truck.

The man in charge of the crane, Mr Yabsley, was riding in the van with the guard, Mr Ellis. Ellis got down to the track and went forward to release the wagon hand-brakes which had been pinned down to assist the engine's brakes on the descent of Dainton bank, leaving Yabsley in the brake-van.

Signalman Saffin replaced his up main signals 1, 2 and 3 to 'Danger' behind the train, but the up main starting signal, No 9, he left lowered since the train had to proceed on its journey. He gave 'Train out of Section' to Dainton at 8.24 am and Dainton at once offered the 7.10 am Plymouth local passenger train. Saffin was able to accept this since he had an outer home signal providing ample safety distance behind the rear of the stationary freight.

The passenger train - five coaches hauled by No 4909 *Blakesley Hall* - passed Dainton on time at 8.26 am and Dainton sent 'Train On Line' to Aller Junction. At 8.27 Saffin accepted the 8.10 Paignton from Kingskerswell, the road at Aller from the Torquay direction being set safely to the up relief line.

At 8.34 Kingskerswell sent the Paignton 'on line' so Saffin 'got the road' on the up relief from Newton Abbot West and pulled his signal levers for the train to pass. He wanted levers 7, 11, 12 and 6 - the up relief line signals - but in a lengthy period of mental abberation he pulled 3 and 2 , the up main home and starter. He was not even alerted to his mistake by the fact that the up main starting signal lever, No 9, was already reversed, and with all the necessary stop signals lowered he was able to pull his up main distant, No 1.

Aller's up main distant 'dropped down the chimney' of No 4909 and the driver, who was about to begin braking, 'let her run', freewheeling down the 1 in 90 incline. The only slowing required, as far as he knew, was the regulation 50 mph around the bend at the foot of the incline. Both driver and fireman saw the goods ahead as they looked across the

field, inside the chord of the curved track, but quite naturally assumed that it was standing on the up relief line.

As the Plymouth train came under the bridge, about 450 yards from the rear of the goods, Signalman Saffin realised his mistake, threw the main line signal levers over and rushed to the window with a red flag. The driver was very alert and braked instantly, but there was too little distance left and the collision occurred at about 45 mph.

The 20-ton brake-van of the goods was crushed, killing Mr Yabsley. The crane truck, match-truck and ten other wagons were forced sideways out of the train, on to the bank, and the rest of the train and the engine, weighing in all around 450 tons, was forced forwards. The coupling between the 15th and 16th wagons snapped and the front part continued another 120 yards before the driver of No 2857 could bring it to a stand.

Mr Yabsley's widow and children received £307 10s, which seems to have been, at that time, the 'going rate' for dead railwaymen. Miss Kennard, a passenger who hurt her leg in the crash, received £13 3s 0d.

Saffin of course got the blame for this accident. No doubt the mistake was his alone and no doubt, as a thoroughly conscientious man, he was utterly crushed by what he had caused - but if there had been a track circuit in the up main, or if the signal levers had been fitted with the mechanical 'sequential locking' mechanism, the accident could not have happened.

Having blamed Saffin the Company took no remedial action. On August Bank Holiday Monday 1929 there was a derailment at Aller Junction. The Traffic Department's Annual Report gives no details except to say that it had 'caused a great disruption of traffic', but as a result of lightning having struck twice track circuits were installed at Aller on 10 October 1929 and 27 March 1930 at a total cost of £380.

28
Great Western accidents, 1930–37

There was only one train crash with fatal results in 1930. This happened at Lawrence Hill, on the four-track section between Dr Day's Junction, Bristol, and Stapleton Road. The signalman at Lawrence Hill, Mr Toop, was not required to keep a train register and all booking was done by the Lad in Stapleton Road box, ¾ mile away.

At 5.41 am on 9 January, No 3 Transfer Freight, Stoke Gifford to Bristol East Depot, had stopped a little way short of Lawrence Hill's home signal to allow the guard to unpin the wagons' brakes, pinned down to ensure a safe descent of Filton incline. Twenty-seven freights per day stopped at Lawrence Hill for this purpose. Drivers did not pull right up to the signal because there was point rodding there which would have made it difficult for the guard to walk along the train.

The train was therefore out of sight of the signalman, and there was no track circuit to remind him of its presence and to prevent him giving 'Line Clear' to Stapleton Road. The driver of the freight did not sound his whistle nor send his fireman to the box in accordance with Rule 55. Toop was tired, he may well have dozed off after taking the goods 'on line' from Stapleton Road, and the train stood in silence.

Fourteen minutes after sending the goods 'on line' to Lawrence Hill, the Stapleton Road signalman still had it 'on the block' and phoned Toop to ask 'Have you knocked out for the Trip?' Toop said 'No', which was quite true since the train had not yet passed him, but he understood the question as a diplomatic reminder to 'wake up'.

Without further thought Toop then gave 'Train out of Section' to Stapleton Road, who then 'asked the road' for the 2.40 am Shrewsbury passenger. Toop pegged 'Line Clear' and Stapleton Road 'pulled off', but Toop did not 'get the road' from Dr Day's Junction and his signals remained at 'Danger', so the driver of the Shrewsbury, passing Lawrence Hill's distant signal at 'Caution', had braked from 65 mph to 40 when the triple red tail-lamps of the freight came into view. Then the brakes went on in earnest, so that No 4063 *Bath Abbey* crashed into the goods brake van at only about 20 mph. One passenger was killed.

The tragedy was that if the goods had been pulled up close to the home signal, the Shrewsbury would just have had enough room to stop. The GWR was advised to put boards down over the point rodding to encourage drivers to stop close to the signal, and to install a track circuit.

The Shipston-on-Stour branch lost its passenger service in August 1929, and in February 1930 only a single freight train each day traversed the line. The goods was due to leave Moreton-in-Marsh at 1.35 pm and travel sedately to Shipston, calling at Stretton-on-Fosse and Longdon Road stations if required. However, in spite of its minimal use, the 8¾-mile single-track branch was meticulously maintained by two permanent way gangs; economies had not sunk so low as to neglect the hedges, ditches and track.

Ganger Webb was in charge of the Stretton-Shipston length which he patrolled daily on his 'velocipede'. There was no electrical signalling

Just like Ganger Webb and his men on the Shipston branch, here is the Witney permanent way gang - the Ganger with the extra-special hat - on their pump-action 'velocipede' near Witney Goods Junction in about 1928. The perfectly aligned track and tight, well-cut hedges are all their own work. With men like this around, the Company was certain of getting a good job done. (British Rail)

between Moreton and Shipston so to protect the gangs and the trains the understanding was that the train was not to leave Moreton before 1.35 pm and that until that time the branch was considered to in the possession of the Permanent Way Department.

At 1.40 pm on 3 February 1930 Ganger Webb left his men at Stretton cutting hedges - those hedges were still a fine sight in 1953 - and worked away on his velocipede towards Shipston. He ought not really to have been on the line, but perhaps his watch was running slow. Unfortunately the daily goods had left Moreton at 1.25, the tank engine running bunker first, and passed Stretton at 1.45.

Rounding a bend on the approach to Longdon Road, working almost silently at 5 mph, it caught up with Ganger Webb on his velocipede. Owing to the curve the driver's view ahead was virtually nil, although the fireman would have seen the man in plenty of time, had he been looking out. So it was that the engine hit the fragile velocipede at walking speed and Ganger Webb was killed.

The 1.18 pm Paddington-Swansea express was approaching Coychurch level crossing, about 2 miles east of Bridgend, on 20 February 1931. The signals

guarding the crossing were cleared but when the train got to the crossing it met a Willys 'Overland' van belonging to Mr Bryant, a local greengrocer, which was crossing the down main line. The van, which weighed slightly less than one ton, was crushed by the train engine, No 4097 *Kenilworth Castle*, weighing 126 tons and travelling at 60 mph. The occupants of the van, Mr Bryant and Inspector Cooper of Western Welsh buses, were killed.

The accident was due to the negligence of the crossing-keeper, who let the van across the line without a moment's thought. He did not look to see the position of the 'repeater' block instruments and he did not bother to replace the signals to 'Danger' before allowing the lorry on to the track. But it might also be said that the GWR was negligent in not providing basic mechanical interlocking between the gates and the signals. Mr Bryant left a widow and two children. Each widow received a sum not exceeding £2,000 from the GWR.

On 6 January 1932 Signalman Ron Neate was in Didcot East Junction box. Ron was 43, he had been a signalman for 19 years, and had been working Didcot East Junction for 16 months. He accepted the 8.5 pm from Severn Tunnel Junction on the up main from Didcot East End at 3.12 am and set the junctions to cross this train to the up relief line, a movement which would take it across the down relief line.

At 3.21 am Ron gave 'Line Clear' to Freddie Sugar at Moreton Cutting for the 2.30 am from Paddington on the down main and the 1.50 am Ladbroke Grove-Chippenham milk empties on the down relief line. Ron's mistake was to accept the Ladbroke at full 'Line Clear' when he had the up main to up relief junction set for the crossing movement over the down relief. He lowered his signals for the newspaper train but kept them at 'Danger' against the Ladbroke.

Ron Neate ought to have accepted the Ladbroke Grove under the 'Warning Arrangement' which would have warned the driver that the junction ahead was blocked. He may have forgotten that he had the junction set, or he may have known but gambled that the goods would have cleared the down relief before the milk empties 'got handy', thus removing the need to inflict a heavy check on it at Moreton. This was the kind of temptation trap which a signalmen was could fall into.

Unfortunately for Ron, Driver Henley on the Ladbroke was also a bit 'gung-ho'. He heard the ATC's warning siren passing the East Junction distant signal at 'Caution', braked and, by his own admission, could easily have stopped at the home signal - except that he did not see it. Smoke and steam obscured his vision of it, but he *did* see the green lights of the signals through the station on the down *main* and assumed they were for him. So he let his engine, No 2949 *Stanford Court* drift on, with 16 vans behind - six eight-wheelers, seven six-wheelers and five four-wheelers.

The 8.5 am Severn Tunnel, consisting of 51 loaded wagons hauled by No 2808, now decided it was time to be moving on. The engine's tender was on the 'diamond' crossing, where the track crossed the down relief line, when No 2949 scraped in at about 5 mph. Driver Henley had seen the crossing movement and had braked only seconds before impact. His engine gouged along the tender of No 2808 and struck the leading wagon. No 2949 turned on its left side towards the up main at 3.26, just as the 2.30 am from Paddington, usually 'King'-hauled, roared past, at express train speed, on the down main.

The four leading wagons of the goods were batted to the boundary and fell down the embankment; the following seven piled into a heap on top of No 2949, whose own vans piled up from behind.

Luckily no-one was hurt badly, although I imagine there was a fair amount of hurt pride.

The Company's treatment of the two men involved was anything but even-handed. Driver Henley was severely punished by being put on shed pilot duties for the rest of his career, while Ron Neate, who was most at fault, was treated rather leniently - suspended without pay for three days.

There was a crash at Tiverton Junction early on the morning of 12 February 1933. The station had been rebuilt with quadruple track, the platforms served by loops outside the up and down main lines. A new 125-lever signal box to control the layout was brought into use on 25 September 1933.

On the day in question a Paddington-Plymouth excursion was standing on the down platform loop and the signals were lowered on the down main for the 12.45 am Paddington Newspapers. The excursion driver took the main line signal for his own and started. He ran into the blocks and derailed his engine and leading coach, the second coach telescoping into the first. The Travelling Ticket Collector and six passengers were slightly hurt.

On 4 March there was the Vriog tragedy between Llwyngwril and Fairbourne when the 6.10 am Machynlleth- Pwllheli was swept off the track and down to the beach by a landslide which coincided perfectly with the passing train. The driver and fireman were killed but the solitary passenger and the guard were unhurt, the coaches staying on the rails.

On 15 January 1936 there was the dreadful smash at Shrivenham, about 5 miles east of Swindon, when the signalman there, Head, and his mate at Ashbury, Jefferies, both gave 'Train out of Section' for an up coal train, neither of them having seen its tail-lamp. In fact, the brake-van and five wagons of coal had broken away and were blocking the up main, in the darkness and some fog, not far to the west of Shrivenham.

The following express, the 9 pm sleeping car express from Penzance to Paddington (the 'Up Waker'), hauled by No 6007 *King William III* crashed into these trucks and the guard escaped with his life only by diving head first from his van at the last second. Old Oak★ Driver William Starr was less fortunate. He died on the trackside after being

---

★ Not Newton Abbot-based as stated in my book *Grime & Glory*.

impaled on the handles of the reversing screw as his engine lay on its side in the ballast. The two leading coaches smashed on the tender and one passenger was killed.

A great deal was paid out in compensation to injured passengers, including £1,600 to a chicken farmer, Mr Harold Steele, whose skull was fractured. It seems very likely that William Starr's widow received £307 10s, since that was the sum paid out to Mrs Yabsley in 1929 and also to the widow of Oxford Guard Emmens killed in the accident at Dolphin/Langley (Bucks) in March 1937 (see below).

The disgracefully negligent signalmen who caused the Shrivenham crash were treated with great leniency. Minute 11686 of the Superintendents' Meetings 1936 states that each man was suspended without pay for 14 days and sent to work on branch lines. Jefferies was sent as signalman to busy Radstock (Som) where he worked for 25 years, a well known 'character', until his retirement.

Signalman Bonser was on duty at Stourbridge Junction North at 11.45 pm on 17 July 1936. He had 'pulled off' for the 9.50 pm Victoria Basin-Cardiff 'E' headcode freight to pass from the up main to the No 2 up goods loop – the scheduled working – but he failed to notice that the signal routing into the loop was only 'cocked off' and showed no light. However, Bonser expected the train to run into the loop and busied himself with other matters.

He had two engines standing on the down main line, changing crews, he wanted to telephone Stourbridge Engine Shed box, and the shunters were ringing him. He answered this latter call to be told that the shunters wanted one of the engines on the down line returned to the down yard because its crew had escaped without picking up their train. He therefore set the road for this move and shouted instructions from the window. He then tried to phone Engine Shed box.

While he was doing this the up goods, consisting of 37 wagons hauled by No 8332 and driven by Driver Finch, was passing the box about 8 minutes late. Finch saw the No 2 up loop signal 'cocked off' and shouted to Bonser to ask if the road was set safely for the loop. Bonser, with the two engines between him and the up goods, did not hear. Driver Finch quite properly assumed that there was something wrong with the facing points and stopped at the signal, his engine 190 yards beyond the signal

box, the wagons trailing past the box with the brake-van and lamps well to the rear.

Bonser was talking on the phone to Engine Shed box and the man there asked him 'Have you knocked out for the up goods?' Bonser looked out into the darkness and, seeing no triple red tail-lamp, assumed that the goods must have gone far into the loop. In fact, the brake-van had not yet reached him.

He thus gave 'Train out of Section' without having seen the tail-lamp, and accepted the 11.30 pm Dudley-Stourbridge passenger from Engine Shed box. He then re-set the road for the up main instead of for the up loop and lowered his up main signals. Driver Finch saw the bright green light of the main-line signal and sent his fireman, Hopcott, back to the box for instructions.

The Dudley passenger left Brettel Lane 4 minutes late. It was formed with No 4853 propelling an auto-trailer, the driver controlling the steam regulator and the vacuum brake from his cab in the leading end of the coach. The little train galloped downhill past Engine Shed box and over the viaduct at 35 mph.

Off the viaduct the line curved to the right, reducing the forward visibility so that the 'Auto' driver had a maximum of 190 yards braking distance once he caught sight of the triple red tail-lamps on the stationary goods train. He at once blew his brake whistle, braked hard and shut off steam. Fireman Reynolds heard the emergency whistle booming and applied the emergency steam brake, but it was all to no avail – there was insufficient stopping distance.

While the gap between the auto-train and the goods was closing, fireman Hopcott was opening the signal box door at Stourbridge North Junction.

'Is it all right for us to go main line?' he asked, and before Bonser could reply there came the horrible sound of the collision.

Guard Wilkes, on the goods, heard the sound of the hurrying passenger train just in time to leap out of his van. The flimsy auto-coach, with the driver just behind the window, hit the rear of the goods train at not less than 30 mph, hard enough to drive the buffer-beam under the coach, smash the leading bogie off the frames, and demolish the leading end of the coach, forcing the heavy horizontal iron sole-bars out sideways – and killing the driver.

On 1 March 1937 the signalman at Dolphin Junction, between Slough and Langley, put the 7.45

pm Reading–Old Oak Common ballast empties into the up goods loop. The train, 25 steel ballast wagons hauled by No 6320, cleared the up relief into the loop at 9.26, to allow the 20-minutes-late 6.35 pm Oxford–Paddington (via Thame and Maidenhead) to pass.

The empty ballast was drifting along the loop when Langley's up relief home signal cleared for the passenger. There was insufficient clearance between the goods loop and relief line to place this signal between those tracks, so it had been sited to the left of the goods loop, with the loop starting signal, on a much shorter post, alongside.

The driver of the empty ballast train saw the green light in the darkness, took it for his own and put on steam, with the inevitable result that he ran on to 'Olde England' at the trap points at the end of the loop. His engine and four wagons were derailed, and the wagons toppled over, foul of the up relief line. Seconds later the late-running Oxford train, No 6167 hauling four eight-wheelers and a six-wheeled milk truck, crashed into them, killing the assistant guard of the train, Mr B. J. Emmens. His widow received £310 10s compensation from the GWR.

Following this accident the tracks were slewed further apart so that the up relief home could be placed in its proper position.

Two rather unusual accidents must bring this chapter to an end. On 12 July 1937 a 'Metro' Class 2-4-0 tank was hauling the 3.5 pm Newbury–Reading passenger train over Aldermaston troughs when a ball of flames and scorching fumes blew back from the furnace, seriously burning Fireman Foley and singeing his driver somewhat. The downward projecting ATC shoe had dipped into the trough, causing a wash of water which entered the ashpan via the front damper doors which were incorrectly open. Steam erupted off the hot metal and blew the fire through the firehole.

The accident was caused by a triple chain of events. The Aldermaston troughs pumping station engineman, William Bayliss, had allowed the water level in the troughs to be ½ inch higher than was proper, the locomotive was ½ inch down on its springs due partly to wear and partly to the driving effect of the engine, and Foley had mistakenly opened the front dampers, believing that he had the back dampers open, which was normal practise. Foley was badly hurt and off work for a month.

On 17 July the 9.15 am Paddington–Bristol express was hauled by a 'Castle' driven by Mr Payne. As they passed Langley on the down main, the little-end of the right-hand outside connecting rod broke and that end of the rod fell on to the cross-head guide bars. Payne was alert, braked and brought the train to a stand outside Dolphin Junction box, the con-rod still riding on the guide bars. He ensured that his guard went back with detonators to protect the rear, sent his fireman to the signal box to ask for another engine, and recruited the Travelling Ticket Collector (TTC) as a look-out man on the track.

The fireman returned from the box and assisted his driver to remove the rod as their engine roared off steam deafeningly from the safety valves. Having made the engine safe to move, Payne sent his fireman back to the box with that message and told the TTC to get back on the train.

A passenger had been watching driver Payne from the front coach. This man saw Payne take one last look at his work, saw the 8 am Cheltenham express approaching on the up main, saw the white feather of steam from its whistle but heard no sound owing to the noise from the stationary engine's safety valves. Just as the other 'Castle' came up, Driver Payne stepped backwards, directly into its path.

Appendix 1
GWR financial performance, 1913–39

	Income* ($£$)	Expend're ($£$)	Net ($£$)	Dividend† (%)
1913	16,020,995	10,406,109	5,929,035	6½
1921	36,074,692	30,694,993	6,188.433	7½
1923	36,723,331	29,778,508	8,237,023	8 (as 1922)
1924	36,408,336	30,339,505	7,453,094	7½
1925	35,242,137	29,457,722	7,107,759	7½
1926	29,914,515	26,814,052	4,452,541	3
1927	35,976,045	28,820,506	8,441,886	7
1928	35,527,544	29,408,172	7,057,123	5
1929	36,184,053	29,208,791	8,203,274	7
1930	34,346,867	28,226,477	6,987,146	5½
1931	31,139,630	26,052,984	5,682,396	3
1932	28,462,343	24,430,403	4,459,403	3
1933	28,423,656	23,970,743	5,570,023	3
1934	29,280,382	24,311,381	5,410,999	3
1935	29,788,622	24,817,604	5,450,559	3
1936	30,763,033	24,839,821	6,314,830	3
1937	32,586,547	26,121,445	6,886,505	4
1938	31,039,727	26,389,483	5,043,753	3

1939 'Net revenue for 1st 8 months considerable improvement over 1938. But for outbreak of war final results would have approached those of 1937.' (Chairman's Report to GWR AGM)

* Income from railway business but not including interest from investments, rents and leases. The difference between 'Income' and 'Net' is the amount earned from these other sources.

† Paid to holders of 'Consols' – 'Ordinary' shares.

Appendix 2
Automatic Train Control

What became known as 'Automatic Train Control' began life as the 'Audible Distant Signal'. A metal contact strip on a ramp between the rails was connected to a lineside battery, and contacts on the signal arm acted as a connection between the battery and the ramp. When the distant signal was at 'Danger' the battery was disconnected; when it was lowered to 'All Right' the battery was connected to the ramp contact strip.

On the engine there was a pick-up shoe, which contacted with the ramp, and a battery which energised a solenoid which closed a steam valve. The shoe was raised whilst passing over the ramp and in being raised broke the circuit between the battery and the solenoid. If the ramp contact was electrically 'dead', the steam valve opened and blew a whistle close to the driver's ear (how they must have cursed that!). If the ramp was 'live', current from it passed to the solenoid, maintained the magnet and thus kept the steam valve closed while at the same time ringing a bell.

This 'Audible Distant Signal' system was installed experimentally on the double-track Henley branch in January 1906, between Reading and Slough in November 1908 and to Paddington in November 1910. A very few top-rank engines were fitted with the pick-up gear in 1908: 'Star' Class Nos 4000, 4003 and 4006, for instance. A modified version for single-line use was brought into operation on the Fairford branch in December 1906, and the Lambourn branch in September 1909.

In 1913 the system was developed into 'Automatic Train Control', when the solenoid was made to open not a steam valve but an opening to the vacuum brake system. If a distant signal was passed at 'Danger', air rushed into the vacuum brake pipe, causing a siren to sound as it commenced to apply the brakes. If the driver did not cancel this siren the brakes were fully applied to bring the train to a stand before the first 'stop' signal.

The ATC system was further improved in 1927. Until that time the battery remained connected to the electro-magnet until it became completely run down. This was wasteful when an engine was standing for hours on shed between turns, so a special switch was introduced which allowed air to enter a vacuum chamber until the vacuum was destroyed, after about one hour, thus operating a switch to disconnect the battery from the magnet. When the driver 'blew off' the brakes, the vacuum was recreated and the switch resumed its connection.

GWR drivers were always very proud of and very thankful for ATC on their engines.

Appendix 3
Express train punctuality

(Source: GWR Divisional Superintendents' Reports, PRO: RAIL 250)

Average minutes late arriving at destination for the four weeks ended 11 February

	1932	1933	1934	1935	1936	1937	1938
Express trains							
West of England	5.0	5.8	4.7	2.7	8.8	5.1	11.1
South Wales	3.8	6.0	5.7	3.8	9.0	6.7	14.3
Northern	3.9	6.4	5.8	3.0	7.0	5.7	9.4
Cross-country	6.4	5.6	5.6	4.6	7.6	7.7	17.1
Local trains	1.9	2.2	2.3	1.7	3.1	2.5	4.5
Branch trains	1.0	1.0	1.2	0.8	1.6	1.3	2.6

Percentage of all express passenger trains right time
55.1 51.8 53.0 58.4 46.3 50.4 39.0
Percentage of all express passenger trains 1–5 minutes late
32.2 32.6 32.7 31.0 32.0 32.6 30.4

Average minutes late arriving at destination for the four weeks ended 3 June

	1932	1933	1934	1935	1936	1937	1938
Express trains							
West of England	5.0	3.4	3.0	3.7*	2.5	3.76	3.76
South Wales	3.5	2.9	2.6	4.8	4.5	5.8	3.65
Northern	5.5	3.8	3.4	3.7	3.7	3.08	3.62
Cross-country	6.9	4.9	5.7	6.2	5.1	5.59	5.35

*King George V's Jubilee: very heavy excursion traffic affected running

	1932	1933	1934	1935	1936	1937	1938
Local trains	1.9	1.6	1.8	1.5	2.0	1.75	1.87
Branch trains	0.9	1.0	0.9	0.9	1.1	1.0	1.00

Percentage of all express passenger trains right time
58.8 61.1 49.0 57.3 58.6 60.0 59.67
Percentage of all express passenger trains 1–5 minutes late
28.9 28.5 28.2 28.0 28.5 28.5 28.0

Appendix 4
Ocean liners calling at Plymouth

	Liners calling	Passengers landed	Mailbags landed	Revenue (£)*	Ocean Spec'ls
1913	502	26,741	197,875	31,942	304
1927	628	34,000	213,378	51,000	231
1929	674	37,199	237,063	56,215	242
1930	308†				

Steamship lines using Plymouth 1926

Company	Calls made
Cunard	84
French Line	80
Peninsular & Oriental	62
British India Steam Navigation	41
United States Line	38
Elder Dempster	37
American Merchant	35
Holland America	32
Norddeutscher Lloyd	31
Hamburg America	27
Red Star	26
Royal Nederland West Indian Mail	25
Union Castle	24
Ellerman's City & Hall Lines	19
Henderson	18
Orient	14
White Star	9
Ocean, Aberdeen, Australian Commonwealth, Blue Funnel, Bullard King, Harrison, Johnson	28
Total	639

* Not including revenue for mails
† Total only for 4 months June–September

Appendix 5
GWR Tenders at Plymouth, Millbay

Smeaton
Built Preston 1883; 369 tons; 125 ft x 35 ft x 11 ft; two-cylinder compound, twin screw.
Ceased work at Millbay 1929.

Sir Richard Grenville (I)
Built Birkenhead 1891; 420 tons; 132 ft x 30 ft x 12.5 ft; two-cylinder compound, twin screw.
Ceased work Millbay 1931.

Sir Francis Drake
Built Birkenhead 1908; 478 tons gross; 145.8 ft x 38.5 ft x 14 ft; triple expansion, twin screw.
Worked from Millbay until 1953.

Sir Walter Raleigh
Built Birkenhead 1908; 478 tons gross; 145.8 ft x 38.5 ft x 14 ft; triple expansion, twin screw.
Worked until 1947, then sold to French.

Sir John Hawkins
Built Hull 1929; 939 tons; 172.5 ft x 43 ft x14.6 ft; oil fired. 14 knots. Worked until 1962.

Sir Richard Grenville (II)
Built Hull 1931; 901 tons; 172.5 ft x 42 ft x 14.7 ft. Worked until 1963.

From 'The Port of Plymouth' series: *Millbay Docks* by Edwina Searle and Martin Langley.

Appendix 6
Timings for up 'Ocean Specials' from Plymouth, 1929

(Source: GWR Working Book)

Code	'Star' (tons)	'Castle' (tons)	Time to Padd (hr min)	Route
PLYM A	max 175	max 200	4 00	1
PLYM B	176-288	201-305	4 10	1
PLYM C	over 288	over 305	4 18	1
PLYM D	max 175	max 200	4 08	2
PLYM E	176-288	201-305	4 14	2
PLYM F	over 288	over 305	4 22	2
PLYM G	max 175	max 200	4 29	3
PLYM H	176-288	201-305	4 38	3
PLYM K	over 288	over 305	4 49	3
PLYM L	max 175	max 200	4 34	4
PLYM M	176-288	201-305	4 43	4
PLYM N	over 288	over 305	4 54	4
PLYM P	max 176	max 176	4 29	5
PLYM R	176-288	201-305	4 38	5
PLYM S	over 288	over 305	4 48	5

Route 1: non-stop to Paddington via Westbury
Route 2: Calls Taunton and via Westbury
Route 3: Calls Bristol Temple Meads
Route 4: Calls Exeter St David's and Bristol Temple Meads
Route 5: Calls Bedminster, detach, via St Philip's Marsh

Appendix 7
Standardised rates of pay for enginemen, 1919

Cleaners

Age	Per day (shillings pence)
16 and under	4s 0d
17	5s 0d
18/19	6s 0d
20 and over	7s 0d

Firemen

Year	
1st/2nd	9s 6d
3rd/4th	10s 6d
5th-onwards	11s 0d

Drivers

Year	
1st/2nd	12s 0d
3rd/4th	13s 0d
5th-7th	14s 0d
8th-onwards	15s 0d

These rates were not improved upon until July 1939.

Appendix 8
Staff censuses, 1929–37

March 1929–March 1930

Department	1929	1930
Traffic	26,254	26,665
Goods	13,358	13,639
CME	39,129	41,167
Total all grades	106,429	110,729

26 May 1932–26 May 1937

Department	1932	1933	1934	1935	1936	1937
CME	37,348	33,929	34,420	35,945		36,944
Traffic	25,415	24,354	24,199	24,521		24,836
Engineer		16,032	14,418	13,596	14,152	14,467
Goods	12,825	12,180	12,261	12,450		12,913
Docks	4,373	4,086	3,914	3,785		3,869
S&T	2,505	2,305	2,036	1,959		2,008
Other	5,341	5,173				5,577
Total	103,839	96,436	96,642	95,729	98,290	100,614
	-7,403	+1,073	-113	+2,561		+2324

Appendix 9
A diary of troubles, 1929

January
21-23   Dense fog
February
6   Dense fog
11-March 15   Intense frost causes serious delays. Locomotive injectors and water hoses, brake gear, water columns, troughs, signals and points freeze.
26-27   Heavy snow and freezing fog
27   Derailment at Tiverton Junction
March
11   Derailment at Birkenhead
18-27   Dense fog
April
8   Dense fog
12   Heavy snow
July
31-13 Aug   International Boy Scouts Jamboree at Birkenhead. 10,000 Boy Scouts conveyed: 14 special trains run for 6,200 scouts, the remainder by regular services.

August
5 (Bank Holiday
Monday)   Derailment at Aller Junction
September
28   Continuing very fine weather produces extremely heavy passenger traffic all this month after the end of the normal summer timetable. Regular trains run in two or more parts and many excursions and specials are run.

November
1-2   Dense fog
15, 18   Dense fog
19   Landslide at Skewen. Strong gales cause flooding in many places in South Wales.

Index